# The Undeserving Poor

MICHAEL B. KATZ

# THE UNDESERVING POOR

## From the War on Poverty to the War on Welfare

Pantheon Books 🏛 New York

**Library of Congress Cataloging-in-Publication Data**
Katz, Michael B., 1939–
   The undeserving poor: from the war on poverty to the war on welfare /
Michael B. Katz.
      p.   cm.
   Bibliography: p.
   Includes index.
   ISBN 0-394-53457-3
   1. Poor—United States.   2. Poverty.   3. Discrimination—United States.
4. Economic assistance, Domestic—United States.
I.  Title.
HC110.P6K28   1990
362.5'8'0973—dc20                                                      89-42676

*Book design by Gina Davis*

Manufactured in the United States of America

First Edition

# Contents

FOR MICHAEL HARRINGTON
1928–1989

# Acknowledgments

IN 1983, André Schiffrin and Sara Bershtel of Pantheon asked me to write this book. They have been patient and supportive as I have finished intervening projects and repeatedly altered the book's outline. Sara's meticulous and creative editing improved my original manuscript greatly. Many people have helped me with this project in discussions, casual conversations, formal meetings and seminars, or through their writing. I want to acknowledge many of them and hope that those I have neglected will forgive me.

During the past two and a half years, I have helped coordinate an interdisciplinary faculty seminar on work and welfare at the University of Pennsylvania. It is one of a group of seminars sponsored by the Mellon Foundation through a remarkably successful and enlightened program: Program for the Assessment and Revitalization of the Social Sciences (PARSS). The semi-

nars have educated and stimulated me, and I want especially to
thank the following participating colleagues and seminar guests
from outside the University: June Axinn, Fred Block, Gene
Burns, Greg Brooks, Peter Gottschalk, Judith Gueron, Deborah
Harris, Amy Hirsch, David Hollenbach, Jerry Jacobs, Martha
Minow, John Noakes, Mark Stern, Deborah Stone, and Susan
Sturm. The PARSS program arranged for my release from
teaching one course in the fall semester, 1988, to begin reading
aspects of law and philosophy relevant to poverty and social
welfare. This opportunity, which whetted my appetite, also en-
abled me to complete this book.

For a little more than a year, I have been privileged to serve
as archivist and project historian to a new Social Science Research Council Committee on the Urban Underclass. Participation in the committee and attendance at its meetings have
broadened and deepened my understanding of the issues. I am
particularly grateful to the committee's exceptional staff: Martha
Gephart, Robert Pearson, and Raquel Ovryn Rivera.

I also learned a great deal at a series of seminars on the applicability of the European experience in social welfare to America
funded by the Ford Foundation and organized by Ethel Klein at
Columbia in 1986. In April 1988, a conference organized by the
New York Review of Law and Social Change showed me how
important Legal Services lawyers have been for poor people and
stimulated my interest in the role of law in social change.

Others with whom I have discussed aspects of this book include: David Abraham, Mary Jo Bane, Ivar Berg, Barry Bluestone, Amy Cohen, Ellen Eisenberg, David Ellwood, Michael
Frisch, Frank Furstenberg, Norman Glickman, Theodore
Hershberg, Gerald Neuman, Alice O'Connor, Ann Shola Orloff, Frances Fox Piven, Elaine Simon, Theda Skocpol, William
Julius Wilson, Lou Winnick, Komozi Woodard, Viviana Zelizer,
and the students in History/Sociology 532 during the spring semester, 1988.

A number of librarians and archivists have been very helpful.
I want especially to thank the reference staff at the University of
Pennsylvania Library and the archivists at the Ford Foundation,

Minnesota Social Welfare History Archives, and the John Fitz-gerald Kennedy Library. The Ford Foundation has kindly granted me permission to quote from material in its archives.

Two undergraduate research assistants have provided essen-tial help. Eva Moskowitz worked with me in my first year of bibliographic research; James Sparrow has assisted me greatly since the fall 1986. As always, Edda Katz and Sarah Katz have been patient and supportive, as have been my friends and neigh-bors at Clioquossia in Oquossoc, Maine, where most of this book was written. The simultaneous visits to Clioquossia of my son Paul from Spain and my daughter Rebecca and granddaughter Melody from Brazil proved not only a wonderful diversion, but a special inspiration in writing the last part of this book.

*August 1989*

# The Undeserving Poor

# Introduction

T HE VOCABULARY of poverty impoverishes political imagination. For two centuries of American history, considerations of
productivity, cost, and eligibility have channeled discourse
about need, entitlement, and justice within narrow limits
bounded by the market. In every era, a few people have coun-
terposed dignity, community, and equality as standards for policy. But they have remained outsiders, unable to divert the
powerful currents constraining the possibilities for social
thought and public action. In this book, I show how these historic preoccupations have shaped and confined ideas about poor
people and distributive justice in recent American history.

Although poor people always are there, only periodically do
we rediscover or think about them very much. One of those
moments happened in the early 1960s. The reawakened concern
with poverty, embodied in the War on Poverty and the Great

Society, lasted through the early 1970s. The conservative reaction peaked in the early 1980s. The years that span the presidencies of John Fitzgerald Kennedy and Ronald Reagan, therefore, constitute one episode in the recurring dialectic of reform and reaction that punctuates American history. I believe the era of reaction is over. Despite the election of another Republican president, all over the country signs point to a new concern with poverty. George Bush's support for social programs, modest as it is by liberal standards, would have been unthinkable for Ronald Reagan in 1980. So would the announced intention of his Secretary of Housing and Urban Development, Jack Kemp, to launch a new war on poverty.

It's time. By every measure, poverty increased dramatically during the Reagan era (the appendix gives an overview of contemporary trends). Part of the blame rests on cuts in benefits that began in the mid-1970s and accelerated during the Reagan years. Part rests on a legacy of policies that fail to attack the roots of poverty in employment, income distribution, and discrimination. Underlying both policies and cutbacks was the economy. After 1973, real wages declined; income inequality widened; productivity dropped; inflation soared; and unemployment increased. Extraordinary numbers of black men remain out of work.

Economic recovery did not wholly reverse the impact of these trends. Although the number of jobs grew, they consisted disproportionately of badly paid jobs in the service sector. As a consequence, poverty rose dramatically even among those who work. Without the minimal safety net that exists, hunger, homelessness, infant mortality, and disease would be catastrophes unimaginable to most Americans.

Shop-worn ideas still hamper attempts to remove the scourge of poverty from American life. Three major issues have dominated both conservative and liberal poverty discourse for centuries: the categorization of the poor; the impact of poor relief (welfare) on work motivation, labor supply, and family life; and the limits of social obligation. In this book, I trace their impact on the debates about poverty and social welfare from the War on Poverty in the 1960s through Ronald Reagan's war on welfare in the 1980s.

Public officials in the early nineteenth century attempted to distinguish between the able-bodied and the impotent poor; a few decades later, officials transmuted these categories into the moral distinction between the worthy and the unworthy, or the deserving and the undeserving poor.[1] Like their counterparts in England, early nineteenth-century American reformers also argued that badly conceived and administered poor laws had hurt people by increasing pauperism and its attendant costs. Others emphasized the sanctity of private property and the limits of social obligation by arguing that taxation for poor relief was theft and that social classes owed each other very little. These issues remain as alive in the late twentieth century as they were two centuries earlier. Consider, as examples, the current fixation on the underclass; the widespread argument that Great Society antipoverty programs harmed the poor; and the obsession with forcing welfare recipients to pay for their benefits through work.[2]

Why have these concerns remained so prominent? What purposes do they serve? How have they shaped contemporary thought and action? What is their relation to the findings of modern research? These are the key questions this book addresses. It shows that poverty discourse has maintained only a tenuous relation to the origins and demographics of poverty and the results of public policy. How we think and speak about poverty and what we do (or don't do) about it emerges as much from a mix of ideology and politics as from the structure of the problem itself.

Because the language of poverty is a vocabulary of invidious distinction, poverty discourse highlights the social construction of difference. Some ways of classifying people, such as undeserving—or even poor—are so old we use them unreflexively; others, such as homeless or underclass, though much more recent, quickly become unexamined parts of discourse. The problem with this language of difference is both philosophic and practical. We assume that verbal distinctions reflect natural or inherent qualities of people. By mirroring natural divisions, we think the language of difference represents objective distinctions. In fact, it does not. For reasons of convenience, power, or moral judgment, we select from among a myriad of traits and then sort people, objects, and situations into categories which we then treat as real. As Martha Minow shows, this process of reification defines the line between normality and deviance, ignores the perspective of the powerless, and accepts existing social and economic arrangments as natural. Its consequences are serious: "When we identify one thing as like the others," claims Minow, "we are not merely classifying the world: we are investing particular classifications with consequences, and positioning ourselves in relation to those meanings. When we identify one thing as unlike the others we are dividing the world; we use our language to exclude, to distinguish—to discriminate." By mistaking socially constructed categories for natural distinctions, we reinforce inequality and stigmatize even those we set out to help.[3]

One of the most enduring and invidious social categories is "stranger." We engage the world as a series of concentric circles based on degrees of relation: family, friends, neighbors, community, strangers. The composition of the circles shifts over time, but strangers remain always on the outside. Not surprisingly, they are the primary objects of a continuing debate about, to use Michael Ignatieff's evocative phrase, the "needs of strangers." As in England, colonial American poor laws were clear about the limits of social obligation. Parents and children remained responsible for each other; communities were to ease the suffering of their members. But the public owed nothing to strangers, who were to be shunted back to their community of origin. This was the message of the ubiquitous and infamous settlement laws in both Britain and America.[4]

Within cities, poor people have almost always remained strangers. We pass their houses on a train or in a car; read about them as individual cases; study them as abstract statistics; and encounter them asking for help in public places. Even our welfare state, as Ignatieff writes, represents the "bureaucratized transfer of income among strangers." Most of the writing about poor people, even by sympathetic observers, tells us that they are different, truly strangers in our midst: Poor people think, feel, and act in ways unlike middle-class Americans. Their poverty is to some degree a matter of personal responsibility, and its alleviation requires personal transformation, such as the acquisition of skills, commitment to the work ethic, or the practice of chastity. This "supply-side" view of poverty, often despite powerful evidence, has coursed through American social thought for centuries. Because this way of talking about poverty so pervades American history, I have titled this book *The Undeserving Poor.*

When Americans talk about poverty, some things remain unsaid. Mainstream discourse about poverty, whether liberal or conservative, largely stays silent about politics, power, and equality. But poverty, after all, is about distribution; it results because some people receive a great deal less than others. Descriptions of the demography, behavior, or beliefs of subpopulations cannot explain the patterned inequalities evident in every era of American history. These result from styles of dominance, the way power is exercised, and the politics of distribution.

Poverty no longer is natural; it is a social product. As nations emerge from the tyranny of subsistence, gain control over the production of wealth, develop the ability to feed their citizens and generate surpluses, poverty becomes not the product of scarcity, but of political economy. Yet with few exceptions (such as some of the discussions during the Great Depression of the 1930s or the internal colonialism debate of the 1960s), this is not the way Americans have talked and written about poverty.

The question is, Why? Although I will touch on it in various places throughout this book, two lines of explanation are worth mentioning here, even briefly. First, the culture of capitalism measures persons, as well as everything else, by their ability to produce wealth and by their success in earning it; it therefore leads naturally to the moral condemnation of those who, for whatever reason, fail to contribute or to prosper. It also mystifies the exploitive relations that allow some to prosper so well at the expense of so many.

Second, the silence about poverty as a product of political

economy reflects the language of politics in America. As Ira
Katznelson has pointed out, by the late nineteenth century,
American working-class politics at the local level swirled around
issues of family, neighborhood, and ethnicity. Mobilized by
trade unions at work and political machines at home, American
workers failed to develop a language of class that included both
economics and community. As a result, for over a century
American political discourse has redefined issues of power and
distribution as questions of identity, morality, and patronage.
This is what happened to poverty, which slipped easily, unreflectively, into a language of family, race, and culture rather than
inequality, power, and exploitation. The silence is therefore no
anomaly; rather, it is the expected outcome of the way American
political discussion has ignored, deflected, or framed issues of
political economy for a very long time. To transcend this historic
division in the way we talk about public issues, to pull poverty
discourse away from family and toward power, requires sur-
mounting the strongest conventions in Americans' social vocabulary. I offer this book as a modest toehold for the struggle.[5]

# From the Undeserving Poor to the Culture of Poverty

ONE

T HE UNDESERVING POOR have a very old history. They represent the enduring attempt to classify poor people by merit. This impulse to classify has persisted for centuries partly for reasons of policy. Resources are finite. Neither the state nor private charity can distribute them in unlimited quantities to all who might claim need. On what principles, then, should assistance be based? Who should—and, the more difficult question, who should not—receive help? Answering the questions means drawing lines, separating individuals into categories, and defending arbitrary distinctions that discriminate among people none of whom can survive by themselves with comfort and dignity. In practice, honest and perceptive officials have recognized the impurity of all distinctions: No classification can be applied easily or satisfactorily to real people. For reasons of convenience, policy has collapsed into artificial categories the continuum on which poor people have been arrayed. However, scarce resources have been only one reason for classifying poor people. For in poverty discourse, moral assessments have nearly always overlain pragmatic distinctions. The issue becomes not only who can fend for themselves without aid, but more important, whose behavior and character entitle them to the resources of others.[1]

The preoccupation with classifying poor people persists. Contemporary politicians, moralists, and editorial writers still frequently refer to the deserving and the undeserving poor. Social scientists who prefer more neutral language refer to the culture of poverty or the underclass. All these terms serve to isolate one group of poor people from the rest, and to stigmatize them. The undeserving poor, the culture of poverty, and the underclass are moral statuses identified by source of dependence, the behavior with which it is associated, its transmission to children, and its crystallization into cultural patterns.

Empirical evidence almost always challenges the assumptions underlying classifications of poor people. Even in the late nineteenth century, countervailing data, not to mention decades of administrative frustration, showed their inadequacy. Since the 1960s, poverty research has provided an arsenal of ammunition for critics of conventional classifications. Still, as even a casual reading of the popular press, occasional attention to political rhetoric, or informal conversations about poverty reveal, empirical evidence has remarkably little effect on what people think. Part of the reason is that conventional classifications of poor people serve such useful purposes. They offer a familiar and easy target for displacing rage, frustration, and fear. They demonstrate the link between virtue and success that legitimates capitalist political economy. And by dividing poor people, they prevent their coalescing into a powerful, unified, and threatening political force. Stigmatized conditions and punitive treatment are powerful incentives to work, whatever the wages and conditions.

# THE ORIGINS OF THE UNDESERVING POOR

Before the twentieth century, it would have seemed preposterous to imagine the abolition of poverty. Resources were finite; life was harsh. Most people would be born, live, and die in poverty. The questions, then, were who among the needy should be helped? What should they be given? How should relief or charity be administered? The answers by and large were not moral, because poverty entailed no disgrace. Rather, from the time of the Elizabethan poor law, policies in England and America reflected two other ways of classifying poor people. Of primary importance was the division between neighbors and strangers. Responsibility extended to family and community; there it ended. This was the point of the settlement provisions in both English and American poor laws, which required communities (defined variously as parishes, towns, or counties) to assist their permanent members. Others who might fall into need within their borders should be shipped to their places of origin. Settlement laws reflected a state of limited mobility in which most people belonged clearly to some identifiable community. They reflected, too, the permeable and blurred boundaries between family and community in agricultural villages where markets and wage labor had not hardened distinctions and redefined relations.[2]

No aspect of the poor laws caused as great confusion and litigation as the settlement provisions. The restriction of public and private charity to neighbors resonated with deep cultural preferences, but in practice it proved almost impossible to do. As migration and mobility increased, as people wandered from town to town in search of work, who could say with authority to what community someone belonged? The complex attempts at definition all failed, and the result was cruelty and expense. In winter, local authorities shunted sick or old poor people from one town or county to another, and the expense of transporting them, or of defending against their claims in court, consumed a

large share of the tax money raised for relief. Indeed, the modification of the settlement laws became a primary goal of poor
law reform in the early decades of the nineteenth century. Still,
despite the modification, settlement continued as both a legal
and emotional issue, as in the resistance to national welfare standards today and the resentment of dependent outsiders allegedly
drawn to states with relatively generous benefits.[3]

Another distinction originally attempted to separate the genuinely needy from rogues, vagabonds, and sturdy beggars. It
translated over time into the restriction of aid to the impotent
and the exclusion of the able-bodied. This principle, so transparently reasonable on the surface, also proved administratively
impossible to implement. In both England and America, rising
costs for poor relief in the late eighteenth and early nineteenth
centuries convinced critics that in fact the able-bodied had penetrated the relief rolls, and a great object of poor law reform in
both countries became to remove them. This task remained far
more difficult than theorists assumed.

In his major report on the poor laws of the Commonwealth of
Massachusetts in 1821, Josiah Quincy pointed out that the principle on which the laws rested divided the poor into "two
classes": first, "the impotent poor; in which denomination are
included all, who are wholly incapable of work, through old age,
infancy, sickness or corporeal debility." Second were "the able
poor . . . all, who are capable of work, of some nature, or other;
but differing in the degree of their capacity, and in the kind of
work, of which they are capable." No one disagreed about helping the impotent, but the able poor were another matter: "From
the difficulty of discriminating between this class and the former, and of apportioning the degree of public provision to the
degree of actual impotency, arise all the objections to the principle of the existing pauper system." The problem could not be
solved by legislation, because

> There must be, in the nature of things, numerous and minute
> shades of difference between the pauper, who through impo-
> tency, can do absolutely nothing, and the pauper who is able to

do something, but that, very little. Nor does the difficulty of discrimination, proportionally, diminish as the ability, in any particular pauper, to do something, increases. There always must exist,
so many circumstances of age, sex, previous habits, muscular, or
mental, strength, to be taken into the account, that society is
absolutely incapable to fix any standard, or to prescribe any rule,
by which the claim of right to the benefit of the public provision
shall absolutely be determined.[4]

Quincy's language points to another enduring classification:
the distinction between the poor and paupers. Paupers originated as an administrative category. They were recipients of
public relief. Although by itself poverty carried no stigma, pauperism did. During the early nineteenth century, the distinction
between poverty and pauperism hardened, and commentators
increasingly attributed the latter to moral sources. A few years
after Quincy had written his report, a Philadelphia committee of
the Guardians of the Poor, reporting on poor relief in other
cities, asserted: "The poor in consequence of vice, constitute
here and everywhere, by far the greater part of the poor. . . .
From three-fourths to nine-tenths of the paupers in all parts of
our country, may attribute their degradation to the vice of intemperance."[5] In 1834, the Reverend Charles Burroughs,
preaching at the opening of a new chapel in the poorhouse in
Portsmouth, New Hampshire, admonished his audience:

In speaking of poverty, let us never forget that there is a distinction between this and pauperism. The former is an unavoidable
evil, to which many are brought from necessity, and in the wise
and gracious Providence of God. It is the result, not of our faults,
but of our misfortunes. . . . Pauperism is the consequence of wilful error, of shameful indolence, of vicious habits. It is a misery
of human creation, the pernicious work of man, the lamentable
consequence of bad principles and morals.[6]

The transmutation of pauperism into a moral category tar-
nished all the poor. Despite the effort to maintain fine distinc-

tions, increasingly poverty itself became not the natural result of misfortune, but the wilful result of indolence and vice. As Walter Channing pointed out in 1843, to the "popular mind" poverty "is looked to solely as the product of him or of her who has entered its dreadful, because dishonored, uncared for, or unwisely cared for, service. Let me repeat it, the causes of poverty are looked for, and found in him or her who suffers it. . . ."[7] Before the middle of the nineteenth century, the unworthy poor had become a fixture in "the popular mind."

The redefinition of poverty as a moral condition accompanied the transition to capitalism and democracy in early nineteenth-century America. It served to justify the mean-spirited treatment of the poor, which in turn checked expenses for poor relief and provided a powerful incentive to work. In this way the moral definition of poverty helped ensure the supply of cheap labor in a market economy increasingly based on unbound wage labor. The moral redefinition of poverty followed also from the identification of market success with divine favor and personal worth. Especially in America, where opportunity awaited anyone with energy and talent, poverty signaled personal failure. The ubiquity of work and opportunity, of course, were myths, even in the early Republic. The transformation in economic relations, the growth of cities, immigration, the seasonality of labor, fluctuations in consumer demand, periodic depressions, low wages, restricted opportunities for women, industrial accidents, high mortality, and the absence of any social insurance: together these chiseled chronic poverty and dependence into American social life.[8]

Persistent and increasing misery did not soften the moral definition of poverty. Neither did the evidence available through early surveys or the records of institutions and administrative agencies, which showed poverty and dependence as complex products of social and economic circumstances usually beyond individual control.[9] Instead, the definition hardened until nearly the end of the nineteenth century. As a consequence, public policy and private charity remained mean, punitive, and inadequate. Predispositions toward moral definitions of poverty found support in the latest intellectual fashions: in the antebellum period, in Protestant theology; after the Civil War, in the work of Darwin and early hereditarian theory; and in the twentieth century, in eugenics. So deeply embedded in Western culture had the distinction between the deserving and undeserving poor become that even writers on the Left invoked it automatically or translated it into their own vocabulary. Marxists wrote about the "lumpenproletariat," and even the Progressive reformers who, starting in the 1890s, rejected individual explanations of poverty, unreflectively used the old distinctions. Robert Hunter, a socialist, whose widely read book *Poverty* (published in 1904) traced dependence to its structural sources, used the hoary distinction between poor people and paupers ("Paupers are not, as a rule, unhappy. They are not ashamed. . . . They have passed over the line which separates poverty from pauperism"). He asserted that "the poverty which punishes the vicious and the sinful is good and necessary. . . . There is unquestionably a poverty which men deserve. . . ."[10]

The moral classification of the poor survived even the Great Depression. Poverty lost much of its moral censure as unemployment reached catastrophic levels, but the idea of relief remained pejorative and degrading. The unemployed turned to the state for help usually only as a last resort, after they had exhausted all other possibilities. President Franklin Delano Roosevelt could hardly wait to move the federal government out of the business of relief, which it had reluctantly and temporarily entered in 1933. The foundation of the social welfare edifice erected by his administration became a distinction between public assistance and social insurance (relief based solely on need versus universal programs such as Social Security) that assured public policy would continue to discriminate invidiously among categories of dependent people.[11]

During World War II and the prosperous fifties, poverty received little explicit attention from social scientists. However, the rhetoric surrounding controversies about Aid to Dependent Children and other aspects of public assistance showed that the moral classification of poor people had persisted.[12] In the nine-

teenth century, asking for relief became a sign of individual
failure; no label carried a greater stigma than pauper. By the
second half of the twentieth century, some groups in need of
help had been moved out of the pauper class. Most old people,
workers disabled in accidents, and the unemployed (not to mention veterans, always a special category) could claim help as a
right through social insurance. Others, notably women who
headed families with children, remained dependent on public
assistance—morally tarred, as always, by their association with
relief.

## THE CULTURE OF POVERTY

In the early 1960s intellectuals and politicians rediscovered poverty. Sustained economic growth and myths of affluence had
hidden the stubborn persistence of deprivation and dependence;
Americans appeared shocked to discover that between 40 and 50
million among them were, by any objective measure, poor.[13] To
interpret the meaning of these no longer avoidable and dis-
heartening facts, social scientists drew on a new concept: the
culture of poverty. The culture of poverty did not have the classification of poor people as its primary purpose. Still, it served
the same end. For most writers observed that the culture of
poverty did not capture all poor people. Rather, it placed in a
class by themselves those whose behaviors and values converted
their poverty into an enclosed and self-perpetuating world of
dependence. Although some of its exponents located the sources
of poverty in objective factors such as unemployment, the new
concept resonated with traditional moral definitions. The culture of poverty could not quite sanitize the poor; their ancient
odor seeped through the antiseptic layers of social science. They
remained different and inferior because, whatever their origins,
the actions and attitudes of poor people themselves assured their
continued poverty and that of their children.

Not surprisingly, by the 1970s the culture of poverty had become a conservative concept, thought of as a justification for mean and punitive policies, harshly and sometimes unfairly attacked from the Left. But its political history is much more complex, for the culture of poverty originated among liberals who advocated more active, generous, and interventionist policies on behalf of the poor. As such, the concept reflected a larger strand in the liberalism of the time: the assumption that dependent people were mainly helpless and passive, unable, without the leadership of liberal intellectuals, to break the cycles of deprivation and degradation that characterized their lives.

The anthropologist Oscar Lewis introduced the idea of the culture of poverty in his ethnographic portraits of Mexicans and Puerto Ricans.[14] The culture of poverty, he stressed, differed from "economic deprivation . . . or the absence of something." Rather, it was a "way of life . . . passed down from generation to generation along family lines." It could be found in both urban and rural settings and in different regions and nations because it represented a series of "common adaptations to common problems."[15]

Those problems flourish in cash economies where wages are low, unemployment high, social and political organization for the poor undeveloped, kinship bilateral, and dominant class values stress "the accumulation of wealth and property, the possibility of upward mobility and thrift, and . . . personal inadequacy or inferiority" as the source of low economic status. In these settings, the lower strata of rapidly changing societies became likely candidates for the culture of poverty because of their alienation and marginality.[16] Lewis stressed the adaptive role of the culture of poverty: It serves to "cope with feelings of hopelessness and despair which develop from the realization of the impossibility of achieving success in terms of the values and goals of the larger society." Nonetheless, its perpetuation "from generation to generation" cripples children because it leaves them psychologically unprepared "to take full advantage of changing conditions or increased opportunities which may occur in their lifetime."[17]

For Lewis, the culture of poverty had several key features.

Among the most important was "the lack of effective participation and integration of the poor in the major institutions of the larger society" and their consequent apathy, hostility, and suspicion. Nor do the members of the culture of poverty form very many organizations of their own. Indeed, he wrote, "the low level of organization . . . gives the culture of poverty its marginal and anachronistic quality in our highly complex, specialized, organized society. Most primitive people have achieved a higher level of socio-cultural organization than our modern urban slum dwellers."[18]

Other characteristics defined family life within the culture of poverty: "the absence of childhood as a specially prolonged and protected stage in the life cycle, early initiation into sex, free unions or consensual marriages, a relatively high incidence of the abandonment of wives and children," and maternal dominance. Dominating individual psychology were a "strong feeling of marginality, or helplessness, of dependence, and of inferiority" coupled with a battery of other traits:

> a high incidence of maternal deprivation, of orality, of weak ego structure, confusion of sexual identification, a lack of impulse control, a strong present-time orientation with relatively little ability to defer gratification and to plan for the future, a sense of resignation and fatalism, a widespread belief in male superiority, and a high tolerance for psychological pathology of all sorts.[19]

Lewis stressed the distinction between poverty and the culture of poverty. (In the United States, he argued, only 20 percent of the poor were trapped within the culture of poverty.) Both anthropological and historical evidence gave many examples of impoverished peoples untouched by the latter. For the most part, they escaped for one of a variety of reasons: the lack of stratification within their societies (as with hunting and gathering tribes); their integration into the larger society through formal organizations (as with castes in India); an emphasis on literacy and voluntary associations (as with the Jews of Eastern Europe); or, Lewis speculated, political leaders who inspired confidence and hope: "On the basis of my limited experience in one socialist country—Cuba—and on the basis of my reading, I am inclined to believe that the culture of poverty does not exist in the socialist countries." When poor people became class-conscious or joined trade unions, when their outlook became "internationalist," they were no longer part of the culture of poverty because "Any movement . . . which organizes and gives hope to the poor and effectively promotes solidarity and a sense of identification with larger groups, destroys the psychological and social core of the culture of poverty."[20]

Lewis understood the culture of poverty's "positive adaptive function," but he did not romanticize it. He found it "a relatively thin culture. There is a great deal of pathos, suffering and emptiness among those who live in the culture of poverty."[21] Lewis understood how this portrait of the culture of poverty among Puerto Ricans could offend those who have dedicated themselves to eliminating poverty and who are trying to build a positive public image of an often maligned minority group. He knew too the "danger that my findings might be misinterpreted or used to justify prejudices and negative stereotypes . . . which, unfortunately, are still held by some Americans." Clearly, his intent was otherwise. To improve the conditions of people trapped within the culture of poverty, "the first step is to know about them," he asserted, quoting a popular Puerto Rican saying: " 'You can't cover up the sky with your hand.' Indeed, you can't cover up slums, poverty, and ugliness."[22]

Despite his intentions, Lewis's definition of the culture of poverty lent itself easily to appropriation by conservatives in search of a modern academic label for the undeserving poor. At the same time, it also pointed in a radical direction. For the quickest and surest way to eliminate the culture of poverty was through the organization of its members. Lewis' stress on the pivotal role of organized militance links the culture of poverty to the stress on the "maximum feasible participation" of the poor that characterized the War on Poverty in the early 1960s. For him, pride, organization, and class (or racial) consciousness led swiftly away from the culture of poverty. In the United States, the great example for Lewis was the civil rights movement. In the Third World, it was revolution.[23]

Michael Harrington was the first major author to apply the culture of poverty concept to America, although, wrote Lewis, "he used it in a somewhat broader and less technical sense than I had intended."[24] In *The Other America,* a pivotal book in the rediscovery of poverty in the 1960s, Harrington defined the contemporary poor in the United States as "those who, for reasons beyond their control, cannot help themselves." "Poverty in the United States," he wrote, "is a culture, an institution, a way of life. . . . The family structure of the poor . . . is different from that of the rest of the society. . . . There is . . . a language of the poor, a psychology of the poor, a world view of the poor."[25] Harrington's call to action against poverty lacked Lewis's appreciation of the potential of organized militance and assumed the passivity of the poor. Only the intervention of sympathetic elites could begin to lift poor people out of their degraded and helpless condition. The first step was to arouse the conscience of the nation, and this was the purpose of his book.

As the culture of poverty entered the lexicon of American social science, it framed interpretations of public policy issues. Most notable was educational discourse in which the culture of poverty concept, redefined as cultural deprivation, explained the learning disabilities of economically disadvantaged youngsters. Again, in the beginning, the culture of poverty and its synonyms underlay liberal definitions of the problem—for instance, in *The Culturally Deprived Child* by Frank Riessman. Reissman wanted to challenge the widely held notion that the "culturally deprived" child is not interested in education, and to present a new "cultural" approach to teaching these children. He seemed eager to distance himself from the larger implications of the culture of poverty thesis. Although poor people lacked "many of the advantages (and disadvantages) of middle-class culture," he did not think it appropriate to describe them as "culturally deprived" because they possessed "a culture of their own, with many positive characteristics that have developed out of coping with a difficult environment." He wanted to confine cultural deprivation "to those aspects of middle-class culture—such as education, books, formal language—from which these groups have not benefited."[26]

Nonetheless, Riessman's version of cultural deprivation echoed Lewis's delineation of the culture of poverty. Both believed that poor people had developed a distinctive culture based on strategies for coping with hardship. Riessman's "portrait of the underprivileged" resembled Lewis's description of the "culture of poverty." For instance, among other traits, Riessman asserted (in a definition in which the average "underprivileged person" was male) that "the deprived individual feels alienated, not fully a part of society, left out, frustrated in what he can do." Nor, on average, was he "individualistic, introspective, self-oriented, or concerned with self-expression. It is unlikely that he will embrace an outlook that prefers moderation, balance, seeing all sides of an issue." Although he wanted to improve his standard of living, "he is not attracted to a middle-class style of life, with its accompanying concern for status, prestige, and individalistic methods of betterment." The average underprivileged person was also poorly informed, authoritarian, conventional in moral and social opinions, "pragmatic and anti-intellectual," and committed to an ideal of masculinity that stressed ruggedness, action, and "physical prowess."[27]

To liberal educators, cultural deprivation necessitated major changes in schooling. They ranged from "readers and materials more attuned to the experiences and problems of lower socio-economic groups" to methods of instilling "school know-how" in which culturally deprived children were especially deficient, pedagogy that drew on their "physical approach," techniques for combatting their anti-intellectualism, and balancing the " 'female school' " with masculine influences.[28] Cultural deprivation was the foundation for the single most successful program of the 1960s War on Poverty: Operation Headstart, which sought to counteract the familial and environmental disadvantages of poor children through intensive preschool education.

Other liberal social scientists shared some of the same key assumptions. Most important was the image of dependent people in both past and present as passive, lacking the will and organizational capacity to attack the sources of their exploitation and degradation. Historian Oscar Handlin wrote of the Irish immigrants to mid-nineteenth-century Boston: "No other contemporaneous migration partook so fully of this poverty-stricken helplessness." Indeed, "degradation by poverty was almost inevitable under the circumstances of Irish life in Boston." Want "insinuated itself into personal habits, perverting human relations and warping conceptions of right and wrong." Boston's Irish, moreover, reflected the impact of Ireland's harsh agrarian economy and Catholic religion: "Their utter helplessness before the most elemental forces fostered an immense sadness, a deeprooted pessimism about the world and man's role in it. . . ."[29]

Stanley Elkins compared slaves to the inmates of concentration camps. The force of oppression disintegrated their personalities and transformed them into "Sambos," passive grinning subhumans who tried to please their masters. The "Elkins interpretation of slavery," writes John Cell, "was part of the American liberalism of the postwar era. . . . Under segregation, though obviously not so rigidly as during slavery, a closed-behavior system has supposedly continued. And, especially in the South, black people on the whole had continued to submit to it."[30] Psychologist David C. McClelland argued that "achievement motivation is in part responsible for economic growth." Most characteristic of middle-class Americans, "$n$ achievement" (an intrinsic motivation toward achievement) revealed itself in "thoughts of doing well with respect to some standard of performance, of being blocked in the attempt to achieve, of trying various means of achieving, and of reacting with joy or sadness to the results of one's efforts." A "society with a generally high level of $n$ achievement will produce more energetic entrepreneurs who, in turn, produce more rapid economic development." Underdeveloped societies (as the Third World was referred to at the time) lacked $n$ achievement; no one encouraged their entrepreneurs, and as a consequence, their economies failed to grow.[31]

By defining dependent people as passive, in the 1960s liberal social science enhanced its own role. Without the assistance of liberal intellectuals, dependent people would remain mired in their own degradation. These views also fit easily into the chauvinistic assumptions of the Cold War and American penetration of the Third World. For, as with their support of Manifest Destiny in the mid-nineteenth century or America's imperial activities a half century later, liberal intellectuals used American middle-class culture as the standard by which to measure not only their own poor, but the rest of the world as well. The culture of poverty solved another intellectual problem: how to account for the failure of the poor to rise up in protest on the streets or through the electoral system. The false consciousness offered by Marxism appeared increasingly facile and patronizing. The culture of poverty, by contrast, offered a complex and subtle interpretation of the process that connected the objective sources of exploitation with the psychology and behavior of everyday life. Its emphasis on the development and transmission of adaptive coping strategies preserved some dignity and rationality for the poor even as it deplored the culture that resulted and stressed the importance of intervention by sympathetic elites.[32]

## FROM THE CULTURE OF POVERTY TO THE BLACK FAMILY

In the early 1960s, the resurgent interest in poverty did not focus on cities or on race. Michael Harrington's *Other America*, for instance, paid most attention to rural poverty, and the Kennedy administration's early concern with poverty was concentrated on Appalachia. However, after 1964 the civil rights movement and urban riots refocused the meaning of poverty. Now in most discussions, poverty appeared as an urban problem that most seriously afflicted blacks. The fusion of race, poverty, and cities became the tacitly accepted starting point among radicals, liberals, and conservatives for debates about policy and reform.

President Lyndon B. Johnson's commencement speech at Howard University on June 4, 1965, signaled the shifting connotation of poverty. The "great majority of Negro Americans—the poor, the unemployed, and the dispossessed," said Johnson, "are another nation. Despite the court orders and the laws, despite the legislative victories and the speeches, for them the walls are rising and the gulf is widening. . . . The isolation of Negro from white communities is increasing, rather than decreasing, as Negroes crowd into the central cities and become a city within a city. . . . Negro poverty is not white poverty. Many of its causes and many of its cures are the same. But there are differences—deep, corrosive, obstinate differences—radiating painful roots into the community, the family, and the nature of the individual." [33]

Johnson based his remarks on a hitherto confidential report, *The Negro Family: The Case for National Action*, which had been submitted to him in March 1965; its principal author was Daniel Patrick Moynihan, then assistant secretary of labor in the Office of Policy Planning and Research of the Department of Labor. Moynihan's report, published in the fall, became one of the most controversial documents in the history of American social science. [34] His explanation for the worsening poverty among urban blacks did not refer to the culture of poverty. The major intellectual influences on his work were early black sociologists, especially E. Franklin Frazier, and the recently completed *Dark Ghetto* by black social psychologist Kenneth Clark. [35] Nowhere did he mention Oscar Lewis or Michael Harrington. Nonetheless, informed readers could not miss the striking parallels between Lewis's culture of poverty and Moynihan's cycle of poverty; "subculture . . . of the Negro American"; and "tangle of pathology" (a phrase borrowed from Clark). [36] Moynihan's report outraged black leaders and a great many of their white supporters. Because most critics distorted the report, the debate generated more passion than insight. One result was to accelerate the burial of the culture of poverty as an acceptable concept in liberal reform. [37]

Moynihan argued that the Civil Rights Act of 1964 had fulfilled "the demand of Negro Americans for full recognition of their civil rights." Now, Negro Americans would press "beyond civil rights." They would want their equal opportunities to produce "equal results, as compared with other groups." This would not happen without a new and special effort. Two forces undermined blacks' legitimate aspirations for equal results. One was "the racist virus in the American bloodstream that still afflicts us"; the other was the toll of "three centuries of sometimes unimaginable mistreatment." The most difficult fact for white Americans to understand, emphasized the report, is that conditions within "the Negro American community in recent years" had not been improving. On the contrary, they were becoming worse. The fundamental problem with black communities was "family structure." The evidence, still a bit tentative, admitted the report, was "that the Negro family in the urban ghettos is crumbling." A middle class had managed to save itself, but "for vast numbers of the unskilled, poorly educated city working class the fabric of conventional social relationships has all but disintegrated. . . . So long as this situation persists, the cycle of poverty and disadvantage will continue to repeat itself." Only a massive federal effort could reverse the pathology afflicting the lives of black Americans. Its goal should be "the establishment of a stable Negro family structure."[38]

Moynihan used several indexes to demonstrate the disintegration of the black family: "Nearly a quarter of urban negro marriages are dissolved"; "Nearly one-quarter of negro births are now illegitimate"; "Almost one-fourth of negro families are headed by females"; "The breakdown of the negro family has led to a startling increase in welfare dependence."[39] As Rainwater and Yancey point out, Moynihan's dismay at trends in black family structure reflected the influence of the Catholic social welfare philosophy emphasis on "family interests" as the "central objective of social welfare and of social policy in general."[40] The influence of the family in "shaping character and ability," wrote Moynihan, "is so pervasive as to be easily overlooked. The family is the basic social unit of American life; it is the basic socializing unit. By and large, adult conduct in society is learned as a child."[41] By definition, children raised in female-headed families could not learn conduct appropriate to American life. "Ours is a society which presumes male leadership in private and public affairs," asserted Moynihan. "The arrangements of society facilitate such leadership and reward it. A subculture, such as that of the Negro American, in which this is not the pattern is placed at a distinct disadvantage."[42]

The current condition of black Americans resulted from a variety of forces. The unique brutality of American slavery, Moynihan argued, had destroyed family life among blacks and crippled black males, and trends after the Civil War had reinforced the assault on black masculinity. "The very essence of the male animal, from the bantam rooster to the four-star general, is to strut. Indeed, in 19th century America, a particular type of exaggerated male boastfulness became almost a national style. Not for the Negro male. The 'sassy nigger' was lynched."[43] The rapid transformation of American blacks from a rural to an urban population had accentuated the deterioration of black family life. When urbanization occurs "suddenly, drastically, in one or two generations," as it did among blacks, observed Moynihan, "the effect is immensely disruptive of traditional social patterns."[44]

Black male unemployment dramatically heightened the disorganizing impact of slavery's legacy and rapid urbanization. "The fundamental, overwhelming fact is that negro unemployment, with the exception of a few years during World War II and the Korean War, has continued at disaster levels for 35 years." Employment affected family patterns profoundly. During the periods when jobs for black men had been relatively plentiful, "the Negro family became stronger and more stable. As jobs became more and more difficult to find, the stability of the family became more and more difficult to maintain."[45] The American wage system added to the other factors eroding black family stability. Although it offers "relatively high incomes for individuals," it rarely insures "that family, as well as individual needs are met." Alone among industrial democracies, America fails to supplement workers' incomes with family allowances. Because black families have the largest number of children and the lowest incomes, "many Negro fathers literally cannot support their families. Because the father is either not present, is unemployed, or makes such a low wage, the Negro woman goes to work." This "dependence on the mother's income" further undermined the position of the father and deprived the children "of the kind of attention, particularly in school matters, which is now a standard feature of middle-class upbringing."[46] For Moynihan, therefore, male unemployment and underemployment remained key issues.

The result of these trends, as Moynihan saw it, was a self-perpetuating cycle of poverty, which he described provocatively as a "tangle of pathology."[47]

> In essence, the Negro community has been forced into a matriarchal structure which, because it is so out of line with the rest of American society, seriously retards the progress of the group as a whole, and imposes a crushing burden on the Negro male and, in consequence, on a great many Negro women as well.

Housing segregation worsened the situation because it prevented stable middle-class black families from escaping the "cultural influences of the unstable ones."[48] Besides matriarchy, the "tangle of pathology" revealed itself in "the failure of youth" (defined by poor school performance and low scores on standardized tests); delinquency and crime; the failure rate on the Armed Forces Qualification Test; and the alienation of black youths, reflected in staggering unemployment rates, "narcotic addiction," and isolation from white society. "The present generation of Negro youth," observed Moynihan, "growing up in the urban ghettos has probably less personal contact with the white world than any generation in the history of the Negro American."[49]

Only a program of national action could begin to undo the "tangle of pathology." Its object should be "to strengthen the Negro family so as to enable it to raise and support its members as do other families."[50] Moynihan purposefully omitted specific policy recommendations. His audience was the administration; he wanted to persuade the president and his advisors to mount a coordinated attack on the forces retarding the economic progress of black Americans. Clearly, this goal influenced his choice of language, his provocative metaphors, and the lack of balanced argument. As Rainwater and Yancey observe, an alternative approach to poor urban black families would concentrate on how "particular family patterns" help individuals adapt to deprivation and survive "in the one world in which they must live." From this point of view, some of the very behaviors that appear "pathological" assist families "to make as gratifying a life as possible in the ghetto milieu." Had he emphasized the positive aspects of black family patterns, Moynihan might have avoided some of the criticism—but probably would have received other criticisms.[51] Whether that criticism would have been as severe remains moot, for the report provoked a major debate on the black family in which Moynihan became the villain.

Major newspaper accounts omitted Moynihan's emphasis on unemployment as the great source of family disorganization. Scholarly commentators relied on newspaper accounts rather than on the original report, distorted Moynihan's arguments, and offered as their own alternatives views Moynihan either explicitly or implicitly shared.[52] Moynihan's report aroused passionate hostility because it intersected the second phase of the civil rights movement, which emphasized black pride and power. In this context, his thesis "deeply embarrassed" advocates of increased black political power, because his stress on social pathology contradicted claims of black achievement.[53]

The attacks on Moynihan highlight the swelling reaction against cultural explanations of poverty and other ideas that assumed passivity and disorganization among the poor.[54] Although Moynihan rarely used the word "culture," clear parallels exist between his report and early descriptions of the culture of poverty. Critics associated his argument with theories of cultural deprivation. Both Moynihan and culture of poverty theorists located the perpetuation of poverty in attitudes and behaviors transmitted from one generation to the next. Both stressed the origins of those behaviors in the legitimate frustration and alienation bred by blocked opportunities; and both used similar indicators to identify the "culture of poverty" or "tangle of pathology": a high proportion of female-headed families, unrestrained sexuality; an inability to defer gratification, and an apathetic withdrawal from social involvement.

Moynihan did not share Oscar Lewis's emphasis on the adaptive, strategic role of poverty culture. Nonetheless, a casual reading could easily lump both views together as attempts to use cultural explanations to reinforce sophisticated versions of the old idea that poverty resulted from individual behavior. To their critics, Lewis's families caught in the culture of poverty, Riessman's culturally deprived children, and Moynihan's black families all seemed mid-twentieth-century euphemisms for the undeserving poor. The ironic outcome of Moynihan's report, therefore, was to sweep the black family off the agenda of policy research and to hasten the culture of poverty's amputation from its liberal origins. The idea of such a culture, however, did not disappear. Instead, it became a conservative rationalization for cutting welfare.

## CULTURE AS A CONSERVATIVE IDEA

Even in the late 1950s and 1960s, liberal social scientists did not have a monopoly on cultural approaches to poverty. Among the more conservative writers who also developed cultural interpretations of dependence, the political scientist Edward Banfield was prominent. At the same time that Oscar Lewis first described Mexican villagers as trapped in a culture of poverty, Banfield used culture to explain the failure of economic development and modernization. Banfield did not share Lewis's belief that political mobilization could destroy the culture of poverty, and when he extended the fatalistic implications of his interpretation of a "backward society" to American cities, Banfield stressed the fu-

tility of liberal reform. Published shortly after the Moynihan
report, Banfield's book helped cement the association of culture
with conservatism. It foreshadowed the major themes in conservative writing about poverty and welfare during the next two
decades.

In 1958, Banfield published an account of the Southern Italian
village called Montegrano as *The Moral Basis of a Backward Society*.[55] In Montegrano he found a cultural pattern, which he
labeled "amoral familism," that inhibited corporate action and
perpetuated the miserable lives of its peasants. Banfield identified "amoral familism" as behavior consistent with a simple rule:
"Maximize the material, short-run advantage of the nuclear
family; assume that all others will do likewise."[56] Montegranesi
never joined together to sponsor projects such as the improvement of roads; the village had no voluntary charities; most residents said that no one was "particularly public-spirited"; there
was no "stable and effective [political] party organization; villagers remained reluctant to help one another; and friends were
"luxuries" they felt they could not affford. The example of Montegrano showed that "technical conditions and natural resources" did not inevitably result in the formation of economic
and political associations which sponsored development. Instead, the intervening force of culture caused people to live and
think in "ways . . . radically inconsistent with the requirements
or formal organization."[57]

Because their family-centered ethos prevented them from acting "concertedly or in the common good," better incomes, argued Banfield, would do little to "make the atmosphere of the
village less heavy with melancholy." Indeed, it would probably
worsen the situation, because without "accompanying changes
in social structure and culture, increasing incomes would probably bring with them increasing frustration."[58] By 1970, Banfield
had extended his pessimistic forecast for social and cultural
change to American cities.[59] Like the Montegranesi, the American urban lower class remained trapped by a culture that inhibited advancement and perpetuated pathology. Without

transgressing against democratic and constsitutional rights, government could do little to alter the situation. In fact, most of its well-meaning interventions had been ineffective or harmful.

Banfield belittled the then fashionable despair about American cities and argued that no urban crisis in fact existed. On most measures, conditions within cities had improved. Even the number and "relative disadvantage" of "the poor, the Negro, and others who stand outside the charmed circle" had decreased. As a result, "a great many so-called urban problems" were really conditions that we either "cannot eliminate or do not want to incur the disadvantage of eliminating."[60] One reason those conditions remained intractable was, as in Montegrano, their anchor in lower-class culture.

To Banfield, class exerted a major influence on "the city's form and the nature of its problems." To whatever source they traced class, he argued, all definitions stressed its expression in a "characteristic patterning that extends to all aspects of life: manners, consumption, child-rearing, sex, politics, or whatever." No agreement existed on the core principle that unified each cluster of traits. For his purposes, and from a policy standpoint, "the most promising principle seems to be that of psychological orientation toward the future."[61] Banfield located four classes in America: upper, middle, working, and lower. The distinction between the working and lower class played a pivotal role in his analysis, because he wanted to separate the poor into groups defined by their psychology and behavior. "The reader is asked to keep in mind," he wrote, "that members of a 'class' as the word is used here are people who share a 'distinct patterning of attitudes, values, and modes of behavior,' *not* people of like income, occupation, schooling, or status. A lower class individual is likely to be unskilled and poor, but it does not follow from this that persons who are unskilled and poor are likely to be lower class."[62]

Banfield defined the lower class person by his "time-horizon." (Note the use of the male pronoun. Banfield describes class behavior almost exclusively in male terms.):

The lower-class person lives from moment to moment, he is either unable or unwilling to take account of the future or to control his impulses. Improvidence and irresponsibility are direct consequences of this failure to take the future into account . . . and these consequences have further consequences: being improvident and irresponsible, he is likely also to be unskilled, to move frequently from one dead-end job to another, to be a poor husband and father.[63]

The lower-class person was also impulsive: "Bodily needs (especially for sex) and his taste for 'action' take precedence over anything else—and certainly over any work routine." With a "feeble, attenuated sense of self," suffering from "feelings of self-contempt and inadequacy," he remained "suspicious and hostile, aggressive yet dependent," lacking the ability to maintain a stable relationship with a mate, without attachment to community, neighbors, or friends, and with no interest in voluntary organizations or politics. Because the women who headed the characteristically female-headed lower-class households were usually impulsive and incompetent, boys drifted into gangs where they learned the "extraordinarily violent" style of lower-class life. Lower-class life, in fact, was not normal, and lower-class people emerged from Banfield's account as less than fully human: "In the chapters that follow, the term *normal* will be used to refer to class culture that is not lower class."

Banfield's interpretation of the origins of the lower class reflected a common version of American urban and ethnic history usually called the "last of the immigrants" thesis. The "*main* [emphasis in original] disadvantage" of the contemporary Negro, wrote Banfield, was "the same as the Puerto Rican's and Mexican's: namely, that he is the most recent unskilled, and hence relatively low-income, migrant to reach the city from a backward rural area." As with other immigrants, blacks had been attracted to cities by a "job, housing, school, and other opportunities." As poor as facilities in cities were, they were "better by far than any he had known before." Cities were "not the end of his journey but the start of it." Indeed, "Like other immigrants, the Negro has reason to expect that his children will have increases of opportunity even greater than his."[64]

Banfield did not deny the force of race prejudice, but he argued that its intensity and institutional embodiment had lessened. As a consequence, the problems facing contemporary blacks had more to do with class than race. Indeed, he expected that "under favorable conditions Negroes can be expected to close the gap between their levels of welfare and those of whites much faster than most people would probably imagine." He predicted that "the movement of the Negro up the class scale appears as inexorable as that of all other groups."[65]

Casting blacks as the last of the immigrants has important consequences for policy. It links their advancement to patience, not government intervention or special policies that favor them over others. Cities, Banfield argued, develop according to their own internal logic—determined by the three "imperatives" of rate of population growth, transportation technology, and distribution of income—which place "stringent limits on policy." Government interference might speed up or slow down the process of growth, but it cannot change it.[66] In fact, it often has made problems worse.

One of those problems Banfield wanted to clarify was poverty. He argued that urban poverty seldom originated in cities. Cities attracted poor people, and migrants imported poverty. Poverty, however, was a condition with "four degrees": destitution, want, hardship, and relative deprivation. No one within cities was destitute any longer. That is, no one lacked "income sufficient to assure physical survival and to prevent suffering from hunger, exposure, or remediable or preventable illness." Even the amount of want had nearly disappeared, and in only a few decades there would "almost certainly" be none.[67] The modern problem of poverty, therefore, had more to do with relative deprivation, with "income *level* [rather] than . . . income *distribution.*"[68] Even though the contemporary poor remained no more relatively deprived than their counterparts a decade before, they thought "the gap to be wider." This accentuation of discontent resulted largely from the well-meaning, though misguided, liberalism of the War on Poverty, which, by focusing on income differences, "probably engendered and strengthened feelings of relative deprivation."[69]

Banfield realized that absolute poverty still existed among the people once called "undeserving." Now, as he observed, new terms, "troubled," "culturally deprived," "hard to reach," "chronically," or "multiproblem", carried the same connotation. This poverty reflected both lack of money and the "extreme present-orientation" of the lower class. Beyond the boundary of the lower class, "poverty in the sense of hardship, want, or destitution" now generally resulted from "external circumstance— involuntary unemployment, prolonged illness, the death of a breadwinner, or some other misfortune." Among the lower class, however, its proximate cause was "ways of thinking and behaving that are, in the adult, if not elements built into personality, at least more or less deeply ingrained habits."[70]

All the problems of the lower class were in fact one problem: "the existence of an outlook and style of life which is radically present-oriented and which therefore attaches no value to work, sacrifice, self-improvement, or the service to family, friends, or community."[71] The Italian peasants of Montegrano at least showed a fierce loyalty to their immediate family. The American urban lower class lacked even this small, redeeming virtue.

Not surprisingly, therefore, none of the programs directed toward lower-class reformation in recent years succeeded; only policies unacceptable in a constitutional democracy (such as semi-institutional care, separation of children from parents, or preventive detention based on the statistical probability of criminal behavior) could even begin to eradicate it. In their absence, the lower class would replenish itself and continue to generate serious urban problems at a rate far exceeding its size.[72] Government, Banfield feared, would only exacerbate the problem, because its "growing multitude of programs" created an unstoppable "bureaucratic juggernaut" that had no effect on the reality of the problem. If the government needed a symbol for its policies, what was preferable "in every way" to a Freedom Budget or Marshall Plan was a "useless dome."[73]

Banfield's work revealed the conservative potential within cultural theories of poverty. Without Lewis's faith in the transforming power of political mobilization, the culture of poverty led neither to socialism nor to a liberal war on poverty. Instead, its logical outcome was the "benign neglect" advocated as a response to urban problems by Daniel Patrick Moynihan when he served in the Nixon administration.[74] In fact, Banfield's argument contained all the essential themes of the conservative attack on poverty and welfare launched in the 1980s: the "last of the immigrants" thesis as a description of American history; the gradual disappearance of physical want; the damage done to the poor by liberal government policy; and the preeminent role of culture and behavior in the perpetuation of misery. In the 1960s and early 1970s, these ideas conflicted with proud and militant independence movements that fought for civil rights and national liberation; in the cynical, conservative, and anxious 1980s, they rapidly gained favor.

# Poverty and the Politics of Liberation | TWO

In THE 1950s and 1960s, events challenged the image of poor people that then dominated American social science. In the same years that social scientists described them as passive, apathetic, and detached from politics, all over the world previously dependent people were asserting their right to liberation. Wars of independence attacked the vestiges of colonialism in Africa, Asia, and the Near East; guerrilla movements organized against dictatorships in Central and Latin America; in the United States, southern blacks mobilized to claim their civil rights. After 1965, northern blacks transformed their movement into a militant assertion of racial pride and demand for social and economic justice. And by the late 1970s a resurgent feminism had incorporated women's poverty into its own politics of liberation.

# THE CULTURE OF POVERTY: THEORETICAL WEAKNESSES

Theories of cultural poverty and deprivation or lower-class pathology offended the advocates of liberation. Despite the differences among individual writers and their protestations of liberal goodwill, American social scientists collectively seemed to sanction an image of poor people that denigrated their culture and personality, belittled their capacity for self-mobilization, and reinforced direct or indirect colonial rule. It offered them social work and therapy when they needed economic justice and political mobilization.[1] By the late 1960s and early 1970s, social scientists who supported independence movements in the Third World and civil rights, black power, and affirmative action in the United States had challenged culture of poverty theories. Their assaults took three main forms: political exposé; empirical refutation; and theoretical criticism.

The implicit politics of cultural theories disturbed many critics. Social scientists sympathetic to national liberation movements argued that, as an idea, the culture of poverty reinforced colonial domination and obscured the structural sources of exploitation. Randolf S. David, writing from the Philippines, claimed that culture of poverty researchers, "having decided that poverty has reduced people into a sub-species of the human race, proclaim the emergence of a unique and fascinating way of life associated with such extreme deprivation." With a prurient interest in the more lurid aspects of the lives of the urban poor, social scientists had become "well-equipped peeping toms." Despite their liberal good intentions, their "romantic interest" cast the condition of the poor "as an *unalterable* given which we can only cope with, adjust to, or build our whole life around."[2] To Alessio Colombis, Banfield's portrait of a Southern Italian village reflected the influence of the Cold War on American social science: "His thesis offers a pseudo-scientific cover justifying relations of exploitation and subjection resulting from the situations of domination and inequality that still exist

today."[3] Alejandro Portes identified the culture of poverty as
one of three major theories that portrayed Latin American slum
radicalism as irrational, a "simplistic emotional response to
irrational psychological needs." These theories attributed
the radicalism of the poor to their cultural backwardness: "Ex-
tremism permeates these groups to the extent that they are also
permeated by ignorance, social isolation, and irrational
aggressiveness."[4]

David, Colombis, and Portes each proposed an alternative
explanation. Portes's research on a Chilean slum showed the
poorest residents most active in neighborhood councils, and he
argued for the fundamental rationality of social conduct.[5] Colombis contended that Banfield neglected the constraints on villagers' behavior, misunderstood class structure, and ignored the
exercise of power. His interpretation stressed their "economic,
political, administrative, cultural and social subjection" and emphasized the importance of placing the local situation in context, which meant analyzing it within the framework of Italian
society.[6] David also urged the replacement of cultural explanations with structural analyses that linked the roots of poverty to
forces within the white society: Urban poverty "implies a relationship of dependence—a relationship which produces further
underdevelopment for the poor and continued development for
the affluent."[7]

Critics who focused on America offered similar objections.
Walter Miller underlined the political significance that conceptions of poverty had assumed in the charged atmosphere of the
1960s. Discussions of poverty touched most of the major domestic issues of the time: the urban crisis, welfare, the crisis in education, the black revolution, the white backlash, a culture of
violence, and crime in the streets. Unsuccessful attempts to
cope with these great domestic issues revealed a consistent conceptual failure in discourse about poverty and undercut attempts
to formulate a coherent national policy.[8] In one way or another,
most of the terms used to describe poor people stressed the behavioral and cultural aspects of poverty. As a result, according
to Chandler Davidson, researchers and advocates had "built a

one-sided case against an entire social class—the poor."
Whether they were aware of the fact or not, social scientists'
descriptions served the interests of the affluent and justified the
inequitable distribution of wealth and income.[9] Most writing
about American working-class people by sociologists, psycholo-
gists, and anthropologists, claimed Eleanor Leacock, contributed to a "picture of a people who, lacking family organization
and reared without consistent and close relations with adults
. . . are passive, have difficulty with abstract thinking and com-
munication, seek escape from problems through relatively un-
inhibited expressions of sex or aggression, lack ego strength and
are unable to plan for the future." This image supported programs that attempted to solve poverty-related problems within
the present socioeconomic structure by transforming workers
into "solid middle-class citizens."[10]

Political criticism of the culture of poverty often did not define
its target with precision. Instead, it abstracted a series of conservative implications (often from writers who considered themselves liberal) and identified them with a broad range of writing
in the social sciences. Some critics lumped Oscar Lewis, Michael Harrington, Frank Riessman, Daniel Moynihan, and Edward Banfield into one category.[11] Clearly, by the late 1960s, the
very act of writing about cultural aspects of poverty had assumed
political significance. By escalating the war on the culture of
poverty, militant social scientists enlisted as professionals in
some of the great international and domestic battles of their
time.

Many of the culture of poverty's professisonal critics chose to
fight more limited engagements. Instead of sweeping political
attacks, they attempted to disprove some aspect of the theory
with empirical research. The result was a raft of case studies.
For example, Leonard Davidson and David Krackhardt studied
a large manufacturing firm's special employment training program for poor blacks. They found that employees' behavior reflected "situational realities" rather than the personalities of
minority workers.[12] Frederick Jaffe and Steven Polgar lamented
the cooptation of the culture-of-poverty concept as an explana-

tion for slow progress in family planning programs. Using data
from American cities, they argued the opposite case: Accessibil-
ity, rather than culture and motivation, determined the success
of family planning programs.[13] Harland Padfield, who examined
an industrial training program for hard-core unemployed men
in San Diego, also asserted that his research results undermined
the culture of poverty thesis.[14]

Some of the most important empirical studies that tried to
chip away at one of the culture of poverty's major themes drew
on Hyman Rodman's influential notion of "value stretch", which
asserted that lower-class people, without abandoning the general
values of the society, developed an alternative set of values
which helped them adjust to their circumstances.[15]

Elliot Liebow's *Tally's Corner*, an ethnography of streetcorner
men in Washington, D.C., portrayed a "shadow system" of values that qualified Rodman's and others' concepts of "an alternative system of lower-class values" in two ways. First,
alternative or stretched values differed from the general system
of values because they are "derivative, subsidiary in nature, thin-
ner, and less weighty, less completely internalized." Second, its
users could not automatically invoke the alternative value system; instead, it was "a shadow cast by the common value system
in the distorting lower-class culture." Liebow explained the behavior of poor black men "as a direct response to the conditions
of lower-class Negro life rather than as mute compliance with
historical or cultural imperatives." The streetcorner man did not
carry an independent cultural tradition; rather, his behavior reflected his attempt to achieve many of the goals and values of
the larger society and his attempts to conceal his failure from
others and himself.[16]

Although other scholars added empirical evidence that contradicted the culture of poverty thesis by discovering indigenous
organizations and a capacity for political mobilization among
the very poor, their work shared the limitations common to most
case studies: their general applicability remained uncertain. Ingenious defenders could reinterpret their data, dismiss them as
exceptions, or incorporate them as subtle modifications within a

general pattern. By itself, the empirical evidence was too limited, fragmentary, and sparse to support either side in the controversy. Therefore, theoretical and methodological criticism became all the more important. Could the assumptions, logic, and procedures of the culture of poverty thesis withstand intense scrutiny? Critics said no.

Several arguments distinguished most theoretical and methodological criticism of the culture of poverty: [17]

1. Most discussions lack a satisfactory definition of culture and subculture. What does the culture of poverty mean by culture? Critics point to the absence of a uniform or consistent definition and argue that culture usually becomes a synonym for subculture, itself a slippery concept whose ambiguities culture of poverty theorists do not avoid. Of what is the subculture of poverty a subset? What are its boundaries? Does it evolve from a larger culture or arise as a reaction to it? Is there more than one subculture of poverty? Advocates of the culture of poverty, according to their critics, answer none of these questisons adequately.
2. The culture of poverty literature includes no uniform set of characteristics. Even more, the long lists of traits usually offered have an *ad hoc* quality. They do not separate indexes of material deprivation from behavior and personality, and they do not, by and large, identify the core characteristics that give shape and coherence to the whole.
3. Assumptions about the mechanisms perpetuating the culture of poverty are inadequate because they assume the primacy of socialization. In other words, families pass on the culture of poverty to children. A situational explanation is equally plausible: That is, each generation may re-create parallel subcultural patterns as it adapts to similar constraints. The policy implications of this issue are very important, for its resolution leads to social work and therapy or to politics and redistribution as the method for breaking up a culture of poverty.
4. Culture of poverty theories are tautologies. The pathological

behavior of poor people causes their poverty, which is the source of their pathological behavior. This lack of clearly specified independent and dependent variables leaves the reasoning circular. Most expositions of the culture of poverty, therefore, leave cause and effect hopelessly tangled.

5. The purpose of culture of poverty theories often remains ambiguous. Are they intended as descriptions of a subculture or as explanations? What exactly are they supposed to explain? Family patterns? The persistence of poverty? Political apathy? The answer is usually unclear, and theories become catchalls for a loosely associated set of behaviors and material conditions.

6. Links between subcultures, social institutions, and social structures remain unspecified. The culture of poverty, if it exists, does not float in a vacuum. How is it shaped by the distribution of power and resources? How is it affected by the political and institutional structure in which it is embedded? These are questions culture of poverty theorists usually do not pursue.

7. The boundaries between culture, class, and ethnicity remain vague in most writings. Is the culture of poverty synonymous with the lower class? Does it penetrate other classes? What distinguishes the definition of a class from the definition of a culture of poverty? Are some of the behaviors identified with the culture of poverty in fact attributes of ethnic groups? Are there distinct subcultures of poverty among different ethnic groups, or does ethnic variation in the behavior of very poor people contradict the idea of a culture of poverty?

8. The culture of poverty is an ethnocentric idea. It takes one set of standards—usually white, middle-class American—and applies them to the evaluation of other groups. In the process it defines differences as pathologies, thereby failing to appreciate their positive, adaptive significance and the validity and coherence of other cultures or subcultures.

9. Because it is based on instances of doubtful generalizability, culture of poverty theory rests on a weak evidential base. Its methodology therefore suffers from the limits inherent in all case studies.

10. Most culture of poverty research is static: It examines its

subjects at one point in time or throughout a period in which the structures that define and constrain their behavior do not alter. As a consequence, its assumptions about how poor people will react to a change in their circumstances rest on deductions, not evidence.

11. Most culture of poverty research focuses on families. It neglects careful examination of other contexts and social interactions. Instead it generalizes from domestic behavior to work, politics, and social organization.

Despite frequent weaknesses in their own arguments, critics of the culture of poverty raised fundamental questions. They did not, however—and many did not want to—discredit attempts to link culture and poverty. Rather, they showed weaknesses in existing formulations and pointed to questions left unanswered. Politics also shaped these debates about theories and methods, as the participants knew well. Those who believed that the unequal distribution of power and resources shaped and constrained the behavior of poor people wanted to redirect research and policy. For them, culture remained at best a tangent, interesting and in some vague way important, but a distraction; at worst, it justified the perpetuation of colonialism abroad and inequity at home. In the 1960s and early 1970s, the political climate favored the critics. Daniel Patrick Moynihan's report gave them the ammunition they needed. With an outraged civil rights movement behind them, the critics drove cultural questions out of poverty research for about fifteen years. However, sociologists and anthropologists concerned with poverty failed to replace culture as an organizing concept. As a consequence, their disciplines became marginal to the policymakers and scholars who led the emerging national debate. Instead, leadership in poverty research passed to the economists, whose capture of the issue remains scarcely challenged to this day.

# THE MOYNIHAN REPORT UNDER FIRE

Conventional ideological labels fail to capture the complex political response to Daniel Moynihan's report, *The Negro Family: The Case for National Action*. Moynihan, after all, identified himself with liberal causes, and he wanted to encourage the Johnson administration to devote more attention and resources to the problems of northern blacks. Although some of his critics believed his report would divert attention from the great structural forces afflicting blacks, organizational issues, as Rainwater and Yancey contend, shaped the response of others. Many of the critics on Moynihan's left, they point out, were themselves trying to modify the way government treated blacks and poor people. As much as Moynihan, they wanted to influence the president. Had the report suited their interests, these critics "would have swallowed their ideological distaste and used the report as an argument for their programs." The opposition of the Permanent Government (a loose synonym for the civil service, here officials concerned with welfare and labor), appeared conservative when contrasted with Moynihan's "subdued welfare socialism (or welfare capitalism, as you please)." Here, as with civil rights leaders, opposition stemmed "from organizational threats to their existence and tactical requirements" instead of ideology.[18]

Civil rights leaders applauded President Johnson's Howard University speech with its reference to "the breakdown of the Negro family structure," and they welcomed the idea of a national conference devoted to the needs of black Americans.[19] They became increasingly uneasy, however, as rumors about Moynihan's report and the conference circulated in Washington. Was it, in fact, to be a conference about the black family? Press commentary on the report, which had not been released, only fueled speculation. Then, in the summer of 1965, the Watts riot riveted attention on black ghettoes and signaled the end of one phase of the civil rights movement. Its exclusive focus on the legal foundations of discrimination had to end. A new generation challenged the movement's leaders and questioned both their goal of integration and their nonviolent tactics. Newspaper and magazine writers fueled anger among blacks by invoking Moynihan's report (still not released) as an explanation of the riot, which they attributed to the deterioration of the black family.

Civil rights leaders could not subscribe to an interpretation which substituted family pathology for unemployment, inadequate housing, poor schools, and police brutality. Nonetheless, the reactions of the leaders to Moynihan's thesis were not uniform. Younger, militant leaders were most critical. Floyd McKissick, CORE's new director, observed that Moynihan's report "assumed that middle-class American values are the correct ones for everyone in America." McKissick accused Moynihan of thinking that "everyone should have a family structure like his own," and of blaming individuals "when it's the damn system that needs changing."[20] Older leaders stressed the report's strengths as well as its dangers. In a speech on October 29, 1965, Martin Luther King, Jr., stressed the opportunity afforded by public awareness of problems with black family structure "to deal fully rather than haphazardly with the problem as a whole —to see it as a social catastrophe and meet it as other disasters are met with an adequacy of resources."[21]

Civil rights leaders increasingly distrusted the administration, which did not include them in the conference planning. In fact, the president threatened to leapfrog over civil rights leaders and take leadership of the movement himself.[22] Shaken and surprised by the Watts riot, increasingly concerned about the implications of the administration's activities, civil rights leaders began to attack the Moynihan Report and to try to redirect the forthcoming conference. The black family, they argued, should not even be on the agenda.

Clearly, this reaction to the family issue worried the administration. At the November planning conference, only one of eight agenda papers focused on the black family. One government official quipped that "he had been reliably informed that no such man as Daniel Patrick Moynihan existed"; and speakers attacked Moynihan (who responded vigorously). At the general conference in February, the black family did not appear on the agenda, and Moynihan's report did not appear in a bibliography that included fifteen references to Department of Labor documents.[23]

The Permanent Government's interests differed from those of the civil rights leaders. Moynihan's report threatened the reputation and influence of the welfare establishment, which emphasized improving existing programs. For Moynihan's not-so-hidden message was "that existing federal programs in labor and in welfare were inadequate to deal with the problems of the Urban Negro." The report also challenged the welfare establishment's approach to civil rights, which acquiesced in "subtle and blatant discrimination and inadequate labor and welfare services to Negroes." Welfare officials tried to obscure their complicity in discriminatory treatment by stressing their "color-blind" viewpoint; they called Moynihan's emphasis on color "reactionary rather than radical."[24] Government officials, unlike civil rights leaders, could not publicly denounce the report. They used other tactics. One was to circulate criticisms within government circles and to develop alternative statistics. Another was to turn to their contacts in universities. Government officials sent summaries of the report to faculty members and solicited critical replies, which they then used to reject the validity of the report. They also leaked accounts of the report to the press.[25]

It would be wrong to dismiss the controversy surrounding the Moynihan Report as simply ideological differences and organizational politics, for it raised substantive issues of great importance. One set of questions was empirical. Was Moynihan correct about the trends in the black family? He had tried to show an explosive growth in the proportion of black female-headed households, out-of-wedlock births, and teenage pregnancy. Elizabeth Herzog, chief of the Child Life Studies Branch, Division of Research, in the Children's Bureau countered that exaggerations had distorted much less alarming patterns revealed by the data. Black families, it is true, were about 2.5 times as likely as whites to be "fatherless," but the statistics did not reveal a rapid increase in those rates in recent years. After a gradual increase from 1949 (19 percent) to 1959 (24 percent), the rate remained relatively stationary at 23 percent in 1964. Therefore, contrary to Moynihan's claims, the statistics showed that "during the past twenty-five years there has been a gradual rise, preceded and followed by a plateau, but not an acute increase in the over-all proportion of broken homes among Negroes."[26]

The question, of course, was how to interpret a rise of 5 percentage points. To Herzog it was a minor increase, but as Moynihan later replied, it could also be construed as a 25 percent leap. Had the issue been unemployment, this would have been considered catastrophic. Other critics, such as William Ryan, argued that undercounting, racial biases in statistical reporting, the differential availability of birth control, and the limited options available to poor, black, pregnant young women so qualified official rates that the trends Moynihan reported could be fictitious. In any case, events soon would undermine arguments that Moynihan had misread the trends: If he had overstated what had happened in the recent past, he was sadly prescient about the future.

Nonetheless, as critics pointed out repeatedly, Moynihan's exclusive focus on black domestic pathology obscured the rise in female-headed families, divorce rates, and out-of-wedlock births among whites. Nor did he control for income. References to "the Negro family" casually glossed over the varieties of black families, and did not compare the incidence of female heads (or other indexes) among whites and blacks of comparable economic standing. Had he done so, critics argued, he would have discovered more similarities than differences. As it was, critics contended, Moynihan's report fueled an ideology that condemned black families in general and displaced blame for their problems from segregation, discrimination, and poverty to cultural pathology. Circumstances, in fact, dictated the critics' position on the important issue of relation between class and race. Critics on the Left argued in opposite ways when they attacked Moynihan and Oscar Lewis. Moynihan, they claimed, confounded class and race by failing to observe the similar family patterns of blacks and whites within the same social classes. Lewis, they asserted, had erred because he assumed universal cultural patterns within social classes, when in fact they varied by ethnicity.[27]

Curiously, critics neglected a slightly different empirical problem. Moynihan showed that trends in unemployment rates and AFDC cases had diverged after 1962. Although nonwhite male unemployment had declined, the number of new AFDC cases had increased. Moynihan assumed this showed the emergence of a self-perpetuating tangle of pathology: "The steady expansion of this welfare program, as of public assistance programs in general, can be taken as a measure of the steady disintegration of the Negro family structure over the past generation in the United States." The relation, however, was far more complex. Until recently, the number of AFDC cases did not reflect the size of the population eligible for assistance. In the late 1950s and early 1960s, in fact, only a relatively small proportion of eligible families received AFDC. During the years about which Moynihan wrote, advocates of welfare rights led a campaign to extend public assistance to eligible families and to broaden eligibility requirements. As a consequence, the proportion receiving AFDC began to increase dramatically. Moynihan did not consider the extent to which the rising number of cases opened reflected an extension of AFDC to previously eligible families. In fact, though, changing rates of use and eligibility standards undercut any attempt to use AFDC rates as an index of increased family disintegration.[28]

Moynihan's report also raised normative issues. It assumed but by no means proved that the matriarchal family structure and the absence of a father were "pathological." As Herbert Gans pointed out, sociologists had demonstrated an extended and surprisingly stable kinship system of mothers, grandmothers, aunts, and other female relatives among blacks. Many women who headed families, moreover, raised boys who adapted successfully and contracted stable marriages. Indeed, a family headed by a "capable if unmarried mother" could provide a healthier environment than "a two-parent family in which the father is a marginal appendage." Nor should out-of-wedlock births among blacks be evaluated in the same way as among whites, because they carried different meanings for the different populations.[29]

Both Moynihan and most of his critics assumed that black families increasingly were female-headed by choice. Moynihan wanted to find ways to break up a matriarchal culture; critics asserted its validity and strength. Few, however, asked, as did Christopher Jencks, whether in fact "the families in question are matriarchal by necessity or by choice." Jencks could find little evidence that poor blacks preferred matriarchal families; on the contrary, "there is considerable reason to suppose that they eagerly adopted the more patriarchal middle-class norm whenever they can."[30]

In her influential study *All Our Kin*, anthropologist Carol Stack developed the most influential alternative view of poor black families. Moynihan, she wrote, like most other social scientists, remained trapped within conventional definitions of family that failed to capture the domestic experience of poor black Americans. Stack's ethnographic study of families supported by welfare found "extensive networks of kin and friends supporting, reinforcing one another—devising schemes for self-help, strategies for survival in a community of severe economic deprivation." As she studied these kin networks, Stack argued for the inadequacy of the conventional definition of a family as the husband, wife, and their offspring. She defined family "as the smallest, organized durable network of kin and non-kin who interact daily, providing domestic needs of children and assuring their survival." In this sense, families extended across "several kin-based households." Her definition, Stack asserted, made possible the identification of supportive kin networks and offered insight into how the people she studied actually "describe and order the world in which they live." Indeed, her study of kin

networks convinced Stack not of the weakness or pathology of
black families supported by AFDC, but rather of "the stability
and collective power of family life."[31]

Controversy also swirled around the sources of the trends
identified by Moynihan. Critics argued that he had substituted
the effect of matriarchal culture for unemployment, discrimination, and racism. Benjamin Payton, director of the Office of
Church and Race of the Protestant Council of the City of New
York, wrote that Moynihan's greatest error was his "analysis of
the Negro family as 'the fundamental source of the weakness of
the Negro community at the present time.' " Payton located the
root of the problem in urbanization, "its conflicts, inadequate
resources and injustices."[32] One reason critics blamed Moynihan for neglecting unemployment and related structural sources
of black problems resulted from early press reports. These, based
on leaks from officials and summaries of the report, highlighted
the stress on family pathology and ignored its analysis of the
social forces underlying the trends in black domestic life. In fact,
Moynihan agreed with his critics' stress on unemployment, but
his rhetorical emphasis on family structure, combined with the
unavailability of the actual text, obscured any potential consensus. As a result, much of the public debate surrounding the
report reflected not what it said, but what people thought it said.

Within the next several years, historians undermined Moynihan's reliance on the legacy of slavery as a partial explanation of
the so-called matriarchal structure of black families. (More recently, Jacqueline Jones's superb history of work and family
among black women has shown how inappropriate the term
"matriarchy" is as a designation for their role.) In the process,
they also demolished the "last of the immigrants" thesis as a basis
for interpreting modern black urban history. Slavery did not
destroy blacks' sense of family. To the contrary, slaves made
heroic efforts to preserve family ties; during Reconstruction,
freedmen traveled to find mates from whom they had been separated by slaveowners, and thousands greeted the opportunity
for legal marriage, denied under slavery, by solemnizing long-
standing relationships. Herbert Gutman showed a high propor-

tion of two-parent families among blacks in the post–Civil War South and in early-twentieth-century cities. Theodore Hershberg and his associates demonstrated parallel structures among black and white families of similar wealth in late nineteenth-century Philadelphia. They traced increasing rates of female-headed black families to the early death of black men forced into unhealthy and dangerous work and to the inability of poor black women to remarry.

Conditions within the cities to which they had migrated, not slavery, strained blacks' ability to retain two-parent families. Within those cities, blacks faced circumstances that differed fundamentally from those found earlier by European immigrants. They entered cities in large numbers as unskilled and semiskilled manufacturing jobs were leaving, not growing. The discrimination they encountered kept them out of the manufacturing jobs into which earlier immigrants had been recruited. One important goal of public schools had been the assimilation and "Americanization" of immigrant children; by contrast, they excluded and segregated blacks. Racism enforced housing segregation, and residential concentration among blacks increased at the same time it lessened among immigrants and their children. Political machines had embraced earlier immigrants and incorporated them into the system of "city trenches" by which American cities were governed; they excluded blacks from effective political power until cities had been so abandoned by industry and deserted by whites that resistance to black political participation no longer mattered.

All the processes that had opened opportunities for immigrants and their children broke down for blacks; their situation differed in every important way. By itself, public policy could not relax and assume that time would work for blacks as it had for immigrants. The last of the immigrants joined the legacy of slavery as another myth that had diverted attention from the origins of black poverty and excused the inaction of government.[33] The intellectual politics of liberation, however, were not solely negative. They did more than drive cultural explanations of poverty and black families off the research agenda of social

science. They also offered alternate explanations for ghetto poverty in the United States and mass poverty in the Third World.

## THE GHETTO AS COLONY

"Whether one is talking about the fantastic changes taking place
in Africa, Asia or the black communities of America," wrote
Stokely Carmichael and Charles Hamilton in 1967, "it is necessary to realize that the current, turbulent period in history is
characterized by the demands of previously oppressed people to
be free of their oppression."[34] The modern black American
struggle against oppression began in the South in the 1950s and
swiftly escalated into a national movement for civil rights. Its
first targets were the legal bases of discrimination: segregation in
public facilities, schools, and housing, and barriers to voting.
With the passage of the Civil Rights Act in 1964 and the Voting
Rights Act a year later, the civil rights movement reached its first
goals. For the first time in American history, the federal government committed itself to extending the full rights of citizens to
all black Americans.

The historic achievements of the civil rights movement did
not end discrimination or racism. Southern states mounted massive resistance to school integration; northern cities balked at
busing students to reduce racial imbalance; whites fled to suburbs, whose exclusionary zoning ensured that all but a handful
of affluent blacks would remain outside their boundaries; and,
in myriad ways, the institutional racism of the world of work
checked black occupational progress. Nonetheless, in every area
formal racial barriers crumbled before the most dramatic and
successful social movement in American history. Still, the civil
rights movement could not rest content with its magnificent
achievements. For its participants knew that racism continued
to infect America's institutions and, especially in cities, that
growing numbers of blacks lived in terrible poverty whose roots
lay in racism and exploitation.[35]

After 1964, events accelerated the transformation of the civil rights movement into a struggle against the poverty and exploitation of northern ghettoes. One catalytic event, the great Watts riot of 1965, followed by ghetto revolts in cities around the country, impelled civil rights leaders as well as politicians to reassess their strategies. Militant young blacks rejected the emphasis on integration and nonviolence at the core of the civil rights campaigns. As they argued that older civil rights leaders had ignored the forces that sustained the systematic oppression of blacks, they drew support from the young, poor blacks in northern ghettos and, as a consequence, shifted the social base of the black liberation movement away from its earlier anchor in an alliance between middle-class blacks and liberal whites. The "most significant indication of the middle class nature of the civil rights movement," wrote one militant black scholar in 1969, "was the fact that it did absolutely nothing to alleviate the grim plight of the poorest segments of the black population." The black rioters of the 1960s, he argued, "were vigorously repudiating the civil rights Negro leaders" and calling for new leadership willing to confront the problems arising from "oppression and powerlessness" and capable of speaking to the needs of the black masses.[36]

Stung by the urban uprisings, aware of the limits of integration as a strategy, challenged by new contenders for power, older civil rights leaders began to refocus their attention on urban poverty. Although they retained their commitment to integration and nonviolence, they too helped transform the black struggle into a quest for economic justice and political power. This new phase of the black liberation struggle had three overlapping components. Established civil rights leaders advocated economic redistribution, job creation, and housing reform. A new and militant Black Power movement asserted American blacks' kinship with anticolonial struggles around the world, rejected integration as a goal, and hoped to restructure American social and economic institutions. Black economists debated the source of ghetto underdevelopment and poverty, the accuracy of colonial analogies, and strategies for economic development.

In 1967, Martin Luther King, Jr., summed up a decade's

achievements and outlined the tasks that remained. "In assault after assault," he said, "we caused the sagging walls of segregation to come tumbling down. During this era the entire edifice of segregation was profoundly shaken. . . . today, Civil Rights is a dominating issue in every state, crowding the pages of the press and the daily conversation of white Americans." Nonetheless, he stressed, "the deep rumbling of discontent in our cities is indicative of the fact that the plant of freedom had grown only a bud and not yet a flower."[37] Blacks, King pointed out, still lived "in the basement of the Great Society." Half of them lived in substandard housing; they had half the income of whites; twice as many were unemployed; their infant mortality rate was double that of whites; and twice as many blacks were "dying in Vietnam as whites in proportion to their size in the population." Blacks, as a consequence, faced a set of difficult and interrelated tasks. First was to "massively assert our dignity and worth." Another was "to discover how to organize our strength in terms of economic and political power." A third was the development of a program to "drive the nation to a guaranteed annual income." Black poverty had nothing to do with "want of industrious habits and moral fiber"; rather, "dislocations in the market operations of our economy and the prevalence of discrimination thrust people into idleness and bind them in constant or frequent unemployment against their will." The task was clear: "We must create full employment or we must create incomes." Joining his call for economic justice to his increasing criticism of the Vietnam War, King argued that if the nation can spend "35 billion dollars a year to fight an unjust, evil war in Vietnam, and 20 billion dollars to put a man on the moon, it can spend billions of dollars to put God's children on their own two feet right here on earth."[38]

King linked the struggles of black Americans to movements against colonialism throughout the world. "The deep rumbling of discontent that we hear today," he wrote, "is the thunder of disinherited masses, rising from dungeons of oppression to the bright hills of freedom. . . . All over the word like a fever, freedom is spreading in the widest liberation movement in history." As in America, freedom required not only political rights but economic justice. "Like a monstrous octopus," poverty stretched "its choking, prehensile tentacles into lands and villages all over the world. . . . The time has come for an all-out world war against poverty." [39]

Still, King retained his commitment to nonviolence and criticized urban riots: "At best, the riots have produced a little additional anti-poverty money allotted by frightened government officials, and a few water-sprinklers to cool the children of the ghettos. It is something like improving the food in prison while the people remain securely incarcerated behind bars." In no instance had riots gained any concrete improvement. No violent revolution would find sympathy and support from either the white or the majority of the black population, and "romantic illusions and empty philosophical debates about freedom" distracted energy from a tactical strategy for change. Here, as in his commitment to integration, King challenged the new, militant philosophy of liberation, Black Power. [40]

In the summer of 1966, three leading civil rights organizations —SCLC, CORE, and SNCC—jointly sponsored a civil rights march in Mississippi. On June 17, state troopers in Greenwood ordered marchers not to pitch their tents on the grounds of a black high school. When one of SNCC's leaders, Stokely Carmichael, defied their order, the police arrested him. Released from jail only minutes before a major rally, Carmichael told an angry, militant crowd: "The only way we gonna stop them white men from whuppin' us is to take over. We been saying freedom for six years and we ain't got nothin'. What we gonna start saying now is Black Power!" His cry, writes Jack Bloom in his study of the civil rights movement, reflected "the experience and disillusionment of the civil rights workers in the South, but it was fueled by the ghetto uprisings [which started in Harlem in 1964]." By calling for "social transformation," Carmichael and other Black Power advocates rejected both the strategies and analyses of the old civil rights coalition. One result was a new explanation for the poverty of black America: The colonialism of white America had trapped blacks in an ever-worsening poverty from which militant solidarity offered the only escape. [41]

Others had used the colonial analogy earlier, but the advocates of Black Power transformed it into the basis of a national
movement.[42] Black Americans, wrote Carmichael and Hamilton, formed "a colony, and it is not in the interest of the colonial
power to liberate them." Although blacks were legal citizens,
they stood as "colonial subjects in relation to the white society."
Colonialism, they argued, operated in three areas: political, economic, and social. Like other colonial masters, whites made the
key political decisions that affected blacks' lives and governed
them through indirect rule by coopting selected blacks to administer their decisions. As in other colonial situations, the colony
existed "for the sole purpose of enriching, in one form or another, the 'colonizer.' " Outside "exploiters" entered the ghetto,
bled "it dry," and left it "economically dependent on the larger
society." As a result, the economic depression of black communities worsened. Here, then, was the source of black poverty.[43]

In the rhetoric of Black Power, the colonial analogy became a
brilliant and powerful strategy for galvanizing blacks into a militant national movement. As an explanation of poverty, it broke
radically with liberal discourse, whether expressed as the culture
of poverty, the residue of discrimination, or the lack of human
capital. But was it correct? Was Black America truly a colony?
Could its persistent and deepening poverty be explained by the
dependency theory with which radical scholars of the Third
World had begun to challenge mainstream theories of economic
development? These questions animated a vibrant debate among
black social scientists and the few white colleagues who shared
their concerns.

The colonial analogy rejected the core premise of conventional development economics: the benefits of economic growth.
Critical scholars argued that wealth created by economic growth
did not automatically trickle down from rich to poor. In Third
World countries, poverty had spread even as economies mod-
ernized and grew. Without changes in political control, the benefits of growth always failed to reach those most in need. In fact,
growth had widened the gap between rich and poor. Nor did
conventional economic theories explain the economic failure of

black ghettos. American economic growth had not decreased poverty among blacks. Indeed, black unemployment remained high even during a period of economic expansion. Similarly, explanations of black poverty that stressed only the role of discrimination or the low educational achivement of blacks overlooked some uncomfortable facts. The passage of civil rights legislation had not ended ghetto poverty, and blacks achieved far less than whites with comparable educations.[44]

As they applied the colonial model to America, black scholars drew especially on dependency theory as developed by Andre Gunder Frank and other Third World economists. In a series of Latin American case studies, Frank illustrated his theory that conventional analyses of development and underdevelopment ignored the "economic and other relations between the metropolis and its economic colonies throughout the history of the world-wide expansion and development of the mercantilist and capitalist system." The expansion of the capitalist system had "effectively and entirely penetrated even the apparently most isolated sectors of the underdeveloped world." One result was relations of dependence that prevented development and fostered growth inequality and poverty. Ron Bailey argued that Tanzanian economist Justinian Ryeyemamu's definition of dependence could be applied to the status of Africans in the United States. Dependence meant that economic development and expansion in metropolitan economies retarded growth among peripheral economies. Dominant nations used their power to monopolize markets and transfer surplus wealth from dependent nations to themselves, just as powerful white economic interests extracted and appropriated surplus wealth from black ghettoes.[45]

Particularly through the work of Baran and Sweezy on monopoly capital, Marxism also influenced colonial models of ghetto economic development, although black scholars criticized conventional Marxist analyses for their lack of attention to race. The history of capitalist development, contended Baran and Sweezy, confirmed again and again that "capitalism everywhere generates wealth at one pole and poverty at the other." This was "a law of capitalist development . . . equally applicable

to the most advanced metropolis and the most backward colony." Within capitalist economies, they stressed, poverty always
remained rooted in unemployment and underemployment, or
the industrial reserve army, which in America concentrated in
"the decaying centers of the big cities. . . ."[46]

Applied to America, the colonial model was straightforward:
Ghettoes export their unskilled labor and import consumer
goods. Most capital within them remains in the hands of outsiders who control local businesses and export their profits. Unable to import capital, ghettoes neither produce the material
needed for their own subsistence nor accumulate the capital
essential to development. Blacks who work outside the ghetto
bring back wages too low to offset the drain of their energy and
resources. The result is exploitation and dependency, or what
some called "domestic colonialism." Wilfred David summarized
the model clearly:

> Unskilled labor is the basic productive resource of the ghetto,
> which is "exported" to the outside economy. Consumer goods
> and services are largely "imported" from outside, and with a few
> exceptions, the ghetto is unable to produce its needed materials.
> Further, it is difficult to import capital into the ghetto for use by
> its residents, and where such capital is employed it is largely "for-
> eign-owned." Thus, wealth is extracted by "outsiders" as profits
> from the sale of consumer goods and returns to invested capital.
> The outward flow of cash is partially offset by the wages of "ex-
> ported" labor, but the result is that no net financial accumulation
> takes place within the ghetto. This creates a situation of depen-
> dency. Much as a colony is dependent on its "mother country,"
> so too is the ghetto dependent on the larger society for most of its
> material needs.[47]

Poverty among American blacks, writers pointed out, had special features. The economic forces generating black poverty,
claimed Frank Davis, differ from those that create white poverty. Demand for black labor, he argued, did not increase when
discrimination lessened; in both boom and depression, unem-

ployment rates remained high among unskilled ghetto laborers. Indeed, technological change had rendered black unskilled workers "redundant." Demand for their labor in high-paying industry would decrease, thereby perpetuating low wages and poverty in the black ghetto. Urbanization as well as automation had worsened their situation. In subsistence economies, agricultural economist Frank Parsons pointed out, agriculture provided one "refuge for the poor—for all the people who can't find anything else to do." But in the United States—especially for blacks driven from the land by the mechanization of southern agriculture—refuge in a subsistence economy ceased to be "a feasible (or acceptable) alternative." The intersection of race with a dual labor market also sustained black poverty. According to Wilfred David, black workers face a dual labor market, with primary-sector jobs reserved for whites and blacks relegated to a secondary or "low-paying low-status jobs." This arrangement protects workers in the primary sector from layoffs due to business cycles. And because secondary-sector jobs offer almost no opportunity for advancement, the dual labor market reinforces the subordinate position of the ghetto worker.[48]

Colonial powers always confront the problem of control; they must discover how to prevent protest and rebellion. Writers advocating the colonial analogy contended that America had two strategies: One was to distribute back to the ghetto a small part of the surplus extracted from its residents. The major examples were welfare and Great Society programs. One critic labeled Model Cities programs "liberal pacifiers." The other strategy was tokenism, or the selective promotion of a few blacks to positions of influence within ghetto communities. As with colonies elsewhere, internal imperialists chose when possible to govern through indirect rule. Within ghettos, according to William Tabb, "acculturated natives" acted as "middlemen between other natives and the colonist businessmen who . . . reside 'abroad.' " Not only did they serve the colonial power, they also exemplified the rewards of "working hard within the system." Indeed, tokenism's true purpose, according to Baran and Sweezy, was securing the loyalty of the black bourgeoisie: "If

this loyalty can be made secure, the potential revolutionizing of
the Negro protest movement can be forestalled and the world be
given palpable evidence—through the placement of loyal Negroes in prominent positions—that the United States does not
pursue a South African policy of *apartheid* but on the contrary
fights against it and strives for equal opportunity for its Negro
citizens."[49]

Although critics of the colonial analogy often argued that true
colonies formed geographically separate states, most black scholars rejected strict geographic separation as irrelevant. "The concentration made of a given population on a single land area,"
claimed Ralph H. Metcalf, Jr., only made colonization "more
convenient as a result of centralization." But an oppressive
country could colonize its oppressed population by exploiting
them "economically, politically, and militarily, with almost the
same machinery it would use with a centralized population."
Although not a national political unit, wrote Wilfred David, the
black ghetto exists "as a geographical, economic, and social unit
within its own unique psycho-pathology. . . . The black ghetto
is an economic entity covered by a glacier of poverty."[50]

Not a colony in a conventional sense, black America formed
a new type of settlement, which writers labeled an internal colony. African Americans, they explained, had lived as colonized
people before the development of urban ghettos. Indeed, from
its inception, their colonization ran as a bitter stream through
American history. To J. H. O'Dell, the American Revolution
had been incomplete because it left slavery intact. Capitalist
institutions and racist psychology had developed within a colonial framework that continued to constrain American blacks.
For Wilfred Davis, blacks' contemporary status also derived from
their history in America. Study of the black ghetto, therefore,
became "in essence a study of *de facto* slavery, i.e., the black
ghetto economy is a *de facto* slave economy." (The argument
that internal colonialism represented the legacy of slavery, of
course, reflected the legacy of slavery argument that some black
scholars and liberal whites angrily rejected when Moynihan and
others applied it to black culture and family life.)[51]

Black settlement and migration patterns, argued Ron Bailey, also reflected their colonial status. Like other colonial populations, they usually concentrated in areas where their labor was most needed: the antebellum rural South; late nineteenth-century industrializing southern cities; and twentieth-century Northern manufacturing cities badly in need of semi- and unskilled labor. Now, however, automation and deindustrialization had left American blacks concentrated in urban ghettos with no vital economic function. Like other African states, American blacks now formed a colony no longer really needed by its colonizers. They were what some writers called a "neocolony." ("Neocolonialism" is a term coined by Kwame Nkrumah, who used it to refer to the way in which imperialist powers switch tactics—that is, substitute foreign aid and other indirect measures for repression as a means to "perpetuate colonialism while at the same time talking about 'freedom.' "[52])

Exploitation was the central and most controversial concept in theories of black colonialism. Based on Marxist definitions of surplus value, exploitation referred to the use of blacks to produce wealth of which they received only a small, inadequate share. "The rate of exploitation," explained Ron Bailey, "is the ratio of surplus value to wages." All capitalists tried to increase their share of workers' daily production. "When the share going to the worker is decreased, the rate of exploitation increases." Although capitalism meant the exploitation of all workers, some suffered more than others. The question was the basis of differential exploitation, or, as Donald Harris asked it, "whether there is a systematic pattern of under-payment of black labor relative to whites *for the same task, same level of skill, and same level of productivity*." Black proponents of internal colonization answered, resoundingly, yes. Indeed, Bailey claimed that only the concept of "super-exploitation" could describe the labor market situation of American blacks throughout their history. Blacks had been barred from many jobs, relegated to the "least skilled, lowest occupational categories," and paid less than whites with similar education and training for comparable work. Almost everywhere, they remained the last hired and first fired. The result of these "mechanisms, once by law and now more by custom," was black super-exploitation and impoverishment.[53]

Not all black economists agreed. Thomas Sowell, for one, traced black disadvantages to discrimination rather than exploitation. Because of discrimination, argued Sowell, a black man "born with the native ability to be a chemist and earn $20,000 a year" easily could find himself a "ditch-digger making $3,000 a year." He would be "worse off than if he were in fact exploited," and policies directed toward raising his wages as a ditchdigger only would worsen his situation. For the net result likely would be that machines would replace ditchdiggers, thereby reducing his already meager income. Nor were black people robbed of very much by white America: "The real problem is that deliberate discrimination, unconscious racism and general neglect have left black people too poor to be robbed of anything that would make a difference on a national scale." For Sowell the source of oppression was not the conjunction of capitalism and racism. "Whenever one group oppresses another, it almost invariably does so by denying them opportunities for self-realization, *not* by allowing them to develop their potential and then taking away what they have produced." The answer to black poverty, therefore, lay in the hard task of developing their own human capital.[54]

Nor did all radical black scholars accept the colonial analogy. Joseph Seward, who taught for seven years in Ghana, argued that the analogy usefully aroused American blacks to "our kinship to our African and Caribbean brothers-in-oppression." Nonetheless, it was wrong on several counts, for it failed to point out that whereas African and Caribbean neocolonies could break with monopoly capitalism if they chose to, American blacks could not. Seward worried that the internal colonial analogy would end up another source of black oppression because of its increasing acceptance in "liberal ruling class thinking." One trick of the ruling class, he argued, was the use of the colonial analogy to promote black capitalism; that is, the capitalist development of ghettoes by blacks themselves. Black capitalism, he predicted, would only transfer resentment of Jewish landlords and merchants to the black middle class. "Black capitalism, if it ever gets off the ground, can be expected to make black workers and slumdwellers even more anti-black bourgeoisie." American monopoly capitalism had made black people poor, and "black capitalism isn't going to change that."[55]

Like Seward, though with very different politics, Sowell rejected black capitalism as an answer to ghetto poverty. "Capital," he pointed out, "is the most fluid of resources." It flows wherever profits are highest, and it had avoided the ghetto because businesses there had "on the whole done poorly," as had "the community banks which . . . financed them." Black capitalism, with its emphasis on artifically supported markets, was a new form of mercantilism, which had been discredited historically as a strategy of economic development. In Europe and America, generations had elapsed before "repeated disasters" finally led to the abandonment of mercantile policies, but black people could not afford to repeat the same process.[56]

Unlike Sowell, advocates of the colonial analogy did not rely on markets freed from discrimination for black economic advancement. Instead they rejected liberal individualism. By focusing on individuals and individual initiatives, Frank Davis argued, the ideology of free enterprise neglected the group oppression of black people, which called for collective action. "The problem in America," wrote Guy C. Z. Mhone, "is simply that opportunities for blacks are only open to them on an individual level." Any efforts to enhance "the group upward mobility of black people only results in a redefinition of status such that blacks will remain at the bottom."[57]

Above all, blacks needed power, and power rested on institutional control. The solution to black poverty therefore depended on blacks' seizing control over the institutions that dominated their lives. Academic analysts of internal colonialism and champions of black power (the line between the two was often blurred) reached the same conclusion. As James Turner wrote: Any serious attempt at liberation required "a plan to create political cadres" dedicated to organizing black people in the great metropolitan areas and developing strong, independent political

organizations directed toward capturing control of all the institutions that touched their lives and livelihoods. Even liberal
white remedies for black poverty, claimed economist Charles
Sackrey, failed to advocate changing the distribution of power."
Whites would still own and control the productive equipment of
the economy, even in areas . . . predominantly black; whites
would also continue to make most of the laws, would still run
the schools, the cities, and the counties."[58]

By the late 1970s, debates about the ghetto as colony, like the
black power movement with which they were so intimately connected, had faded. Neither the literature of internal colonialism
nor black power left a strong institutional legacy or influenced
mainstream American economic and political thought. Alone
among major scholars in the 1980s, Ira Katznelson showed how
internal colonialism helps account for the object and form of
ghetto conflict in the 1960s.[59]

Internal colonialism's brief prominence was nonetheless a significant moment in American discourse about poverty, because
it offered the only major alternative to the liberalism of the time.
As we will see, even liberal approaches that avoided the culture
of poverty concentrated on microeconomic issues: how to get
people off welfare, how to train the unemployed, how to prevent
children from failing in school. They avoided the macroeconomic questions posed in the literature of internal colonialism: Why does America generate so much poverty? How does
poverty relate to the dynamics of capitalism? Is American poverty linked to the world economy? Do the same mechanisms
perpetuate poverty among American blacks and among people
of color in the Third World?

Whether or not theorists of internal colonialism offered correct answers, these remain questions of profound importance.
Their neglect has impoverished American discourse on poverty.
What accounts for the lack of attention they have received? Why
did internal colonialism never enter the mainstream of American debates about poverty? The easy answer is the quality of the
literature. By and large, it lacked the polish found in major academic journals, nor did it use the advanced econometric tech-

niques that began to dominate poverty research in the 1960s. In method as well as theory, its advocates remained outside the prevailing research tradition. Still, they formulated critical questions, and their work bristled with insights unavailable elsewhere. They might have laid the foundation for a generation of rigorous empirical, theoretical, and historical research. Their work led to an intellectual open road, not a dead end. But they suffered fatally from their association with black power and Marxism. Because black power seemed to sanction violence, outside black academic circles it faded quickly as a respectable, debatable political alternative. Nor, despite the emergence of an extraordinarily gifted group of radical economists, did most economists modulate their hostility to Marxist theory or expand the questions that underlay their research. The colonial analogy raised issues of class and power usually avoided by American social science, including the new branch of research on poverty, and its advocates lacked the cultural authority to force these issues onto the agenda of academic liberalism.[60]

At the same time, public policy deflected the potential power of the colonial analogy. Community action, as Katznelson argues in *City Trenches*, was in part a mimetic response to demands for black power. Its limited devolution of authority absorbed the energy of local leaders, bred factions within neighborhoods, and linked militants to the state. Civil rights laws and affirmative action also weakened the colonial analogy by opening jobs and neighborhoods. Individual mobility, as so often before in American history, undercut group solidarity. The theory of internal colonialism lost its institutional and social base. With its intellectual legitimacy also eroded, it became another missed opportunity to break through the barriers that have channeled American discussions of poverty and wealth in its narrow course.[61]

## WOMEN AND POVERTY

The modern feminist movement emerged in the late 1960s. Like the civil rights movement that nurtured it, in its first decade modern feminism concentrated on discrimination and the denial of rights and opportunities to women, and the concerns of primarily white, highly educated, and affluent women. In the late 1970s, the movement began to consider the problems of working-class women and women of color. One result was the discovery of women's poverty and the appearance of "the feminization of poverty" as a feminist issue. Feminist writers not only documented the increasingly female component of poverty, but developed explanations for women's persistent poverty. Through its association with feminism, as well as through its role in civil rights and the struggles against colonial domination, poverty became an issue in the politics of liberation. By the 1980s many writers had described the extent of poverty among women, but the use to which they put the alarming statistics varied. Some incorporated them into a comprehensive analysis of poverty intended to stimulate a broad array of public programs; others integrated poverty into a feminist agenda; and one major public figure drew on the statistics of women's poverty to reassert his alarm at their implications for family stability and the precarious state of what feminists would call patriarchy.

Women always have borne more than their share of poverty. Except for major depressions when vast numbers of men found themselves suddenly out of work, basic themes in the feminization of poverty could be applied to almost any period in the modern history of Western societies. Consider the situation of women in early and mid-nineteenth-century America. Most women lived on farms, where their labor was essential to the family's economy. Some supplemented farm income with the household manufacture of clothing and other articles, but the value of household manufacture declined steeply in the first decades of the nineteenth century.[62] Almost none worked for wages after they had married. Before marriage, most employed women were domestic servants; others worked in mills; a smaller number taught school; many labored as seamstresses; others were prostitutes. All these occupations paid very little. After marriage, women supplemented family income in various ways: by helping their artisan or shopkeeper husbands, taking in boarders, or sewing and washing at home.[63] They depended on their husbands for their primary income. When working-class husbands died, they usually left almost no savings and no life insurance. Their widows, often with children, could earn only the most meager income at customary women's work. Even farmers' widows often found themselves destitute or dependent on their children. No public programs existed on which women could draw as a right. Instead, they depended on family and charity. As a consequence, women, even single women trying to support themselves, often suffered terrible, absolute poverty.[64]

Many contemporaries understood the source of women's poverty, even if they could do little to alleviate it. Most poor women, even harsh critics of relief admitted, had not fallen into poverty through indolence or intemperance. Upright widows with children and old women remained the quintessential worthy poor. But where could they turn for help? They looked first to their families. Children much more readily housed and cared for their mothers than their fathers. Men never evoked as much sympathy as women. They should have saved enough for their old age; they were cantankerous and difficult to live with; and they could not help with housework and childcare. Women with young children or without families to care for them turned to private and public authorities. Most large towns and cities in the early nineteenth century had female benevolent societies that made small gifts to widows, and widows more often than widowers received outdoor relief from public sources. But in both cases the amounts were small and their continuation uncertain. Neither benevolent societies nor overseers of the poor offered help as a right; it always remained charity. (Unemployed and older men, who could not tap the same well of sympathy as women, more often depended on indoor relief—that is, the poorhouse.)[65]

Women's prospects did not improve very much until the twentieth century. Life insurance became more widespread, and late in the nineteenth century, widows of northern Civil War veterans received pensions. Industrialization opened more semi- and unskilled jobs to women. Still, a very small fraction of married women worked for wages outside the home. After 1911, state governments began to introduce mothers' pensions. These very small grants for worthy widows with children, though they represented an important extension of government responsibility, never reached more than a tiny fraction of eligible women. Nor did the constitutional right to vote, won in 1920, directly alleviate the hardships experienced by poor women.[66]

Energetic women reformers from the federal government's Children's Bureau managed quietly to nationalize the mothers' pension concept in the Aid to Dependent Children provision of the 1935 legislation creating the Social Security system. Its sponsors thought that ADC would be a small program supporting widows with children, but after World War II its demography started to change. By the 1960s, AFDC (Aid to Families with Dependent Children, as it was renamed) supported growing numbers of women whose husbands had deserted or divorced them, or who had never married. Increasing numbers of them were women of color. Hostility to the program and its recipients mounted: Southern states tacked on punitive regulations, and a welfare backlash swept northern cities. In the early 1960s, the program still supported only a modest number of women, largely because most of those eligible did not apply or because officials arbitrarily denied them relief. A combination of forces—the civil rights movement, the War on Poverty, and the welfare rights movement—helped increasing numbers of women onto the AFDC rolls, whose size exploded. Even though the cost remained a small and shrinking fraction of the total budget for social welfare, it bore the onus of public hostility, which inflated popular conceptions of its relative cost and generosity (AFDC never lifted women over the official poverty line) and fueled myths about the poor women who turned to it for survival. AFDC clients fueled sexuality and welfare into a powerful image that touched deep, irrational fears embedded in American culture. As they refused to be grateful and demanded public assistance as a right, they provoked a transformation in the historic relation between women and welfare. Poor women now became the undeserving poor.[67]

Today, more eligible women than ever before receive public assistance, and income from other programs also helps alleviate women's poverty. These include Social Security extended to survivors in 1939; Supplemental Social Security in 1974; Medicare and Medicaid in 1965; the increase in Social Security benefit levels; federal housing programs; nutritional grants to women and children with infants; and the transformation and expansion of the food stamp program after the late 1960s.[68] Women now can draw on an unprecedented array of income supports. Even though women still earn lower wages for comparable work, experience employment discrimination, and find themselves the object of sexual harassment, legislation and the courts now try to guarantee their civil rights. As their labor force participation has soared, women have entered an unprecedented variety of occupations. During the last two decades, the position of American women has improved along most of the major routes charted by the early feminists. What, then, explains the discovery of women's poverty now, rather than twenty, thirty, or fifty years ago?

Part of the answer is demographic and statistical. Modern povery statistics date from 1959, but in the decades for which relatively consistent measures exist, the proportion of women among the poor has risen dramatically. The increases are especially large among women who head households. In 1960, women headed 24 percent of all poor households; in 1984, they headed 48 percent. In the same period, the number of poor female family heads had increased 83 percent, from 1.9 million to 3.5 million. The changes affected both white and black women, but black women fared worst. In 1960, women headed 20 percent of poor white families and in 1984, 38 percent. By contrast, they comprised 42 percent of poor black families in 1960 and 73 percent in 1984. After 1970, the number of house-

holds headed by women began to rise sharply. Among all families, female-headed households rose from 11 percent to 16
percent in 1984. For whites, the increase was from 10 percent to
12 percent and for blacks from 28 percent to 43 percent. By 1986,
for the first time women headed more than half of all poor families. In 1979, cash programs removed 19 percent of female-
headed families from poverty; by 1984, they lifted only 10 percent above the official poverty line. (Frances Fox Piven and
Richard Cloward argue that the real increase in the number of
female-headed households is much, though an indeterminate
amount, lower. The reason, they contend, is that changes in
census categories artificially inflated the increase.)[69]

Still, dramatic as these figures are, they do not by themselves
account for the intensity of the concern with women's poverty.
Surely, if comparable figures existed for the years before World
War II, poverty rates among female-headed families and among
unmarried women would have been even higher. Even in 1980,
only 37 percent of all poor people lived in female-headed families. Among white women, the official poverty rate fell from 24
percent to 22 percent between 1973 and 1983; for black women,
the decline was from 50 percent to 49 percent. In fact, the rate
of poverty excluding income from public transfer payments (a
better index of earnings) for both white and black working-age
women declined between 1973 and 1983.[70] Although the proportion of persons below the poverty line living in female-headed
households increased 16 percent between 1979 and 1982, the
share in married-couple households rose 46 percent.[71] Between
1978 and 1983, the proportion of white men less than 65 years
old with children who lived in poverty prior to government income transfer programs rose 66 percent. In 1978, the transfer
programs removed 27 percent of them from poverty; by 1983,
the proportion had fallen to 21 percent.[72] One of the most dramatic developments of the 1980s was the reemergence of the
working poor. "Nationwide in 1986, according to the Census
Bureau," wrote Robert Pear, "two million adults were poor, although they worked year-round in full-time jobs. That is 52 percent more than in 1975 and 22 percent more than in 1980. An

additional 6.9 million poor people worked either part time or full time part of the year." [73]

Part of the concern with women's poverty reflects mounting alarm at the growing proportion of children in poverty. Between 1979 and 1982, the proportion of children under 6 living in poverty increased from 18 percent to 24 percent and of 6- to 17-year-olds, from 16 to 21 percent. In New York City, about 38 percent of all children live below a nationally established poverty line uncorrected for the city's cost of living. Marian Wright Edelman points out: "Children were slightly worse off in 1979 than in 1969. But from 1979 to 1983 the bottom fell out." In 1980, 1981, and 1982 more than 1 million children per year joined the poverty rolls, and the rate of child poverty soared to its highest level since the early 1960s. [74]

The prominence of the feminization of poverty as a social issue results from the interaction of women's real poverty with the energy of modern feminism and recent public policy. Three conditions have been especially important: the identification of the early feminist movement with affluent women; the male bias in discussions of poverty; and the Reagan administration's attack on social programs. To become a mass movement, feminism needed to incorporate working-class women and women of color —which, of course, directed its attention to poverty. As it turned to poverty, feminism confronted a discourse surprisingly male-centered. Despite the historic poverty of women, most writing about poor people (as I have pointed out already) used male pronouns. By implication, the poverty of men appeared more real, urgent, and distressing. After 1980, the Reagan administration's policies worsened the situation of poor women. Cuts in income maintenance programs, food stamps, health care, and even the administration's early tax policy all fell heavily on them. (Of course, male poverty has also increased in recent years.) The conjunction of demographic trends, ideology, and politics transformed women's poverty into a major public issue. [75]

Through its attack on social welfare and affirmative action, the Reagan administration, feminist writers argue, pursued an antifeminist agenda designed to "return society to a former, more explicitly patriarchal mode." (Patriarchal refers to a male-dominated form of social organization in which women are not only systematically subordinated, but excluded from public life.)[76] Kathleen Moran, for example, argues that women are poor because they are women: "The economic subjugation of women exists within a systematic context of group subjugation. The entirety of social relations as well as the mechanisms of social identification are based on male dominance and the maintenance of female dependence."[77]

However, theories of patriarchy risk telescoping history. They imply the continuity of fixed gender relations embodied in a division between public and private spheres that assigns political and economic power to men.[78] Indeed, a version of history that rests on an implicit assumption of unchanging gender relations contradicts one of feminist theory's great contributions, its emphasis on the social and cultural—and, therefore, by definition, always changing—construction of gender, as contrasted with the biological distinction between sexes.[79] The analysis of women's poverty flows most productively from an appreciation of the consequences of shifting patterns of gender relations for women.[80]

Theories of patriarchy also form shaky foundations for the analysis of poverty because they do not always deal convincingly with race. The principal "sources of oppression," contend black feminist writers, differ for black women and white women. The idea of the conventional two-parent family as the source of patriarchal exploitation, so prevalent in feminist literature, ignores the high proportion of single-parent households headed by black women and their high rate of labor-force participation. Indeed, throughout both slave and Reconstruction eras, the two-parent family remained for black women and men one small but crucial symbol of rebellion and autonomy, not a symbol of oppression. Of course, some feminist historians and theorists are developing more contingent, contextual concepts of patriarchy; questioning the rigid public-private dichotomy; and exploring the relations among gender, ethnicity, and inequality. As yet, however, these strands in feminist scholarship remain separate from the policy issues that emerge from the intersection of gender with race and poverty in America's cities.[81]

The data do not wholly support another argument advanced by some feminists: that the Reagan administration tried to "return society to a former, more explicitly patriarchal mode." To be sure, opposition to the ERA and abortion, hostility toward affirmative action, and cuts in welfare programs serving women and children all are antifeminist. However, the re-creation of patriarchy implies encouraging the reconstitution of two-parent families in which women stay at home to care for their husbands and children. It rests on the belief that married women with children should not remain in the work force.

At times, public policy has made the removal of women from the work force one of its goals. Early in the twentieth century, for instance, this was one of the important purposes of mothers' pensions. But it was not a goal of the Reagan administration or of contemporary conservative welfare policy. On the contrary, more than any other goal, conservative welfare reform stresses "workfare," which usually means forcing women with young children into the work force. Most other married women, part of the argument goes, now must work to supplement their family's income. Why should women supported by public aid be exempt? If their wives are to stay at home, husbands need to earn enough money to support their families. Therefore, what used to be called a "family wage" should be a cornerstone of a genuinely patriarchal social policy.[82] (The irony, of course, is that the "family wage" is essential to feminist policy too, because so many women need to support families by themselves.) Current policy and practice, however, have moved in precisely the opposite direction. Attacks on unions, contracts that lower wages and reduce fringe benefits, and the replacement of high wages in manufacturing with low-paying service sector jobs all mean that most families will continue to require more than one wage to sustain even a modest standard of living. Indeed, as other writers point out, trends in the history of the labor market almost guarantee the continued poverty of vast numbers of women.

Labor market mechanisms underlie other analyses of women's poverty. An excellent essay by Joan Smith shows the relations between women's continued poverty and the growth of the service sector of the economy. The feminization of poverty, she argues, has two sources: the increased number of female-headed households and the kind of work women do. Women work primarily in the service sector, whose explosive growth accounts for most of the jobs open to them. Most of these jobs pay lower wages than the manufacturing sector; increasingly they are part time; and they less often carry health insurance or other benefits. In fact, the business environment in the service sector has two key characteristics: a low capital-to-labor ratio and frantic competition. This means that service sector industries strive to increase the size of their labor force (to increase production) and to decrease the wages they pay. In other words, they want lots of cheap labor. Women, willing to work part time for low wages and no benefits, provide the major labor pool. As a consequence, service sector jobs pay less than a family wage, and women who work in them but lack other sources of income remain too poor to live independently of parents, husbands, or government supports. The growth of the service sector thus depends on a supply of workers involved in nonmarket institutions. As a result, women's poverty and continued dependence remain central to the most rapidly expanding sector of the American economy.[83]

Nonetheless, according to Smith, the situation is unstable because of its inherent contradiction. As service industries draw women into the labor force, the pool of cheap labor will evaporate, and they will be forced to pay higher wages. Smith wrote before the current revival of interest in workfare, which is one solution to the service industry's dilemma. By forcing women into low-wage jobs as the price of public assistance, welfare policy could expand the supply of cheap labor which, as Smith predicted, has begun to dwindle. By supplementing their income with health care, housing subsidies, and childcare, welfare policy could also subsidize the service sector by socializing the price of labor and ensuring that profits remain high and private.[84]

The institutional structure of the welfare state also works against the interest of poor women. The American welfare state emerged in the 1930s divided between public assistance and social insurance. Social insurance benefits were entitlements; they reflected the assumption that workers and employers paid into funds on which they drew in times of unemployment or when they retired. (The insurance model, in fact, has been more myth than fact.) Public assistance is means tested. That is, it serves only people who meet strict income and asset requirements. Although early advocates of social insurance included benefits for the elderly, the unemployed, and the poor within their proposals, the split deliberately engineered into policy created two very different types of programs. Public assistance has become synonymous with welfare; it carries the old stigma of relief. Its recipients are the modern paupers. Social insurance benefits, moreover, always were more generous, and the gap between them and public assistance continues to widen. Social Security, for instance, now lifts most of the elderly out of poverty; AFDC boosts no one above the official poverty line. From the beginning, gender biases underscored the distinctions between categories. Federal public assistance, ADC, was a women's program. By consigning most needy women with children to ADC, public policy ensured that they would remain poor. Social Security for decades excluded agricultural and domestic workers, two types of occupations that employed a large proportion of women (and blacks). Social Security also reflected prior earnings, which again favored men. Even more, unemployment insurance contained a structural bias against women because it rested on a male model. That is, its founders assumed it would serve male household heads.[85]

Women's poverty is a political as well as an economic issue, for it links women, the state, and the meaning of citizenship. Barbara Ehrenreich and Frances Fox Piven point out that women have the political potential to extend the welfare state. In 1980, women held 70 percent of the 17.3 million social service jobs. Social service jobs account for about a quarter of all women's employment. Women also receive most welfare benefits: in 1980,

54 percent of Social Security, 60 percent of Medicare; and nearly
all AFDC. Income support programs also protect poor women
who work in the low-wage service sector against abuses by their
employers: "low wages, unpaid overtime work, speed-ups, or personal and sexual harassment." Women remain more likely to
resist when they know the result will not be starvation for themselves and their children. As the principal clients and beneficiaries of the welfare state, women's attitudes toward social welfare
issues, poll data show, remain much more sympathetic than
men's. A majority of women opposed the Reagan administration's cutbacks, for instance. All this points to the material and
ideological preconditions for a powerful political coalition in
favor of redirecting the thrust of recent social policy.[86]

However, argues Barbara Nelson, women "are not natural
citizens of the Western liberal democracies." Liberal political
ideology excluded them from the public sphere. Gender, race,
and, at first, property circumscribed claims to citizenship as "an
individual's productive capacity" became the only legitimate
basis for claiming social benefits. Therefore, claims for women
based solely on motherhood lacked legitimacy. "The reality of
women's poverty and the limits to women's citizenship in a liberal democracy" coalesced to "disempower poor women."[87] Poor
women vote and participate in political activity less often than
others. They support government social programs, but they remain unable to translate their support into effective political
action. As clients of the welfare state, they are despised. They
remain, in truth, less than full citizens, and the obstacles to their
effective mobilization are enormous.


By stressing the feminization of poverty, writers risk slighting the
problems of black Americans, both women and men. Douglas
Glasgow of the National Urban League, for one, points to weaknesses in the feminization of poverty literature. Although he
does not minimize the degree of poverty among black women,
Glasgow contends that the literature overstates it. Between 1959
and 1985, poverty among black women declined from 71 percent

to 54 percent. Morever, he believes, the literature obscures historical differences between the work experience of blacks and white women. Black women remained clustered in badly paid, nonunionized domestic and other service work and, when married, worked for wages far more often than white women. Indeed, their wages constituted a larger share of family income. Emphasis on the feminization of poverty also sometimes "clouds the importance of race as a casual factor in the determination of poverty." As Glasgow observes: "At every level of education and across all family structures, the proportion of black Americans in poverty exceeds the proportion of white Americans in poverty." Of greatest importance, however, contemporary discourse "diverts attention from the staggering dislocation and disconnection of black males from the labor market, income, and, concomitantly, from the family."[88]

Writing about women and poverty serves different agendas. Only one of these is feminism.[89] Other writers, such as Michael Harrington, explore the economic situation of women as part of a broader discussion of poverty. In his *The New American Poverty*, for instance, only one chapter focuses on women's poverty. My speculation is that this is the reason his excellent and accurate book has neither captured public attention nor shaped public discourse as did *The Other America*. With the partial exception of the homeless, poverty has become a source of intense public interest only insofar as it intersects concerns about women, children, and families.[90]

Indeed, the same statistics that inform feminist analyses of poverty have rekindled alarm about the condition of black families. In *Family and Nation*, Daniel Patrick Moynihan argues that trends during the last two decades vindicate his prophecies about the deterioration of black domestic life, and he calls for social policy directed toward promoting stable, two-parent families. Despite his concern with poverty, family stability remains Moynihan's focus. For him only one family form is adequate, and the future of the nation hangs on its restoration. Here, then, are the statistics of women's poverty deployed in the service of patriarchy.[91]

Moynihan stressed one issue that usually does not enter most feminist discussions of women's poverty: adolescent pregnancy, which, were one to trust the media, has reached epidemic proportions.[92] (Adolescent pregnancy is discussed in detail in Chapter 5.) Despite the distortions in most public discussions of the issue, pregnancy among black teenagers has placed the black family back on the agenda of social science and public policy, where its reemergence as a legitimate topic in poverty discourse confronts feminist writers with a dilemma. They cannot deny either the poverty of most unmarried mothers, especially those in their teen years, or the way in which early motherhood circumscribes their life chances (although evidence shows that their achievements exceed what most people would predict).[93] Still largely silent on the issue, feminist writers about poverty have yet to formulate a clear position on adolescent pregnancy. But they cannot avoid the task and still remain leaders in the escalating national debate about poverty and welfare.

As an idea, the feminization of poverty highlights the harsh, often desperate circumstances confronting large numbers of women. It emphasizes the systemic origins of their condition in the distribution of power, discrimination, and the foundations of politics. By removing blame from individuals, it also contributes to a large, if implicit project: the rehabilitation of women as the deserving poor. Whether this project will succeed is uncertain. Public sympathy extends more unconditionally to children than to their mothers, who must earn respect and an entitlement to social benefits not only through good behavior, but increasingly by selling their labor in the marketplace. In fact, poor women, like poor blacks, have received relatively little as a consequence of greater formal equality. As with blacks, the politics of liberation have benefitted the middle class more than the poor. Because of its source in the writing of respectable academics, the feminization of poverty, as a concept, will last longer and diffuse more widely than the model of internal colonialism. Whether its effect will be greater remains, however, moot.

# Intellectual Foundations of the War on Poverty

## THREE

Between 1964 and 1972, the federal government unleashed a barrage of new antipoverty programs. Those most directly associated with the Office of Economic Opportunity fought poverty by trying to expand opportunity and empower local communities. Others radically altered procedures for redistributing income. Even though the former never had resources sufficient to realize their goals, spending on distributive social programs—Social Security, Medicare and Medicaid, food stamps, Aid to Families with Dependent Children—escalated until the end of Richard Nixon's first administration.

Public memory, and much subsequent history, treats the War on Poverty harshly. The nation fought a war on poverty and poverty won, has become a summary judgment assented to without reservataion even by many liberals. These years deserve a more discriminating verdict. Although social policy did not seriously dent the forces that generate want, although many new programs failed spectacularly and others disappointed their sponsors, the federal government did alleviate the consequences of poverty. Millions of Americans, most of them elderly, who would have remained poor escaped poverty; others whose incomes remained below the poverty line found medical care, food, housing assistance, and income security at a level unprecedented in America's past.[1]

The idea of a comprehensive assault on poverty had been formulated by President John F. Kennedy. On November 23, 1963, the day after Kennedy's assassination, President Lyndon Johnson met with Walter Heller, chairman of the Council of Economic Advisors, and instructed him to continue planning the antipoverty program. Johnson used the phrase "unconditional war on poverty" for the first time on January 8, 1964, in his State of the Union message. On February 1, he appointed Sargent Shriver to direct the new antipoverty program. Shriver, along with a planning committee that drew members from various branches of the federal government, developed a strategy for the program and drafted the Economic Opportunity Act (creating OEO), passed by the Senate on July 23, 1964, and by the House on August 8. President Johnson signed it into law on August 20.

For its model, the poverty program drew heavily on Mobilization for Youth, a comprehensive program in New York City organized to combat delinquency by boosting poor minority youngsters over the structural barriers to social mobility. Mobilization for Youth influenced the formulation of the War on Poverty through the President's Committee on Juvenile Delinquency (PCJD), which adopted many of its ideas, especially its emphasis on the role of blocked opportunity and the importance of community participation, and hired some of its key staff. PCJD members, more than any other single group, shaped the poverty program.

Within the poverty war, programs to promote opportunity concentrated on four areas: juvenile delinquency, civil rights, job training, and education. Without doubt, the most popular, and some people would argue the most successful, was Operation Headstart, which funded preschool education for poor children. The most controversial aspect of the program was the requirement in Title II of the Economic Opportunity Act that the new community agencies created to receive and administer federal antipoverty funds be "developed, conducted, and administered with maximum feasible participation of the residents."

## IDEAS, BUREAUCRACY, AND POLITICS

Histories of the War on Poverty disagree about the relative influence of ideas, bureaucratic politics, and political strategy. Was the War on Poverty guided by a coherent response to the nature of inequity and deprivation in American society? Or did it emerge from a struggle for power among federal agencies and between old-line bureaucrats and the new administration? Was its driving force compassion for the poor, or the need to win black votes and quell the riots in America's cities?

It is possible to write a history of the early War on Poverty that stresses the primacy of ideas and goodwill. By the early 1960s, the story would begin, politicians influenced by the small but growing literature on poverty in contemporary America had determined to attack the remnants of destitution in the land of plenty. It is also possible to write about the poverty war as the outcome of bureaucratic maneuvering. Within the federal administration, at least four agencies—the President's Commission on Juvenile Delinquency, the Council of Economic Advisors, the Labor Department, and the Bureau of the Budget —jockeyed to shape and control the new initiative. In the same years, the Social Security Administration quietly pressed for one incremental expansion after another, with the result that benefits increased dramatically. It is similarly possible to portray the poverty program and the expansion of social benefits as a response to great social and political forces: the migration of south-

ern blacks to northern cities and the civil rights movement, or as
a way to meet the political needs of the Democratic Party, and
assuage the unrest within America's cities.

All these stories are correct. The history of the poverty program is incomplete without any one of them. The difficulty is
assessing their relative weight and combining them into a coherent explanation.

Some common stories about the poverty war's origins apparently are apocryphal. John F. Kennedy did not read Michael
Harrington's *The Other America* and suddenly declare war on
poverty. A long essay on poverty in *The New Yorker* by Dwight
McDonald, which reviewed *The Other America*, exerted a
greater impact than Harrington's book on Kennedy and his advisors. Also influential was John Kenneth Galbraith's *The Affluent Society*, which stressed increased investment in the public
sector and in other unmet social needs such as the relief of
poverty. Cloward and Ohlin's opportunity theory of delinquency
(described later in this chapter) influenced the initial design of
the program, and echoes of the culture of poverty thesis also ran
through early discussions, even though Oscar Lewis and his
writings apparently played no direct part. Nor should we forget
that antipoverty measures did not form an explicit part of Kennedy's early urban policy. Indeed, the war on poverty, influenced especially by Homer Bigart's articles in the *Herald Tribune*
on rural Kentucky, at first tilted strongly toward Appalachia.[2]

The poverty program also drew on ideas formulated by reformers during the late nineteenth and early twentieth centuries. At a 1973 conference of former poverty war officials at
Brandeis, David Austin, who had served as planning director of
the Cleveland Demonstration Project funded by the President's
Committee on Juvenile Delinquency, recalled: "There's been a
long tradition . . . based . . . on an assumption that essentially
the poor, in many cases seen as immigrants, essentially were to
be helped up and into a stable position in society by the down-
reaching hands of the well-to-do and the intellectuals." The reforms of the 1960s, he thought, represented "a rediscovery of
many of the innovations of the progressive era, had many of the

same characteristics and in the end were influenced very much by the same scientific philanthropy, which strongly emphasized professionalism, social theory and the idea of incorporating the poor into the society without disruption and on an individual case basis."[3] In the tradition of American liberalism, early poverty warriors defined reform as education, not redistribution, and focused their slim resources on the individual rehabilitation of poor people.

The formulation of the poverty program was also, in part, an exercise in bureaucratic politics, with William Cannon of the Bureau of the Budget mediating among contending units within the Executive Branch. In fact, one of the poverty war's most contentious phrases, "maximum feasible participation," emerged from bureaucratic compromise among the program's planners. Richard Boone had wanted to use the word "involvement," which others found too strong. "To my knowledge," Boone remembered, "at that point and thereafter for some time —at least in our circle—the word 'control' was not mentioned. It wasn't part of that vocabulary. It was 'involve' and 'participate.' Those were the two terms that were used and the compromise was 'feasible.' " Another and more serious conflict erupted over the location of the National Youth Corps and Job Corps, both of which Willard Wirtz believed to have been delegated to the Department of Labor by a "treaty in advance."[4] Bureaucratic politics also shaped antipoverty programs at the great foundations. At the Ford Foundation, for instance, Paul Ylvisaker wasn't "altogether happy" with "that bag of opportunity theory which Pat [Daniel P.] Moynihan and others take off so much at—there's a kind of an ideology to it." Nonetheless, a common goal motivated foundation staff: "what always bound us together . . . we could forgive each other our theology if we knew we were in the same rag-tag group who were taking on this establishment."[5]

Political concerns also fueled and directed the early poverty program. According to Daniel Capron, former official of the Council of Economic Advisors and Bureau of the Budget involved in the planning and administration of the War on Poverty and Great Society programs, Kennedy "was persuaded politically that, having made his major '63 domestic program a tax cut which helps the middle and upper income people, that the next piece had to be something to help people that [sic] didn't have enough income to pay taxes." None of the former federal officials who gathered at the 1973 Brandeis conference to discuss the poverty program dissented from Capron's reminiscence, or, for that matter, from each other's enumeration of influences and tales of bureaucratic compromise. They did, however, disagree sharply about the role of the civil rights movement and race.[6] In part, the disagreements reflected the diverging perspectives of those inside and outside the administration, whose different views have shaped interpretations of the War on Poverty since early in its history.

Disagreement centered on the political impact of racial issues, for no one disputed the impact of demography on reshaping America's cities. More than any other single development, in the late 1950s and early 1960s the massive migration of southern blacks to northern cities framed the formulation of both urban and antipoverty policy. Distinctions between the situation of earlier European immigrants and contemporary black migrants underpinned Cloward and Ohlin's interpretation of delinquent subcultures. The culture supposedly brought by black migrants shaped Moynihan's interpretation of black family structure and the mechanisms by which it helped perpetuate poverty.

The impact of migration likewise determined Paul Ylvisaker's strategy for urban policy at the Ford Foundation: "I came to that sudden perception of the city as the magnet and passage-point of great migrations," he remembered. "It was . . . for me an intellectual breakthrough. . . . But at the same time it was also strategic because if you could conceive of an overarching process within which one could deal with the *Verbotens* of race relations and so forth, and where you weren't talking black immediately, which raised all the hackles, then you had much more chance of getting a program accepted."[7]

Consensus on the intellectual and strategic role of black migration did not reflect agreement on the more direct links between race, politics, and social programs. Did Kennedy and then Johnson plan their attack on poverty in response to mounting black protests? Were the War on Poverty and Great Society devices for cementing black loyalty to the Democratic Party? Opinions among those connected to policy at the time differed sharply. Adam Yarmolinsky, Shriver's deputy in planning the poverty program, denied the role of political concerns not only in the early War on Poverty, but in the Kennedy administration's concern with civil rights as well. The Kennedy administration's stance on civil rights was "99 and 44/100 percent noblesse oblige" with "no concern whatsoever about holding the black vote, about an upsurge of revolt of the masses."[8]

Richard Cloward and Frances Fox Piven, the two major participants at the conference least connected to actual federal policymaking, argued the opposite case. Warning against a view of history in which "the main actors were some intellectuals and some bureaucrats," Cloward reminded other participants of the events surrounding the initial discussions of antipoverty policy in 1963: the Birmingham civil rights campaign; the March on Washington in August; the bombings in September. Throughout, Kennedy commissioned "various groups within the administration to study black unemployment and to come up with plans and so forth in order to begin to respond to what were very large political forces particularly within the Democratic party that were being activated and radicalized to some extent by the civil rights movement and by the insurgency that was beginning to take form in the cities." Daniel Capron, referring to the Council of Economic Advisors, conceded: "We saw, literally, the March on Washington and that sure didn't do anything to cool us off on pushing this embryonic program."[9]

Yarmolinsky disagreed. "During the late winter, spring and early summer of 1964," he asserted, "we were concerned with explaining to the Congress and the public that the poverty program was in no sense a help-the-blacks programs, and not only were we saying this, but we didn't think it was." In fact, planners expected the poverty program to offer "very little for the blacks" because "Most poor people are not black, most black people are

not poor," to cite one slogan that Yarmolinsky repeatedly in-
serted into speeches. In 1964 OEO "hadn't the faintest gray tinge
to it. If anything, color it Appalachian if you were going to color
it anything at all." [10]

Capron, disagreeing with Yarmolinsky, distinguished between
political rhetoric and intellectual understanding. The reelection
campaign of 1964, he recalled, was much on their minds: "We
knew that it would be death . . . to bill any kind of program as a
help-the-blacks program. But that doesn't mean that we didn't
realize that this program was very important in terms of the
black vote. . . . Now, we did not articulate it that way. . . . But
we did understand that this was an important part of what was
going on." [11] On occasion, the poverty program's supporters
dropped their reticence about race. In April 1964, at a symposium on integration, Shriver linked the struggle against poverty
to the civil rights movement as "all part of the same battle," and
explained that in the congressional floor debates, the Economic
Opportunity Act "sometimes was regarded as but the logical
counterpart of the Civil Rights Act which had just been passed
in June." [12]

Piven emphasized that she and Cloward were not claiming
that blacks were the *only* concern of the Kennedy administration. But, she contended, the poverty program represented in
part a strategy of political mobilization designed to ensure Democratic electoral success. Documentary evidence clearly showed
the prominence of black votes among the administration's priorities. Because black allegiance to the Democratic Party had
weakened, even in 1960 Kennedy showed concern for the black
vote. She pointed to his "famous call to Mrs. Martin Luther
King, followed by massive pamphleteering about that fact in the
ghettos."

Piven failed to convince David Hackett, former executive director of the President's Committee on Juvenile Delinquency,
who countered, referring to his program: "We would have run it
completely different [sic] if we had followed your thesis. If it had
been a political program and if the administration wanted to

cater to the black vote, we would have done it completely different [sic]. . . . We did it completely the opposite way."[13]

Nonetheless, Piven continued to press the impact of race and
politics on the early poverty program. All the morning's speakers, she pointed out toward the end of the discussion, had talked
about "very large developments in American society having to
do with race, with class and with politics." However they evaluated them, "we've raised again the question that no one wanted
to discuss, which is the relationship of the specific federal programs to very broad social, economic and political developments
in American society in the 1960's. That relationship, it seems
everybody was saying today, did exist." In the end, even Yarmolinsky agreed: "I guess I'm also agreeing with Frances," he
conceded in his closing remarks, that the poverty program "was
in part a response to profound . . . social movements in the
United States. All I was saying earlier was that it was not . . . a
concession by the executive committee of the ruling class to the
rising demands of the masses."[14]

In part, the argument had revealed inevitable differences in
perspective: outsiders (Cloward and Piven) stressed context;
most insiders remained preoccupied with the day-to-day process
of policymaking and the politics of bureaucracy. Outsiders focused on broad social and political goals; insiders defended their
motives. No one, it should be stressed, denied the influence of
racial politics on the poverty program after 1964. They disagreed, rather, about its origins.

The insiders had based their case on narrow grounds. Although no spokesperson for the civil rights movement joined the
discussions that shaped the poverty program,[15] the image most
insiders tried at first to convey—an intelligent, well-meaning circle of white federal officials uninfluenced by the racial struggle
headlined in newspapers across the country—remains implausi-
ble, as in the end even the most intransigent insider agreed.
Nonetheless, despite its often narrow focus, the insiders' account remains crucial. For insiders described the complex process by which the antipoverty initiative moved from impulse to

program, and without which it cannot be understood. Their perspective also illuminates key strategic decisions: Why did the administration locate the poverty program in a separate agency? Why did it label it a war?

## LOCATION AND RHETORIC

Lyndon Johnson placed his poverty program in a new federal agency and called it a war. Neither decision represented his only alternative. He could have spread antipoverty funds throughout existing federal departments and used his office to stimulate and coordinate new programs. He also could have promised less than total victory or framed the program in terms of inequality, income, or—for that matter—race. His choices had profound consequences. As a separate agency, OEO remained both visible and vulnerable, a target for Congress, a sometimes hostile public, and the federal agencies bypassed in its creation. It lasted only a decade. As an unconditional war, the poverty program raised expectations that even an adequately funded and redistributive initiative could not be expected to meet within a few years. Its own overblown promises became a principal factor in the disillusion it aroused among contemporaries and the unfavorable verdict rendered by many of its historians.

In part, the War on Poverty seemed to its planners to require a separate federal agency because its projected budget was so low. As President Kennedy thought about the 1964 campaign, he planned the War on Poverty and the tax cuts as his major domestic program, Daniel Capron remembered. And although it was not clear what the dimensions of the program would be, the sum of available money was so small that his advisors realized, according to Capron, "if you threw this into the existing bureaucracy. . . . it was political suicide . . . it would be clear to everyone that it was nothing, that it was just window dressing." [16]

The poverty program also required a new agency because it

assumed the inertia and incompetence of the agencies that existed. Antipoverty strategists within the Kennedy and early Johnson administrations lacked confidence that existing federal departments could create bold and effective programs. Two alternatives emerged. The first, favored by Hackett and his associates in the President's Council on Juvenile Delinquency, was to expand the PCJD model. That meant an independent staff with money for experiments backed by the power of the president. Shriver chose a different course. He so distrusted the Department of Labor that he insisted the Job Corps be run from within the Office of Economic Opportunity. By repeating the pattern with every major OEO initiative, Shriver surrendered the possibility of reforming departments and programs within the federal government. Hackett recalled with regret that each OEO program had been built outside the system. Manpower programs, for instance, operated outside the Department of Labor; Headstart never confronted "the educational system head-on." Therefore, OEO never accomplished any basic reform in the federal system.[17]

For William Cannon at the Bureau of the Budget, the "key decision" in the early antipoverty initiative was adoption of the designation War on Poverty. The Bureau of the Budget opposed the label because it raised unrealistic expectations about the amount of money available for the new program. Nonetheless, during the Christmas holiday in 1963, Johnson decided to call the antipoverty program a war. He chose the language deliberately: "The military image carried with it connotations of victories and defeats that could prove misleading. But I wanted to rally the nation, to sound a call to arms which would stir people in the government, in private industry, and on the campuses to lend their talent to a massive effort to eliminate this evil." As David Zarefsky notes in his excellent analysis of the poverty war's rhetoric, the military metaphor solved important political problems confronting Johnson and facilitated the passage of the Economic Opportunity Act. For one thing, it responded to the national mood after the assassination of John Kennedy.

"Aroused by President Kennedy's untimely death," asserts Zar-efsky, "many Americans longed for redemption through sacri-fice."[18]

As an issue, poverty also helped the new president with deli-cate problems of image. Johnson needed to establish a national identity and create a positive impression by shedding his image as a Texas conservative. He also faced the task of managing the "transition between his caretaker role after the Kennedy assassi-nation and his own presidency."[19] For this reason, he needed a program that appealed to Kennedy's supporters but had not yet been publicly labeled a Kennedy effort.

Because poverty had not yet become an important national concern, Johnson began a rhetorical campaign to alter public opinion in which the military metaphor, announced in his 1964 State of the Union message, played an important role. The met-aphor of unconditional war aroused national interest and partic-ipation and placed the administration in a moral position that opponents attacked only at great risk. "When a nation is at war," points out Zarefsky, it has "acknowledged the existence of a foe sufficiently threatening to warrant attack." Characterizing op-ponents as "almost treasonous," the war metaphor "served as a unifying device, rallying the nation behind a moral challenge."[20]

The military metaphor proved to be brilliant political strategy. Other metaphors for the poverty program would have failed to mobilize public opinion or aroused even more hostility among conservatives. Robert Lampman, for instance, advised Walter Heller in 1963: "Probably a politically acceptable program must avoid completely the use of the term 'inequality' or of the term 'redistribution' of income or wealth." As the military metaphor fueled the passage of the Economic Opportunity Act, it aroused the sympathy of the nation. It also aroused its expectations, which proved fatal for an underfunded program addressing a massive and historic social problem with little theory and no proven methods.[21] For despite their rhetorical fanfare, the pro-grams of the Office of Economic Opportunity consumed only a tiny portion of the federal social welfare budget.

# FROM STRUCTURE TO SERVICE

From the start, internal contradictions plagued the War on Poverty. Among the most debilitating was the translation of a structural analysis of poverty into a service-based strategy. As David Austin reflected in 1973: "The issue is really why a service strategy when you had a structural diagnosis." Although the most influential analyses of poverty stressed its roots in unemployment, federal antipoverty planners deliberately avoided programs that created jobs.[22] In his economic report for 1964, Lyndon Johnson summarized the problem of poverty in America in structural terms. His presentation drew on the detailed second chapter of a report by the Council of Economic Advisors (CEA), written primarily by Robert Lampman, an economist from the University of Wisconsin and an expert in poverty statistics.[23] Using the most detailed data yet published, the CEA's report argued that economic growth by itself would not eliminate poverty in America. Despite echoes of the culture of poverty thesis, it anchored poverty in income distribution, employment, discrimination, and inadequate transfer payments by government, and it proposed a comprehensive program for its reduction. "By the poor," asserted the report, "we mean those who are not now maintaining a decent standard of living—those whose basic needs exceed their means to satisfy them." It also firmly rejected explanations based on character or heredity: "The idea that the bulk of the poor are condemned to that condition because of innate deficiencies of character or intelligence has not withstood intensive analysis."[24] Those in poverty lacked "the earned income, property income and savings, and transfer payments to meet their minimum needs." Many employed people earned inadequate wages, while other poor people could not work on account of "age, disability, premature death of the principal earner, need to care for children or disabled family members, lack of any saleable skill, lack of motivation, or simply heavy unemployment in the area." For others, low pay reflected racial discrimination or "low productivity" that resulted from inadequate education and skills.

Property and savings income were most important for the elderly, but many had earned too little to save, and about half of them had no hospital insurance. Without such transfer payments as existed, many more families would have been poor. Nonetheless, only half the poor received any transfer payments at all, and the most generous payments (private pensions and Social Security) offered the least help to those employed irregularly or in the worst-paying jobs. Aside from earnings, poverty's roots, according to the report, lay in a "vicious circle." Poverty bred poverty because of "high risks of illness; limitations on mobility; limited access to education, information, and training." As a consequence, parents passed on their poverty to their children. With discrimination often an insurmountable barrier, escaping poverty proved nearly impossible for "American children raised in families accustomed to living on relief."[25]

Despite its structural diagnosis, the Council of Economic Advisors laid the foundation for a War on Poverty based on economic growth, civil rights, and new social and educational services designed to equalize opportunity. The council stressed removing the handicaps that denied the poor "fair access to the expanding incomes of a growing economy" and introducing new federal programs "with special emphasis on prevention and rehabilitation." As for jobs, the council urged their indirect creation through a tax cut that would stimulate the economy.[26]

The CEA report revealed the hallmarks of American liberalism in the early 1960s: an uneasy mix of environmental and cultural explanations of poverty; a continuation of the historic American reliance on education as a solution for social problems; trust in the capacity of government; and faith in the power of experts to design effective public policies. Notably absent were community action and the creation of new jobs by government.

An early poverty warrior, Adam Yarmolinsky, remembered: "You ask yourself do you concentrate on finding jobs for people or preparing people for jobs. There our tactical decision was let's concentrate first on preparing people for jobs." The strategists thought the 1964 tax cut would create jobs; they believed poor people needed a long process of job preparation; and they knew that "it was less expensive to prepare people for jobs than to create jobs for people."[27]

Like other domestic and international policies of the era, this strategy assumed the continuation of growth and abundance, for an antipoverty plan that stressed increased educational opportunity and work preparation depended on the continued expansion and easy availability of jobs. Because growth would stimulate demand and enlarge the available rewards, the eradication of poverty required no painful reallocation of money and power. In the buoyant economy of the early 1960s this analysis still remained plausible, and an analysis of poverty as primarily a problem of employment reasonably could result in a relatively cheap public policy directed toward equalizing opportunity through education and job preparation.[28]

Not all members of the administration agreed, however. The Department of Labor, led by Secretary Willard Wirtz, proposed a poverty program which stressed employment. Wirtz's objections drew on the Labor Department's commitment to macroeconomic policies based on reducing unemployment, where necessary, through public employment. In 1961, Arthur Goldberg, then secretary of labor, advocated a Full Employment Act of 1961, and Wirtz continued to press this Labor Department position.[29] He "violently attacked" the CEA report, which was "published over his strenuous objection." In a memo to Theodore Sorenson, who had circulated a proposal for a poverty program, Wirtz emphasized: *"The Poverty Program must start out with immediate, priority emphasis on employment* [italics in original]." Because poverty "is a description of income," he argued, the major "single immediate change which the poverty program could bring about in the lives of most of the poor would be to provide the family head with a regular, decently paid job." Job creation did not depend solely on direct action by the federal government. The attack, Wirtz believed, should be launched principally at the *local* level, because *"the private forces are stronger than the public* [italics in original]." The tax bill was "an anti-poverty bill, probably the principal weapon we have." Nonetheless, the problem of unemployment demanded "special programs designed to create useful jobs." Wirtz, in common with other advocates of a poverty program, also stressed health and education, but his emphasis on job creation set the Department of Labor apart from the Council of Economic Advisors.[30]

Wirtz apparently persuaded the staff designing the poverty program, because at the last minute it added a job component. Armed with a proposal for a supplementary tax on cigarettes to finance it, Sargent Shriver presented the plan at a cabinet meeting, where Wirtz also argued vigorously on its behalf. President Johnson, however, wanted neither expanded economic transfers nor direct job creation, and he finessed the question of income transfers by appointing a commission. As for the job creation plan, "I have never seen a colder reception from the president," recalled Adam Yarmolinsky. "He just—absolute blank stare— implied without even opening his mouth that Shriver should move on to the next proposal."[31]

Direct attacks on unemployment never had a serious chance of passage in either the Kennedy or the Johnson administrations. Kennedy did not appoint the most influential advocate of Keynesian policies, John Kenneth Galbraith, to the Council of Economic Advisors. His three appointees, led by Walter Heller, did not share Galbraith's interventionist approach. Instead, they stressed aggregate economic objectives, particularly economic growth. Because they believed tax cuts would achieve their goals most efficiently, the focus of the War on Poverty and the Great Society, as Margaret Weir concludes, "shifted from the structure of the economy to the characteristics of the individual, characteristics that training was supposed to modify."[32] By default, the War on Poverty adopted the culture of poverty.

# FROM EQUAL OPPORTUNITY TO COMMUNITY ACTION

As finally approved by the president, the poverty program linked two major strategies: equal opportunity and community action. As an antipoverty strategy, equal opportunity stressed improved and expanded services, especially those related to education and job preparation—for example, Operation Headstart for pre-school children and the Job Corps for adolescents. (It also led to the massive infusion of funds into the schools attended by poor children, which resulted not from the poverty program itself but from the Elementary and Secondary Education Act of 1965.) Community action refers to an emphasis on the active participation of community residents in the formulation and administration of programs. Community action required the establishment of local agencies to receive and spend federal funds. As a strategy, it deliberately bypassed existing local political structures, empowered new groups, and challenged existing institutions.

In equal opportunity, the poverty program struck a note consonant with conventional American liberalism, which always has defined equality as the absence of barriers to individual mobility. Because policies designed to remove barriers to individual mobility usually have assigned education a key role, the poverty program followed another venerable American tradition by relying on education to attack the roots of poverty. With its focus on the individual and its avoidance of redistribution, equal opportunity appears orthogonal, if not contradictory, to the confrontational politics of community action. In practice, the two pillars of the poverty program remained more or less separate, and for reasons more political than intellectual, community action, at least in its more militant form, crumbled fairly quickly.

At the outset, however, the theory that most influenced the poverty program joined opportunity and action in a coherent

and novel explanation of juvenile delinquency. Recall the for-
mative influence of the President's Committee on Juvenile Delinquency on the poverty program. The theoretical base of
Mobilization for Youth reflected the formulation of its research
directors, Richard Cloward and Lloyd Ohlin of the New York
School of Social Work of Columbia University.[33] Cloward and
Ohlin presented their theory in an influential book, *Delinquency
and Opportunity*, published in 1960. (By 1964, the year of the
poverty program's official creation by the Economic Opportunity Act, the book was in its fifth printing.)

During the panic over adolescent behavior in the 1950s, individualistic and psychological theories had begun to dominate the
literature of delinquency. By contrast, *Delinquency and Opportunity* developed a self-consciously social and cultural approach
closer to the criminology of the 1930s and 1940s. Cloward and
Ohlin wanted to reinsert delinquency into the social and cultural
matrix from which psychological theory had abstracted it.[34]
Much like Oscar Lewis's portrayal of poverty, Cloward and
Ohlin presented delinquency as a subculture. They attempted
to delineate its characteristics; chart its distribution by race,
class, and geography; locate its origins; account for its power;
and explain its relative stability or instability over time. Cloward
and Ohlin differentiated between three delinquent subcultures:
criminal, conflict (gang violence), and retreatist (drug-based).
They then asked why the prevalence and appeal of these three
variants shifted across time.[35]

Usually associated with males, delinquent subcultures, they
argued, concentrated among the lower class, emerged during
adolescence, and occurred most often in cities. In modern
urban America, they believed, unlimited and unrealizable aspirations fueled the practice of placing blame for failure on the
larger social order, which in turn reduced its legitimacy and
hence its restraining power. The result was an explosive discrep-
ancy between aspiration and opportunity. Delinquent subcultures did not represent alternative value systems; rather, the
adolescents within them had internalized conventional goals.
Only they faced limits on legitimate means of attaining them.

"Unable to revise their aspirations downward," frustrated adolescents explored "nonconformist alternatives." [36]

To account for the relative strength of the variations in delinquent subcultures, Cloward and Ohlin turned to the historical interaction between immigrants and cities throughout modern American history. They argued that in recent decades the bureaucratization of crime, the decline of political machines, and slum clearance had intensifed social disorganization. At the same time, the most recent arrivals in northern cities, black migrants from the South, confronted unprecedented conditions that blocked group mobility and frustrated historic processes of assimilation. With traditional social structures crumbling and mobility blocked, urban adolescents turned increasingly to crime, conflict, and drugs. [37]

Although *Delinquency and Opportunity* offered no policy proposals, the importance of both opportunity and community action was one implicit message. Expanded opportunities would close the gap between aspiration and achievement; empowerment would help combat the subcultures of conflict and retreatism that grew out of hopelessness and despair. Cloward and Ohlin, much like Oscar Lewis, offered a cultural explanation that pointed to the need for a redistribution of power downward and outward to communities of the poor. [38]

Mobilization for Youth drew out the implications of *Delinquency and Opportunity* for opportunity and community action. Its 1962 summary proposal argued, "Obstacles to economic and social betterment among low-income groups are responsible for delinquency." No effort to prevent juvenile delinquency could succeed unless it offered young people genuine opportunities to behave differently. At the same time, community participation remained critical. To be really effective, residents must create and participate in programs "rather than have them imposed from without by persons who are alien to the traditions and aspirations of the community." Combatting delinquency therefore required more than the expansion of opportunity: Young people would respond more positively to an adult community which exhibits "the capacity to organize itself, to impose informal sanctions, and to mobilize indigenous resources."[39]

The link between opportunity and community action forged by Mobilization for Youth persuaded the staff of the President's Committee on Juvenile Delinquency. What weight it carried with the president is impossible to know, for community action emerged in practice as an ambiguous concept whose appeal lay as much in practical politics as in theory. Frances Fox Piven captured both the novelty and the threat of community action:

> Some deference to "citizen participation" has always been important in legitimizing governmental action in America. But the Great Society programs went beyond token representation. They gave money to ghetto organizations that then used the money to harass city agencies. Community workers were hired to badger housing inspectors and to pry loose federal welfare payments. Later the new community agencies began to organize the poor to picket the welfare department or to boycott the school system. . Local officials were flabbergasted; one level of government and party was financing the harassment of another level of government and party![40]

Even before Cloward and Ohlin gave it a theoretical base, Mobilization for Youth had emphasized the importance of "indigenous leaders" and the mobilization of community resources. This stress on community, in turn, drew on the traditions of the settlement house movement, which had always encouraged active citizen participation. Early in the twentieth century, Jane Addams, with customary simplicity and eloquence, had stated the premise from which community action eventually grew: "unless all men and all classes contribute to a good, we cannot even be sure that it is worth having."[41]

Despite its historic roots, the term "community action" did not enter the discourse of poverty warriors until late 1963. Within the Kennedy and early Johnson administrations, a group of former federal officials recalled, it assumed several different meanings. Daniel Capron, for example, stressed the utility of community action as a planning mechanism. He recalled how impressed he and his colleagues were with variations in "the situation in each group of the poor" among and within cities. Because this variation required different mixes of resources, each local group should have "a major say in deciding what their highest priorities were in the way of services."[42] Community action also was a method for encouraging social experiments. Shriver's principal deputy, Adam Yarmolinsky, for one, saw it "as a way of attempting to test out a variety of solutions to the poverty problem."[43]

Community action appealed to federal planners as a technique for coordinating policy. Lloyd Ohlin stressed the need at both local and federal levels for "creating a coordinating structure that could funnel money into the new programs and use that as the carrot to bring programs together." A community action agency, continued Fred Hayes, a former OEO official, was "a treaty organization," an effort to bring "the school system, the city and other interests together in a new structure simply because you had no old ones that were both competent and nonsuspect."[44]

For others, community action was a form of social therapy. Community participation overcame anomie and social disorganization by energizing previously apathetic and disaffected poor people to act on their own behalf. At the same time, it promoted the success of new services by capturing the loyalty of their constituents, who had participated in their planning and implementation. This was the meaning of community action in the settlement movement; it was implicit in *Delinquency and Opportunity* (whose authors taught in a school of social work); and it wafted through federal planning for the poverty program. William Cannon, formerly of the Bureau of the Budget, recalled that one "version [of maximum feasible participation] was the fact, almost in psychology, that you don't get programs well done unless you have the participation of those people who you were delivering them to."[45]

Community action had a very practical appeal as well. It was a cheap strategy for attacking poverty. Daniel Capron recalled that officials within the Bureau of the Budget knew the administration would appropriate very little new money for the anti-poverty initiative, and they groped for some way to focus limited funds on a highly visible program. Clearly, a negative income tax, which Budget Bureau officials would have preferred, remained "ahead of its time." Instead, they looked for a "cheap program" that "would show us ways to get . . . lots of federal dollars." For this reason, "community action struck us as very attractive."[46]

Finally, community action offered a way to attack the rigid, self-protective, unresponsive, and interlocking federal and local service delivery network. Yarmolinsky stressed the hostility of the Kennedy and early Johnson administrations to the "old-line" bureaucrats. The heart of the War on Poverty was an institutional critique rather than a program. Community action was the method for "shaking the system" and forcing change on reluctant school administrators, welfare and employment service officials, and even settlement houses and Community Chest leaders, what Yarmolinsky called "the board ladies" and "the bureaucrats." Federal poverty warriors expected to build an alliance between mayors and poor people. They believed (naively, Yarmolinsky admits) that mayors and their constituents, who needed and wanted new services, would join forces to formulate a program "which we from Washington would insist that the bureaucrats carry out." When Frances Fox Piven asked why federal planners expected mayors to join a fight against their own bureaucrats, Henry Cohen and Fred Hayes answered, "Ah, that's the key point." They pointed to the fact that the mayors were dealing with school boards that "were almost totally insulated from them," with welfare agencies that were "run by county governments rather than by the city," with a whole range of "categorical programs," all "administered by special districts, state governments, or county governments." Community action, they believed, would enlist the support of mayors because it offered them the prospect of control over services of immediate concern to their constituents. This was, of course, a costly misreading of American urban politics.[47]

By late in 1963, Hackett, Boone, and other community action advocates had persuaded Capron, Heller, and Schultze of the value of a poverty program based on community action. Sargent Shriver, however, remained unconvinced. He worried about its appeal to Congress and about potential problems in coordinating "agencies, organizations, and disparate interests." Nonetheless, his resistance wore down, although for exactly what reasons remains unclear.

As Yarmolinsky recalled in an exchange with Arnold Gurin, Dean of the Heller School at Brandeis:

YARMOLINSKY: I think I'd have to say that the principal factor was that when someone shows you the stripe down the middle of the road and you're not going to redefine the road, the chances are you'll include the center stripe.
GURIN: So it was really that residual?
YARMOLINSKY: It was being pushed very, very hard. . . . There was no one in the room who said, "That is really a bad idea and we oughtn't to do any of it." . . . after the first day, and the first week when no one had said, "Throw it out," because it was there, we thought about it. We thought about its pros and cons. We didn't think about it on a yes or no basis. We thought about what can be. . . . Look, Shriver thought about it, again, primarily as a salesman. I suppose I thought about it primarily as how you would administer it; it was a fascinating administrative problem.[48]


# EXPANDING SOCIAL WELFARE

Neither community action nor the War on Poverty's new service programs increased the amount of money spent on social welfare. Nonetheless, between the late 1960s and the early 1970s, the federal government expanded public social spending in five major ways. First, the number of persons receiving Aid to Families with Dependent Children (AFDC) exploded. Second, food stamps became more widely available and free to the poor. Third, through Supplemental Social Security, the aged, blind, and disabled received a guaranteed minimum income. Fourth, Social Security benefits increased dramatically and were linked to inflation. Fifth, Medicaid and Medicare created a system of national health insurance for welfare recipients and the elderly. Still, Congress defeated the most dramatic proposal for expanding public school provisions: Richard Nixon's guaranteed minimum income for families. In many ways, Nixon's abortive Family Assistance Plan remains the most interesting part of the story because it was the first major attempt to overhaul the social welfare structure erected in the 1930s. As such, it rested on ideas about antipoverty strategy that differed sharply from the service-based programs of the War on Poverty.

On August 8, 1969, President Richard Nixon proposed a Family Assistance Plan that would guarantee all families with dependent children a minimum yearly income ($1,600 for a family of four). He also proposed that states pay a prescribed federal minimum to disabled, blind, and elderly people eligible for welfare. The House Ways and Means Committee held the first hearings on the bill between October 15 and November 13. At the same time, it examined a bill that would increase Social Security benefits and link them automatically to inflation. In March, the Ways and Means Committee approved the bill, and the House passed it on April 16 by a vote of 243 to 155. The Senate proved more resistant. Throughout the next two years, the Senate sent administration proposals back for redrafting and considered alternatives. It did, however, agree to raise Social Security benefits and to broaden the food stamp program. At last, on October 17, 1972, the Senate passed a welfare reform bill stripped of the Family Assistance Plan. Instead, it created Supplemental Social Security (which folded aid for the blind, disabled, and elderly not eligible for Social Security into one program with a federally mandated income floor) and workfare (an unsuccessful attempt to link welfare to work).

Nixon's plan reflected proposals for a negative income tax or national minimum income advocated by many economists of that period. Its earliest major proponent was conservative economist Milton Friedman. It had also appealed to economists in the Kennedy and Johnson administrations, who considered increasing the income of poor people the most straightforward way to reduce poverty.[49] Johnson himself remained more cautious, and he fended off the advocates of an income-based approach to antipoverty strategy by creating a national commission on income maintenance, otherwise known as the Heineman Commission.[50] Its report, *Poverty amidst Plenty: The American Paradox*, published in November 1969, offered an informed and eloquent plea for a national minimum income. Because commission members included the chairman of the board of IBM, the president of Northwest Industries, the president of the Equitable Life Assurance Society, the chairman of the Westinghouse Electric Corporation, and the chairman of the Republic National Bank of Dallas, as well as professional economists, politicians, and union officials, its advocacy of a strategy anathema to many conservatives (not to mention the president who appointed it) is startling. However, for businessmen able to overcome their resistance to any expansion of government social benefits, the national minimum income meshed with important conservative goals.

The commission's main recommendation was "*the development of a universal income supplement program to be administered by the Federal Government, making payments to all members of the population with income needs* [italics in original]." Most people were poor because they "lack money, and most of them cannot increase their incomes"; only the government had the resources to provide "*some minimum income to all in need* [italics in original]." Poverty, the commission stressed, did not result from personal failing, and it offered a blistering criticism of existing welfare programs, which failed to

provide adequate support or incentives and demeaned recipients. Underlying their inadequacy was an ineffective strategy
and outmoded assumptions. The strategy depended on services,
which could not "substitute for adequate incomes," "pay rent,"
or "buy food for a poor family." The obsolete assumption, which
considered employment and receipt of welfare "mutually exclusive," had become "untenable in a world where many employ-
able persons have potential earnings below assistance payment
standards."[51]

By proposing to supplement wages, the commission staked out
a new position in official American discourse on poverty and
welfare. Nonetheless, despite its radical surface, it rested on
premises compatible with business interests. First, it simply accepted the spread of low-wage labor as inevitable and did not
recommend improving working conditions or wages. Second, it
provided an "alternative to the minimum wage," as University of
Minnesota economist George Stigler had pointed out nearly
twenty-five years before Nixon's proposal. Thus, a negative income tax would help business by socializing the cost of labor and
give economists worried about the effect of the minimum wage
on the market a way to support the needy without risking inflation. Third, in contrast to *in-kind programs*, (ones that provided
goods such as food and housing), which the commission wanted
abolished, income supplements worked on market principles.
The market system, argued the report, "is more effective at dis-
tributing goods and services than direct governmental distribution." Income supplements permitted "greater consumer
choice" and "greater flexibility of family resources." Fourth, income supplements avoided the problems inherent in expanding
social insurance, which performed "an antipoverty function far
less efficiently than programs which pay benefits on the basis of
need." Social insurance, argued the commission, paid disproportionate benefits to the nonpoor and lacked incentives. By
contrast, an intelligently designed income maintenance program
could provide "financial incentives to work, and to limit incentives for family breakup." It also would reduce the administrative
costs associated with direct subsidy by 15 to 30 percent.[52]

Nixon's reasons for supporting a family assistance plan were complex. Influenced especially by HEW Secretary Robert Finch and Daniel Moynihan, who had joined his administration, Nixon reached his decision by stages. He disliked both social workers and the current welfare system, and a bold welfare reform plan offered concrete political advantages. "Why not utterly repudiate the old Democratic-devised welfare system as socially destructive and unfair? Why not insist that a reformed system reward those who work more than whose who could work but don't?" Nixon, assert Vincent and Lee Burke in their history of the Family Assistance Plan, "liked to think of himself as a modern-day Disraeli, a Tory bringing social progress," and his welfare reform "offered a dazzling opportunity to win a place in history." Nixon would gain however Congress acted: "If Congress approved his plan, Nixon would be credited with reforming a despised institution; if Congress balked, Nixon would get a political issue." [53]

Unlike discourse about poverty and welfare in the 1980s, the Heineman Commission said little about race, teenage pregnancy, female-headed families, or an underclass. Its justification of a national guaranteed income with market principles blended sophisticated conservatism with liberalism in a way characteristic of the late 1960s. Nonetheless, as modified in Nixon's plan, the commission's proposals managed to anger not only many conservatives, but potential allies on the Left as well. Conservatives objected to Nixon's plan because it would expand the number of families eligible for aid and because it violated their beliefs about the limited role of government and the harmful effects of welfare. On the Left, opinion divided between those who supported the bill as an important precedent and those who believed its benefits to be woefully inadequate and its workfare provisions punitive.

No such coalition formed to defeat the other expansions of public social provision in the same years. Because everyone grows old, Social Security cuts across class lines and draws on the massive political power of the elderly. As for food stamps, hunger historically has moved Americans more than any form of deprivation. In 1968, after a powerful television documentary on hunger, Senator George McGovern, chair of a new Senate Committee on Nutrition and Human Needs, began public hearings on the issue. By proposing the expansion of the food stamp program, Nixon preempted what otherwise surely would have become a major political issue for the Democrats. Poll after poll has demonstrated that for decades public opinion has favored national health insurance. Without the active opposition of the powerful American medical profession, America would not be the only Western democracy without it. The 1965 passage of Medicare for the elderly and Medicaid for welfare recipients therefore reflected a political compromise, not a major ideological shift.[54]

Unlike the other expansions of public social provision, the explosion of the welfare rolls required only modest legislative changes. In 1960, 745,000 families received AFDC at a cost of less than $1 billion; by 1972, the number of families had become 3 million and the cost had multiplied to $6 billion. The reasons were several. The migration of southern blacks to northern cities increased the number of poor people dependent on cash incomes and reduced the number of subsistence farmers. Starting in 1961, Congress permitted states to extend aid to families headed by unemployed male parents. (As of 1988, only 28 states had taken advantage of this opportunity, which was a minor factor in the increase.) Some states loosened the standards for eligibility. More important, mobilized by the welfare rights movement, the proportion of poor families applying for welfare increased dramatically, as did the proportion of applicants accepted, which skyrocketed from about 33 percent in the early 1960s to 90 percent in 1971. The latter event reflected the efforts of the nascent welfare rights movement to recast welfare as an entitlement, reduce its stigma, and mobilize poor people to claim assistance as a right. Indeed, welfare rights became a social movement acted out in demonstrations that pressured reluctant welfare officials and in courtrooms where lawyers successfully challenged state laws restricting eligibility.[55]

. . .

Welfare rights was a new idea in American social policy. "Prior to the 1960s," writes Rand Rosenblatt in his review of its legislative history, "recipients of benefits under programs such as AFDC were not seen as having 'rights' to benefits or even to a fair process for deciding individual cases." The achievement of welfare rights required both the mobilization of poor people and new legal doctrines. Funded by the poverty program, the Legal Services Corporation for the first time in American history provided poor people with lawyers to act on their behalf. With the example of civil rights victories in the courts, a new generation of welfare and poverty lawyers successfully challenged state laws in the Supreme Court.[56]

Welfare rights advocates won legal victories in three key areas: length-of-residence requirements, invasion of privacy practices, and unregulated state discretion over eligibility conditions and the amount of grants. Three key Supreme Court decisions in the 1960s dented these historic features of welfare law. *King* v. *Smith* (1968) struck down an Alabama rule that effectively denied welfare to any children and their mother if the mother had sexual relationships. (The rule had defined any man with whom a recipient mother had sexual relations as the "substitute father" of her children, regardless of his relation to them.) *Shapiro* v. *Thompson* (1969) declared that a residency requirement—a one-year waiting period before new state residents could receive welfare—"penalized the fundamental constitutional right to interstate travel and thereby denied equal protection of the law." *Goldberg* v. *Kelly* (1970) required welfare agencies to offer clients a hearing that met "minimal due process standards" before stopping benefits.

These cases extended benefits to hundreds of thousands of women and children. According to Rosenblatt, in *King* v. *Smith*, the Supreme Court had estimated that the substitute-father rule in Alabama alone had excluded about 20,000 people, including 16,000 children. In other states similar rules probably excluded over 500,000 children. The Court's reasoning in the King decision prompted many lower court decisions that struck down other exclusionary state rules. Nonetheless, by the early

1970s, a backlash against welfare rights surfaced among voters and within all levels of government as the Court started to change direction. In *Dandridge* v. *Williams* (1970), the court refused to force states to match welfare grants to living needs. In *Wyman* v. *James* (1971), the Court agreed that states could terminate welfare benefits if a client denied a caseworker access to her home, and in 1973, in *New York State Department of Social Services* v. *Dublino,* the Court upheld state work requirements more restrictive than those in federal law.[57]

Legal philosophers buttressed the welfare rights movement by redefining the concepts of property, rights, and entitlements. By far the most important and influential of these redifinitions was Charles Reich's article "The New Property," which appeared in the *Yale Law Journal* in April 1964. Property, stressed Reich, "is not a natural right but a deliberate construction of society. "Because it is created by law, property is not limited to land, possessions, or other forms of material wealth. Property, rather, "represents a relationship between wealth and its 'owner' " sanctioned by law. Therefore, a person with property "has certain legal rights with respect to an item of wealth." In the modern state, governments have created myriad new forms of wealth: income and benefits, jobs, occupational licenses, franchises, contracts, subsidies, use of public resources, and services. Together, these compose what Reich called new forms of "government largesse": "The valuables dispensed by government take many forms, but they all share one characteristic. They are steadily taking the place of traditional forms of wealth—forms which are held as private property." Changes in the forms of private wealth enhanced the significance of government largesse, because "today more and more of our wealth takes the form of rights or status rather than of intangible goods." Thus, a profession or a job is frequently far more valuable than a house or bank account. And for the jobless, "their status as governmentally assisted or insured persons may be the main source of subsistence."[58]

For Reich, the new forms of government largesse had significant costs: They eroded conventional boundaries between public and private, enhanced the power of the state, and threatened individual liberty. Only new procedural safeguards, he argued, could both protect individual liberty and guard individuals' access to this "largesse." "Eventually," he wrote, "those forms of largesse which are closely linked to status must be deemed to be held as of right." And he saw the concept of right most urgently needed with respect to benefits like unemployment compensation, public assistance, and old age insurance. For these forms of largesse rest on a recognition that "misfortune and deprivation are often caused by forces far beyond the control of the individual." Their goal is "to preserve the self-sufficiency of the individual, to rehabilitate him where necessary, and to allow him to be a valuable member of a family and a community; in theory they represent part of the individual's rightful share in the commonwealth."[59]

The conservative judicial retreat of the 1970s circumscribed the influence of Reich's elegant redefinition of property, although his article set off a debate among scholars that still continues. William Simon, writing from a political position to the left of Reich, pointed out that "The New Property" offered no criteria for distribution and reified individual rights and state power as "distinct and opposed entities." Reich's portrayal of welfare benefits as matters of right obscured their role in the transfer of wealth "from one group of right-holders to another." Rights for Simon reflect power; they do not guard against it. For this reason, he found Reich's argument unintentionally conservative. When all wealth is translated into rights, its forced redistribution by government becomes impossible. This was one paradox; the other was the contradiction between Reich's intended legitimation of the welfare state and his portrait of the state as a menace. Simon's final verdict on Reich's new property was harsh: "[Its] view of welfare rights is incoherent as jurisprudence and exhausted as politics. It is irrelevant to what ought to be the two principal concerns of liberal welfare jurisprudence." These were theories and programs based on need as a distribu-

tive principle and an approach to public administration that recognized "the value of a responsible state as well as the dangers
of an irresponsible one."

Moral as well as legal philosophers also began to reconsider
distributive justice in the 1960s. Most important among them
was John Rawls of Harvard. First in a series of articles, then in
his immensely influential A *Theory of Justice*, Rawls challenged
the utilitarian basis of liberalism and, by implication, its translation into the opportunity-based strategy of the War on Poverty
and the Great Society. Rawls argued for a concept of justice
based neither on utilitarianism, which stressed efficiency, nor on
its leading philosophic criticism, intuitionism. Instead, starting
with social contract theory, he returned to first principles: "The
principles of justice," he wrote, "are the object of the original
agreement," or social contract. "They are the principles that free
and rational persons concerned to further their own interests
would accept in an initial position of equality as defining the
fundamental terms of their association." These principles regulated "all further agreements," specifying permissible forms of
"social cooperation" and "government." Rawls called this way of
regarding the principles of justice "justice as fairness."[60]

Justice as fairness depended on liberty and social justice.
"First: each person is to have an equal right to the most extensive
basic liberty compatible with a similar liberty for others. Second:
social and economic inequalities are to be arranged so that they
are both (a) reasonably expected to be to everyone's advantage,
and (b) attached to positions and offices open to all." Rawls's
emphasis on social justice led to the criterion he then applied to
social policies and institutions: They are to be judged by the
degree to which they improve the circumstances of "the least
advantaged members of society."[61]

Although he did not draw the connection, the concept Rawls
labeled "liberal equality" underlay the War on Poverty and the
Great Society. For Rawls, liberal equality intuitively appears
"defective" because its stress on removing barriers to opportunity still "permits the distribution of wealth and income to be
determined by the natural distribution of abilities and talents,"

leaving distributive shares to be "decided by the outcome of the natural lottery," an outcome "arbitrary from a moral perspective." Because of the practical impossibility of securing "equal chances of achievement and culture for those similarly endowed," he continued, "we may want to adopt a principle which recognizes this fact and also mitigates the arbitrary effects of the natural lottery."

His "difference principle," that is, the primary claims of the least advantaged, drew Rawls to an alternative conception of equal opportunity: "To treat all persons equally, to provide genuine equality of opportunity, society must give more attention to those with fewer native assets and to those born into the less favorable social positions." The difference principle rested on values at variance with those at the core of liberal equality. "It transforms the aims of the basic structure so that the total scheme of institutions no longer emphasizes social efficiency and technocratic values." The difference principle was, instead, "an agreement to regard the distribution of natural talents as a common asset and to share in the benefits of this distribution whatever it turns out to be." [62]

Rawls did not intend the difference principle as an argument for the elimination of inequality or of capitalism. "The basic structure can be arranged," he wrote, "so that these contingencies [greater natural capacities or other advantages] work for the good of the least fortunate." As for socialism, "It seems improbable that the control of economic activity by the bureaucracy that would be bound to develop in a socially regulated system— would be more just on balance than control exercised by means of prices." [63]

A "properly organized democratic state," according to Rawls, differed little from other social democratic blueprints for a welfare state. Besides guarantees of liberty, freedom of thought, equal citizenship, and a just, open political process, the government should ensure "fair (as opposed to formal) equality of opportunity," and guarantee "a social minimum either by family allowances and special payments for sickness and employment, or more systematically by such devices as a graded income supplement (a so-called negative income tax)." Rawls offered liberals what they badly needed: a fresh, cogent legitimation of the welfare state. But it came too late, and it veered too sharply from the utilitarianism that now underlay social policy. Within a year after *A Theory of Justice* appeared, the initiative had passed to conservatives, and the War on Poverty, for all practical purposes, was over.[64]

The value of AFDC benefits in real dollars is a reasonable, if rough, index of national generosity. It peaked in 1972. Since then, welfare rights activists have expended more energy protecting earlier gains than on extending them. What, exactly, had they won? How should we assess the outcome of the War on Poverty, the Great Society, and the expansion of public social provision?


# RESULTS

Neither the War on Poverty, the Great Society, nor the extension of public social benefits challenged the structure of the American welfare state. Instead, they reinforced the historic distinction between social insurance and public assistance that has defined welfare in America since the 1930s. Social welfare expanded along well-worn tracks. Social Security benefits increased and were indexed. Supplemental Social Insurance, on the other hand, folded programs into a new form of means-tested relief. Congress added a broadened and liberalized food stamp program to public assistance, whose benefits were lower than Social Security. Health insurance also divided into two programs, one part of the social insurance apparatus and the other part of the structure of public assistance. The benefits they provided, and the reimbursement they offered providers, differed sharply. Social insurance received by far the greatest share of public funds and provided the highest benefits. In 1970, Social Security payments to the elderly, $30.3 billion, already exceeded AFDC payments by about ten times. By 1984, Social Security payments, which were indexed to inflation, had mushroomed to $180.9 billion. AFDC, which was not indexed, had risen to only $8.3 billion.[65]

Although the Great Society did not alter the structure of social welfare, its accomplishments belie contemporary conventional wisdom that either ignores or belittles the great achievements of the era. Between 1965 and 1972, the government transfer programs lifted about half the poor over the poverty line. Between 1959 and 1980, the proportion of elderly poor people dropped, almost entirely as a result of government transfer programs, from 35 percent to 16 percent. Medicare and Medicaid improved health care dramatically. In 1963, one of every five Americans who lived below the poverty line never had been examined by a physician, and poor people used medical facilities far less than others. By 1970, the proportion never examined had dipped to 8 percent, and the proportion visiting a physician annually was about the same as for everyone else. Between 1965 and 1972, poor women began to consult physicians far more often during pregnancy, and infant mortality dropped 33 percent. Food stamps successfully reduced hunger, and housing programs lessened overcrowding and the number of people living in substandard housing.

Of course, there are less sanguine ways to read the evidence: poverty remained unacceptably high; millions of Americans still lacked medical insurance; in the 1980s, housing became a major problem for virtually anyone with a low income; and hunger reappeared as a national disgrace. Indeed, as the rate of poverty before income transfer programs shows, neither public policy nor private enterprise had moderated the great forces that generate poverty in America. At best, they alleviate its effects. Nonetheless, the expansion of public social benefits from 1964 to 1972 transformed the lives of millions of Americans and demonstrated the capacity of government as an agent of social change.[66]

The achievements of some service-based programs also deserve recognition. Operation Headstart helped significant numbers of poor children prepare for school; Upward Bound prepared large numbers of adolescents for college; and financial assistance permitted thousands of young people from families with low or modest incomes to take advantage of higher education. (Of course, as a whole, urban education still remains a disaster.) As Legal Services opened access to litigation by poor people for the first time, lawyers used class action suits to expand the rights of the poor in several key areas: medical aid, landlordtenant relations, state housing laws, consumer credit, and welfare administration. However, despite the success of some Job Corps centers, manpower training and employment programs remained disappointing, although the jobs provided by the Comprehensive Employment and Training Act (CETA) were an important form of work relief. Community action, for all its problems, nourished and intensified a growing citizen's movement, reshaped local politics, and launched a new generation of minority leaders, many of them women, into public life.[67]

The War on Poverty and the Great Society also left a profound intellectual legacy. Part of that legacy was the new stream of legal and philosophic scholarship, represented by Reich, Simon, Rawls, and others, which formulated new approaches to the legitimacy of the welfare state and distributive justice. Another part was a debate about strategies of social change and welfare reform. Especially in two influential books, *Regulating the Poor* and *Poor People's Movements*, Frances Fox Piven and Richard Cloward recast the history of public welfare and challenged liberal approaches to reform through legislation, organization, and reliance on disinterested elites. For Piven and Cloward, welfare's primary historical role was the regulation of the labor market. Until the 1980s, they argue, welfare expanded and contracted with business cycles. Governments, influenced by employers, increased aid in slack periods and then cut it in good times to drive workers back into the labor market. Only through mobilization, they contend, have poor people won significant concessions rather than small and transitory increases in relief. In the 1960s, as in the 1930s, they exploited moments of vulnerability in the political system (the Democratic Party's need for their votes); threatened public order (the Unemployed Workers'

Councils of the 1930s, the riots of the 1960s); or interrupted the work of public bureaucracies (protests in welfare offices). Poor people, according to Piven and Cloward, succeeded primarily through relatively spontaneous mobilization. When their indigenous leaders or well-meaning liberals transformed mobilizations into organizations, they lost both their radical edge and their effectiveness.[68]

Another intellectual legacy of the War on Poverty and the Great Society was a series of new definitions of poverty. The first of these, poverty as a bureaucratic standard, guided concrete policy discussions; a second, poverty as blocked opportunity, underpinned the Economic Opportunity Act; a third, poverty as the absence of power, emerged from the theory and practice of community action. The others were by-products of research and the transformation of American social science that occurred during those years.

The War on Poverty began without an official definition of poverty. The Office of Economic Opportunity, which needed a defensible bureaucratic standard as a yardstick for diagnosing poverty and measuring progress against it, drew on the work of Mollie Orshansky in the Social Security Administration's Office of Research and Statistics. The Orshansky index, as it was called, assumed that poor families spent about one-third of their income on food, so it pegged the poverty line at three times the cost of the Department of Agriculture's low-cost budget for food, adjusted for family composition and rural-urban differences. Reliance on the Department of Agriculture's food budget had precedents in both public and private sectors. "Food plans prepared by the Department of Agriculture," observed Orshansky, "have for more than 30 years served as a guide for estimating costs of food needed by families of different composition." Indeed, for many years welfare agencies had used the low-cost plan to keep down the cost of food allotments to needy families.[69]

Orshansky never harbored illusions about the adequacy of the low-cost food budget. It assumed, she pointed out, "that the housewife will be a careful shopper, a skillful cook, and a good manager who will prepare all the family's meals at home." It

included no "additional allowance for snacks or the higher cost
of meals away from home or meals served to guests." It established, at best, a "crude criterion of income adequacy." In fact,
Orshansky developed the index as a research tool, not an instru-
ment of policy or a criterion for determining eligibility for antipoverty programs. She wanted to determine the demography of
the poverty population and to identify groups at risk. The index,
she wrote, "is not designed to be applied directly to an individual
family with a specific problem. Nor even as a screening device
can it be expected to stand unchallenged as an exact count of
the poor in absolute numbers. But it can delineate broadly the
relative incidence of poverty among discrete population groups
and in this way outline targets for action." The poverty line, she
said, identifies "groups most vulnerable to risk of poverty" even
though it cannot measure poverty precisely. "The best that can
be said of the measure," she wrote, "is that at a time when it
seemed useful, it was there." [70]

Contrary to Orshansky's intentions, the Office of Economic
Opportunity adopted her index as its standard, only it utilized
estimates based on the Department of Agriculture's economy
food plan, which was about 25 percent lower than the low-cost
plan used by Orshansky. In 1968, the Social Security Administration, concerned about the index's adequacy, proposed adjust-
ing it "to conform to the higher general level of living," but the
Bureau of the Budget's Office of Statistical Standards overruled
the proposal. Instead, a Federal Interagency Committee, created in October 1968, reconsidered the poverty line. The committee decided to retain 1963 as the base year but to "switch to
the Consumer Price Index as the price inflates for annual updat-
ing." As Orshansky pointed out: "This meant, of course, that the
food-income relationship which was the basis for the original
poverty measure no longer was the current rationale." Another
important alteration to the poverty index had taken place two
years earlier, when the Census Bureau "quietly dropped its
method of estimation of unreported incomes" and, as a consequence, dropped the number of persons in poverty by about 1.5
million. [71]

As many critics have observed, the official poverty index remains far too low. It rests on unrealistic assumptions about the relation of food to income; it does not vary with regional differences in the cost of living; and it ignores changing standards of consumption. It has also created a new definition of poverty. For the purposes of government policy, poverty is not deprivation; it is a bureaucratic category designed to facilitate the routine collection of statistics and the determination of eligibility for public assistance. It is also a political category, for if nothing else, the history of the poverty line illustrates the politics of numbers. Federal administrators have waged a quiet but persistent campaign against increased standards and, at every junction, have chosen the lowest plausible figure. In this way, they have both checked the expansion of benefits and minimized the problem of poverty in America. Had the Census Bureau updated its thresholds to account for "more recent nutrition standards and consumption practices," asserted Orshansky, the number of poor people in America in 1975 would have risen "from 26 million to 36 million, or from 24 million to 37 million, depending on which census survey you use."[72]

Public policy redefined poverty not only by adopting a bureaucratic standard, but also by its appetite for research. Indeed, the distinguished economist Robert Haveman, former director of the University of Wisconsin's Institute for Research on Poverty, argues that between 1965 and 1980, public policy transformed American social science.[73]

In the early 1960s, anthropologists and sociologists became the first to apply modern social science to contemporary poverty. However, the core concept—the culture of poverty—drew devastating criticism, and their ethnographic methods offered little help to policymakers in need of systematic data. The angry protest following Daniel Patrick Moynihan's 1965 report, *The Negro Family: The Case for National Action*, helped bury both the culture of poverty and the black family as acceptable topics in liberal social science and to pass the leadership in poverty research to economists. Economists met government's need for systematic data, predictive models, and program evaluation. From its "outset," writes Haveman, "the War on Poverty was conceived of as an economic war; the designs, the debates, and the evaluations were all conducted in economic terms. Economics was the central discipline in both the action and the research components of the war."[74]

Massive new government spending on poverty and social welfare (a rise in the share of the federal budget spent on three major social programs from 27 to 53 percent) prompted new research, most of it funded by the federal government. In part, the government stressed research for reasons of political convenience. The "politics of federal antipoverty policy," writes Haveman, "made research spending an attractive option. Research support was clearly less controversial and risky than, say, community action or a guaranteed income program." However, the emphasis on research had other sources as well. From the earliest planning for the War on Poverty, claims Haveman, "the presumption that research and evaluation should guide social policy decisions was a principal tenet." This emphasis reflected "the movement to place government on a more rational and analytic basis" stimulated by Robert McNamara, President Kennedy's secretary of defense, who in turn had been influenced by his experience as president of the Ford Motor Company. McNamara urged the application of systems analysis techniques to public choices and staffed the Defense Department's new and influential Office of the Assistant Secretary for Planning and Evaluation with military analysts from the Rand Corporation. The federal government's chief poverty warrior, Sargent Shriver, first director of OEO, appointed key staff with Defense Department and Rand Corporation backgrounds. As a result, OEO's Office of Planning, Research, and Evaluation "embodied the philosophy of PPBS [planning-programming-budgeting system]" pioneered at Defense.[75]

OEO, which turned to agencies outside the government for most of its research, established the Institute for Research on Poverty at the University of Wisconsin and funded a great deal of other poverty-related research as well. Between 1965 and 1980, in current dollars, annual federal spending on poverty-related research increased from $2.5 to $160 million or from 0.64 percent to 30.12 percent of all federal research and development spending. This increased government spending changed research priorities in the social sciences. Between 1962 and 1964, five leading economics journals published only three articles on poverty-related research; by 1971–1973, the number had increased to fifty-nine. For five leading sociology journals, the increase in the same period was from fifteen to forty-one.[76]

Poverty researchers' first task was descriptive: how to assess and measure changes in economic well-being, poverty, and inequality, and how to incorporate noncash transfers into measures of economic status. Because academic literature on these topics in the early 1960s was nearly nonexistent, the adoption of an official government poverty line became an early priority. This is why OEO seized on Orshansky's index so eagerly and put it to uses for which it was not intended. The unplanned expansion of the nation's income support system also posed urgent research questions: did welfare programs and income transfer policies cause people to work less? Although research showed only very modest work disincentives, it did highlight the inequities that resulted from administrative discretion and benefit variations among states. As a result, most poverty researchers began to advocate a unitary, uniform, and national income maintenance program.

Only the creation of data sets that followed individuals and families over longer periods of time could provide the answer to another important question: Was poverty primarily permanent or transitory? OEO funded the Panel Study of Income Dynamics at the University of Michigan, which in 1968 began to trace a representative sample of the American population. The analysis showed the great differences that emerged from longitudinal, as contrasted with cross-sectional, methods. Sociologists also used new longitudinal data sets for increasingly detailed and sophisticated studies of mobility. (Mobility studies, claims Haveman, had a great influence on sociology but little impact on

policy.) Research on a variety of other topics also shaped thinking about poverty. Studies of the relations among education,
income, and social mobility called into question not only human
capital models, but also the entire educational strategy of the
War on Poverty. In the same years, dual labor market hypotheses forced modifications in neoclassical economic theories.[77]

Poverty research also influenced social science methods. First,
and to Haveman most important, poverty researchers pioneered
large-scale social experiments. Although the implications of poverty research supported a guaranteed national income program,
no one could predict its impact. As a result, OEO sponsored
income maintenance experiments designed to test the effect of
income guarantees on work incentives. These experiments
proved enormously complicated, and their results remain ambiguous. Nonetheless, Haveman feels, the "social policy experiments stand as the clearest example of a breakthrough in the
methodology of social science attributable to the War on Poverty." Other breakthroughs were the development of new methods for correcting bias selectivity (dealing with samples that are
not representative), and the creation of microdata simulation
models to estimate the effects of policies on large populations.[78]

Together with PPBS, poverty research fostered the creation of
public policy analysis as a discipline. New schools within universities trained policy analysts who found work in higher education, government, private research centers, and a burgeoning
evaluation research industry. In the process, poverty acquired a
new definition. It became the property of economists, a technical subject to be discussed only by experts.[79]

The birth of policy analysis and the social research industry
raises critical questions about the sociology of disciplines and
universities. The best social science talent, according to Haveman, did not gravitate to this new field; nor did universities lead
in its major research accomplishments. The reasons reflect the
rigidity of higher learning and the disciplines into which it is
divided. Social science disciplines are recent inventions, conve-

nient ways of carving experience into manageable bites. They do not represent the way the world works. Great issues such as poverty are not problems in sociology, economics, anthropology, or social psychology, or some simple amalgam of them all.

Yet universities remain largely incapable of organizing their resources with sufficient flexibility to facilitate rather than hinder coordinated responses to major issues that transcend conventional disciplinary boundaries. The problem is compounded by the low status of applied interdisciplinary research. Its detractors argue that applied social research lacks theory and fails to advance the disciplines. To the contrary, as Haveman shows, policy research was the energizing source of innovation in social science for at least fifteen years. Poverty research transformed American social science, and poverty researchers tackled questions of enormous complexity. The reasons for the low status of applied research, therefore, lie more in the hubris that leads academics to reify their disciplines and the bureaucratic protectionism that motivates them to guard their turf.

Despite the creation of a new discipline and innovative methods, Haveman, like many others, recognizes the limited impact of research on policy: Policy does not derive from rational analysis, and social science has never found a quick, unmediated path into public policy. Instead, he sees a more modest, although still critical, role for research as a brake on ideology and an arbiter of public debate.[80]

Great Society poverty research proved to be the last hurrah of twentieth-century liberalism. It rested on the expectation that reason, science, and expertise could inform public policy and persuade a benevolent state to engineer social progress. By placing government policy on a scientific basis, poverty researchers hoped to transcend politics and ideology. In the end, although they won several battles, they lost even the intellectual war. They developed new measures with which to chart the contours of poverty; invented dazzling methods with which to experiment, evaluate, and predict; and created a new discipline, a new industry, and a new definition of poverty. But they remained unable to agree on definitive answers to the most important questions (such as the impact of a guaranteed income on work incentives) or to write their conclusions into policy.

From the outset, a variety of factors limited the potential of Great Society poverty research. First, their own enthusiasm and commitment to rationality led poverty researchers to underestimate the influence of politics and ideology and to overestimate the similarities between physical and social science. Large, controlled social experiments with human subjects could not duplicate processes within a physicist's or chemist's laboratory.

Second, the creation of private firms, academic institutes, and huge projects bureaucratized social science and transformed it into a special interest. Survival depended on a steady and copious stream of research dollars. In these circumstances, hype and self-justification became inevitable. Even more, the continued existence of social science as an enterprise depended on its responsiveness to questions posed by the state. This is one reason researchers achieved most in methods and data collection and least in theory or intellectual innovation.

Last, the capture of the social science agenda by government combined with the capture of poverty research by economists to confine the scope of debate within market models of human obligation and interaction. For all its emphasis on innovation, poverty research remained preoccupied by the oldest question in the history of social welfare. For more than two centuries, critics, reformers, and administrators all have asked: Does social welfare leave the poor less willing to work? Although the economists who dominated poverty research disagreed on answers, they asked the same questions. Rarely did they examine their assumptions about the role of market incentives on human behavior or the limits of market models as the basis for public social obligations. In the process, they either ignored or belittled the few alternative frames proposed. It is telling that nowhere in his intelligent, even-handed analysis does Haveman mention the heuristic connection between American poverty and the dependency theory advanced by black scholars in the late 1960s and early 1970s. As a consequence, research failed to shore up the intellectual underpinning of the welfare state. No one noticed that the foundation of liberalism had crumbled, until it was too late.

Interpretations
of Poverty
in the          FOUR
Postindustrial
City

AFTER THE MID-1970s, interpretations of poverty increasingly responded to the emergence of a new urban form: the postindustrial city. The postindustrial American city had emerged as a study in contrasts. New office towers shot up in revitalized downtowns; abandoned factories dotted the rail corridors along former industrial districts. Wealthy professionals who renovated old houses turned seedy neighborhoods into oases of urban charm; poor people increasingly lived in concentrated pockets of poverty. Families on modest incomes could not find affordable housing; arson and neglect destroyed blocks of abandoned homes; and hundreds of thousands of poor people remained homeless. Federally subsidized expressways and commuter trains transported an affluent labor force from federally subsidized suburbs into city cores where, on the streets and subways, they encountered growing numbers of beggars, most of them ineligible for federal welfare, all of them unemployed. Wealthy urbanites spent several thousand dollars each year to send their children to fine private schools from which they entered excellent colleges; children of the urban poor attended decaying public schools whose corridors sometimes required police patrols; many escaped as soon as the law allowed and most of the rest left with minimal skills, unprepared for either higher education or the better jobs offered by the new economy. For the most part, the color of revitalized urban cores and neighborhoods was white; the color of poverty was not. Despite the civil rights movement, in the 1980s American cities remained more racially segregated than at any other time in their history.

Most of the facts about postindustrial cities remained beyond dispute. The question was their interpretation and the response of public policy. By default, intellectual as well as political initiative passed to conservatives, who searched for explanations for continued poverty amid affluence that could justify reducing government aid to cities and social benefits to individuals. In the process, conservative thought about poverty and social welfare passed through two stages and entered a third in the years between the mid-1970s and the late 1980s. It began by denying that poverty remained a real problem. As this argument lost plausibility, conservatives updated some very old ideas that blamed both poor people themselves and the misguided, if well-intentioned, interventions of government.

By the late 1980s, as conditions worsened, only the most intransigent conservatives could disagree that government played a critical role in the alleviation of poverty and social disorganization, and conservative writers increasingly subordinated the libertarian implications of free-market philosophy to a new authoritarianism. The result was a refurbished conservatism that justified big government by advocating the extension of its control over the behavior of millions of Americans. By emphasizing the obligations of the poor instead of their entitlement to public benefits, the appeal of the new authoritarianism diffused beyond conservative circles; in Congress, it even became the intellectual foundation of a bipartisan approach to welfare reform.

Despite the conservative revival, the attempt to recast the intellectual foundation of the welfare state did not end. Philosophers tried to expand the definition of rights and reconstruct the theory of distributive justice; lawyers acting on behalf of poor people argued for the extension of the welfare rights and benefits won in the 1960s; and in the most dramatic rebuttal to conservative social policy, the bishops of the U.S. Catholic Church drew on principles outside conventional liberal discourse about poverty to advocate a massive increase in public benefits. By the late 1980s, in fact, poverty once again became an important political issue, as writers of all political persuasions assessed the cost of the transition to the postindustrial city.

## TRENDS IN URBAN POVERTY

Across the entire country, as we have seen, poverty dropped between the 1960s and early 1970s; then it started to rise again. In 1960, 22 percent of the population had incomes below the poverty line; by 1970 the proportion had dropped to 13 percent; in 1986, it was 14 percent, or 32,370,000 persons. (These and subsequent figures refer to incomes that include government transfers, such as AFDC, food stamps, SSI, and Social Security.) The poverty trajectory differed, however, among blacks and whites. The poverty of whites followed the national pattern: it dropped from 18 percent in 1960 to 10 percent in 1970, and then rose to 11 percent by 1986. Although blacks always had much higher poverty rates, the proportion living below the poverty line decreased from 42 percent in 1960 to 33 percent in 1970 and 32 percent in 1986. Between 1960 and 1986, white poverty decreased by 38 percent and black poverty by 26 percent. Despite the civil rights movement and the Great Society, nearly one of every three black Americans and more than one in four Hispanics still lives below the poverty line.[1]

Children have become the most impoverished age group in

America. Since 1974, their situation has worsened at an alarming rate. Among all children, 27 percent lived below the poverty line in 1960; 15 percent in 1974; and 21 percent in 1986. This represents an increase of 40 percent in just twelve years. More than four of every ten black children live in poverty (their rate rose from 40 to 43 percent between 1974 and 1986), as do 38 percent of Hispanic children. Within central cities, the situation is worse: 29 percent of all children less than 18 years old, or 22 percent of white children and 44 percent of blacks, live below the poverty line. For children less than 6 years old the poverty rates are even higher.

Much of children's poverty derives from the increase in female-headed households. In central cities in 1986, 44 percent of poor persons, 37 percent of whites and 52 percent of blacks, lived in female-headed households. Within them, 60 percent of all children under 18, or 55 percent of whites and 66 percent of blacks, were poor. The situation contrasts sharply with the condition of the age group most impoverished in 1960, the elderly. In central cities in 1986, 7 percent of household heads age 65 or older were poor. Even elderly central city female household heads have a much lower rate of poverty than do children.[2]

Despite the high rates of poverty among blacks and Hispanics, most poor people in the country and in central cities are white. In 1986, 69 percent of the 32,370,000 poor persons were white and about 28 percent were black. This means that blacks, 12 percent of the population, were greatly overrepresented. More than four of every ten persons below the poverty line lived in central cities. Here again, although most of the poor, 57 percent, were white, the 39 percent who were black was nearly double their proportion of the entire population. Across the whole country, 10 percent of families in metropolitan areas lived below the poverty line. Within these areas, 15 percent of the families in central cities and 6 percent outside them (the suburbs) were poor. Poverty, of course, is not just an urban problem: 15 percent of families outside metropolitan areas also lived below the poverty line.[3]

## TRANSFORMATIONS IN
## AMERICA'S CITIES

Three transformations reshaped America's cities after World
War II: the transformation of economy, of demography, and of
space. Each had profound consequences for the nature and extent of poverty. Together, they produced a new configuration,
which may be called the postindustrial city, characterized by
computerized work, the production of services instead of goods,
and more flexibly structured workplaces.[4]

Cities reflect the reshaping of the national occupational structure, especially the decreasing share of employment in manufacturing and the increase in services. Full-time employment in
manufacturing dropped from 27 percent in 1947 to 26 percent in
1969 and 19 percent in 1984. During the same period, service
industries increased their share of full-time employment. The
sectors that grew most were finance, insurance, and real estate,
which increased from 13 percent to 28 percent (to account for
more employment than manufacturing) and government and
government enterprises, which increased from 12 percent to 16
percent. As Emma Rothschild points out, these occupations,
combined with the professions and other services, such as food
and hotels, together account "for all new private jobs in the US
from 1981 to 1986."[5]

The economic transformation away from manufacturing and
toward services occurred even more dramatically within formerly industrial cities,[6] with the result, John Ksarda observes,
that central cities changed "from centers of goods processing to
information processing." Indeed, the proportion of jobs in industries classified as information processing rose, in Rustbelt
cities, by about 35 percent and in the Sunbelt even more, from
about 48 percent to 150 percent.[7]

The consequences of the economic transformation exacerbated poverty for a number of reasons. Jobs increasingly re-

quired more education. The number of jobs where the mean educational level of employees was less than high school had dropped throughout the postwar period, but it declined most during the 1970s: in Philadelphia, Boston, St. Louis, and Houston, it declined between 52 percent and 219 percent. Yet the high school dropout rate in cities hovered around 40 percent, putting increasing numbers of jobs out of the reach of city residents.[8]

A second consequence was dislocation. Between 1979 and 1984, Frank Levy reports, a U.S. Bureau of Labor Statistics study reported that more than half of the 5.1 million adult, previously steadily employed displaced workers it counted had lost manufacturing jobs. By January 1986, although economic recovery had been underway for a year, of every ten of these displaced workers, three worked for wages equal to or better than those in the job they lost; another three were working for "wages lower than those in the job they lost"; and four remained "unemployed or had dropped out of the labor force."[9]

The stagnation of the economy after 1973 compounded the consequences of a shifting occupational structure and displacement. The years after World War II divide into two distinct economic periods. During the first, which lasted through 1973, the average weekly earnings of all 40-year-old men climbed by 2.5 to 3.0 percent annually. In the second period, from 1973 through at least 1985, wages stagnated and often declined. Indeed, between 1973 and 1980, in constant dollars, average family income declined by 7 percent. Declining productivity further reinforced economic stagnation. Between 1950 and the early 1960s, productivity increased about 3.3 percent a year. This healthy rate dropped to about 2.5 percent after 1966 and from 1974 to 1982, plummeted to only 0.8 percent. The result, according to Levy, was a "rapidly increasing *inequality of prospects, an inequality in the chance that a family will enjoy the American dream* [italics in original]."[10]

The characteristics of new jobs also diminished workers' prospects, especially for minorities and the urban poor. According to Rothschild, of the 12 million jobs created during the Reagan

years, 3 million were "services provided by the poor, or poverty
jobs, such as cooks and sales clerks, . . . in industries, such as
retail trade and hotels, that pay poverty wages." The worst paid
of all jobs except agriculture, they also employ the highest concentration of black and Hispanic workers.[11] "Lower-paying industries" within the poverty service sector, Rothschild points
out, accounted for 21 percent of all U.S. jobs in 1987, and 27
percent of new jobs created from 1983 to 1987. These figures are
undoubtedly much too low because they do not include illegal
immigrants, who are concentrated within them. The wages offered by these jobs will not push people out of poverty, and the
frequent absence of fringe benefits (such as health insurance
and pensions) exacerbates the low pay. Indeed, the fastest growing industry has been "personal supply services," or the provision of temporary workers, which grew by 14 percent a year
during the height of the Reagan boom. Personal supply service
jobs last only a short time and provide few benefits. This "expansion of badly paid jobs," concludes Rothschild, "accounts for
much of the increase in poverty in the U.S."[12]

It also is one reason why the number of working poor, which
declined sharply during the 1960s, reversed direction. Between
1978 to 1985, claim Sar A. Levitan and Isaac Shapiro, the number of poor persons working full time year-round, about 2 million, rose by 50 percent, while the number working part time,
about 7.1 million, climbed more than 35 percent. Increased poverty among working people results partly from the quality of the
jobs they can get and partly from the declining real value of the
minimum wage which, in 1987, dropped to its lowest level since
the 1950s. As a result, a person with two children working full
time year-round for the minimum wage earned 23 percent less
than the poverty line.[13]

Economic stagnation, the disproportionate growth of low-
wage jobs, the declining minimum wage, the mismatch between
better jobs and the education of the urban poor, and shifts in
occupational structure have worsened poverty within America's
cities. Most poor people survive by government transfers, not by
what they can earn in the labor market. As early as 1973, families

in poverty received half their income from government payments. In the late 1980s, in nearly half the families in the lowest income quintile, *no one* earned any money in the labor market. There is no reason to expect the situation to improve without dramatic economic growth or unprecedented innovations in public policy.[14]

Transformation stands out as the major theme in the recent history of large, older cities' demography as well as their economies. Their populations, formerly primarily of white European heritage, became predominantly black, Hispanic, and other minority. Recent demographic history is a complex story of competing and sometimes contradictory migration streams. After World War II, the mechanization of southern agriculture drove blacks off the land and into northern cities. Between 1950 and 1980, the proportion of black men working in agriculture dropped from 30 percent to 5 percent. From the end of World War II to 1960, one-third of the southern black population moved to other regions. During the 1950s, the proportion of blacks residing in central cities grew from 41 percent to 51 percent.[15]

As blacks began to move into northern cities, whites, lured by new suburbs easily accessible on new highways and expressways, moved out. So did industry. As a consequence, older cities in the Northeast and Midwest lost population, while southern and western cities grew. Between 1955 and 1960, net migration added 56,000 residents to the South and 1,425,000 to the West. The Midwest lost 842,000 and the Northeast, 639,000. In the following decades the size of these population gains increased, peaking, except for the West, between 1975 and 1980, when the South gained 1,935,000 and the West 976,000, while the Midwest lost 1,302,000 and the Northeast, 1,609,000.[16]

Although the population of older cities declined, black in-migrants partially offset the white exodus. The result was racial transformation. Between 1970 and 1980, New York's population declined by 823,000. However, 1,393,000 whites left as 176,000 blacks, 204,000 Hispanics, and 190,000 of other origins entered. The minority population, as a result, grew from 36 to 48 percent. In the next three years, it rose to 52 percent. Detroit's population dropped by 308,000 during the same years, reflecting the out-migration of 418,000 whites and 1,000 Hispanics and the in-migration of 102,000 blacks and 9,000 of other origins. Its minority population rose from 46 percent to 67 percent.[17]

Racial change was one aspect of urban demographic transformation; a second was family structure. Young adults more often live apart from their parents today than twenty years ago; the aged less frequently live with relatives; and children more than ever before live in households headed by single women. The last of these changes has had the most significant impact on cities. In 1983, single mothers headed almost 6.57 million families, about 19 percent of the total. Among whites, they headed 14 percent of families and among blacks, 48 percent. White female-headed families were spread fairly evenly across cities, suburbs, and nonmetropolitan areas; those headed by a black woman were concentrated (64 percent) in central cities. Families headed by single women grew most swiftly after 1960 among both whites and blacks. Demographers estimate that 42 percent of white children and 84 percent of black children born in the 1970s will live for some time with a single mother before they reach the age of 18.[18]

About half of the families headed by single women are poor, even after income from cash transfer programs. Their poverty has three main sources: The family head earns relatively little; the absent parent fails to provide support; and public transfers remain meager. In 1982, among black families headed by single women, earned family income averaged only $9,128, compared to $23,913 for two-parent black families. The women who headed these families earned an average of $5,383; other family members added only $837; child support averaged a mere $322; Social Security and related payments, $907; and public assistance and food stamps, $2,573. Families headed by a single white woman fared only slightly better, and most of them also lived in poverty.[19]

These demographic transformations have left cities with large numbers of residents unable to take well-paid new jobs and dependent instead on public support and social services. At the same time, financial burdens have risen to nearly intolerable levels, as the flight of industry and affluent whites has decimated the tax base of central cities. The cities now are unable to contribute very much to alleviate the poverty in their midst or its attendant hardships, such as the lack of affordable housing.

Spatial transformations have worsened the shortages of affordable housing and accessible jobs in postwar cities. No one set out to destroy the industrial base of American cities; it eroded as the result of vast changes in the world economy, new transportation and manufacturing technologies, the absence of effective public policy, and the pursuit of short-term profits. The outcome, however, was clear enough. As John Mollenkopf observed, the symbol of American cities shifted from the factory to the office tower. The most fortunate among older industrial cities added a revitalized downtown core of office buildings to miles of abandoned factories, decaying housing, and neglected infrastructure. The least fortunate cities lacked major educational or health complexes, government centers, or corporate headquarters. Not even their cores sprang back to life.

Earlier, the social geography of industrial cities reflected intricate relations between home and workplace. Working-class districts, often with strong ethnic concentrations, clustered near factories. As factories left, more fortunate city workers followed the new jobs to the suburbs. Others, especially those too poor to afford a car, remained trapped, unable to find or afford public transportation that linked their homes with the new geography of work.[20]

Suburbanization did not begin after World War II. Population dispersal has a long history in America and reflects a variety of motives: the desire for space and amenities, access to jobs, exclusivity, upward mobility, and racism. Always, it has depended on transportation: at first, in the mid-nineteenth century, horse-

drawn streetcars and railroads; near the end of the century, electric trolleys; in the twentieth century, buses and automobiles.
Until late in the nineteenth century, public transport remained
too expensive for most working people, and at first only the more
affluent, followed later by the middle classes, could escape beyond city borders. With the introduction of affordable automobiles, suburban growth escalated in the 1920s. The Great
Depression and World War II slowed it to a trickle until the late
1940s.[21]

As late as the end of the nineteenth century, urban downtowns remained fashionable places to live. Workers who served
the urban rich jammed into alleyways or clustered in districts
close to their employers. Other poor people found housing on
the outskirts of cities, where land cost less. Cities remained intri-
cately patterned mosaics of classes, ethnic groups, and races
living in close proximity. Industrial relocation, population dispersal, and suburbanization changed these patterns as people
increasingly sorted themselves residentially by class and race. In
the process, housing prices fell in center cities abandoned by the
affluent as the immigrants and native poor who succeeded them
transformed the social demography of city centers.[22]

After 1945, suburbanization accelerated. Massive increases in
automobile ownership, the federal highway program, and federal housing policies that underwrote suburban mortgages and
redlined cities composed one set of factors speeding its development. Another was the introduction of mass production in the
residential construction industry. Builders such as Abraham,
William, and Alfred Levitt developed techniques for erecting
entire subdivisions of modestly priced homes with lightning
speed. A third was demand. Domestic housing construction had
virtually ceased during the Depression and the war. After the
war, young people, who began to marry earlier than ever before
in American history, created a baby boom that exacerbated the
housing shortage.[23]

Federal policy ensured that housing development happened
in suburbs rather than within cities and favored the white middle
classes rather than minorities and the poor. Although subsidies

of low-income housing remained modest, the actions of the federal government accelerated the exodus to the suburbs. These included a vast postwar expansion of the Federal Housing Administration's (FHA) mortgage guarantee program, the growth of a federally sponsored secondary mortgage market, and the income tax deduction for home ownership. At the same time, zoning ordinances restricted most suburban residential development to single-family housing, and the FHA placed racial restrictions on its mortgages until the 1960s. Together, these policies kept the suburbs white.[24]

Indeed, suburbs have used a variety of exclusionary techniques to block changes in their racial or economic character. Many have centered on preventing the construction of low-cost subsidized housing. Writing the second of two decisions that attacked this use of zoning in Mt. Laurel, New Jersey, State Supreme Court Chief Justice Robert N. Wilentz commented in 1983: "After all this time, 10 years after the trial court's initial order invalidating its zoning ordinance, Mt. Laurel remains afflicted with a blatantly exclusionary ordinance. Papered over with studies, rationalized by hired experts, the ordinance at its core is true to nothing but Mt. Laurel's determination to exclude the poor."

The result, of course, has been the concentration of the poor and of blacks within cities. In 1980, blacks made up only about 6 percent of suburban populations; the suburbs were the modal residence of white Americans; they were home to one in five black households. Even within suburbs, blacks remained concentrated, often in "troubled" areas undergoing economic decline. The process of black suburbanization, according to Gary Orfield, differed from white, and the result could be just the recreation of ghettoes, "with segregated slums, falling population, and effective nullification of everything the early immigrants believed they had won." In some areas, he pointed out, the recreation of the ghetto already had begun.[25]

Federal highway policy reinforced the movement of population and industry out of cities. The 1956 Highway Act creating the interstate highway system reimbursed local governments for

90 percent of the cost of construction and thereby funneled immense sums into cities. Not only did new highways and expressways encourage commuting and population dispersal; they also divided cities into new sections, creating walls between poor or minority neighborhoods and central business districts. They dislocated mainly poor people from their homes with little compensation.[26]

Urban renewal was another great force that reshaped cities in the postwar era. It began with the observation that "blight" had afflicted America's cities. Its charter, the Housing Act of 1949, whose putative intent was to improve the housing of the poor, required redeveloped areas to be primarily residential. However, it defined "primarily" as at least 50 percent residential either before or after redevelopment. In practice, most cities met the requirement by tearing down existing housing and not replacing it. Subsequent legislation broadened even this loose gesture of concern for housing supply.[27] Urban renewal resulted in both revitalized downtowns and the displacement of people from their homes. Nicknamed "Negro removal," it displaced many more than it relocated.

Writing in 1975, John Mollenkopf pointed out: "More than a quarter of a million families have been displaced each year. They have received only $34.8 million in relocation payments, or less than 1 percent of the total." Martin Anderson claimed that between 1950 and 1960, urban renewal destroyed 126,000 homes and built only 28,000 new ones. The average rent on homes destroyed had been about $50 or $60 a month; on new homes, it was $195. As a result, "Housing conditions were made worse for those whose housing conditions were least good." A 1961 study of renewal projects in 41 cities showed that public authorities merely relocated 60 percent of the dispossessed tenants to other slums.[28]

In recent years, gentrification has turned some inner city districts into oases of urban charm. Geographer Brian Berry refers to them as "islands of renewal within the seas of decay." Despite their visibility, they encompass only about 0.5 percent of urban housing stock, and their effects are mixed, for rising taxes and property values drive some people with modest incomes out of their neighborhoods and make it impossible for anyone not affluent to take their place.[29]

Spatial transformation has thus added to the forces worsening the condition of the urban poor, who now live in districts where poverty has concentrated to a degree unprecedented in modern times. The proportion of America's poor living in central cities leaped from 27 percent to 43 percent between 1959 and 1985; among blacks the increase was even greater, from 38 percent to 61 percent. Within cities the concentration of poor blacks (and probably Hispanics) in poverty districts (that is, census tracts designated as poor) also increased dramatically. Between 1970 and 1980, in the 50 largest cities the proportion of poor whites living in census tracts with a poverty rate of 20 percent or more decreased from 36 to 34 percent, and the proportion in tracts with a poverty rate of at least 40 percent remained 8 percent. By contrast, the share of poor blacks in tracts at least 20 percent poor rose from 80 to 84 percent, and in tracts at least 40 percent poor from 27 to 36 percent, or by one-third, in just one decade. In the 50 largest cities, the number of poor persons living in high poverty areas increased 66 percent, from 975,000 to 1,615,000, during the 1970s. This concentration of poverty, however, did not occur uniformly in all cities; three-fourths of all the growth took place in four cities: New York, Chicago, Philadelphia, and Detroit.[30]

## CONSERVATIVES AND POVERTY

Growing poverty in postindustrial cities did not rekindle compassion or renew the faltering energy of the Great Society. Instead, a war on welfare accompanied the conservative revival of the early 1980s. City governments, teetering on the edge of bankruptcy, cut social services; state governments trimmed welfare rolls with more restrictive rules for General Assistance; and the federal government attacked social programs. The result re-

duced the availability of help from each level of government
during the years when the great transformations within postindustrial cities increased poverty and its attendant hardships.[31]

Several sources fed the conservative restoration symbolized by
Ronald Reagan's election as president in 1980. Business interests, unable to compete in an increasingly international market,
wanted to lower wages by reducing the influence of unions and
cutting social programs that not only raised taxes but offered an
alternative to poorly paid jobs. The energy crisis of 1973 ushered
in an era of stagflation in which public psychology shifted away
from its relatively relaxed attitude toward the expansion of social
welfare. Increasingly worried about downward mobility and
their children's future, many Americans returned to an older
psychology of scarcity. As they examined the sources of their
distress, looking for both villains and ways to cut public spending, ordinary Americans and their elected representatives focused on welfare and its beneficiaries, deflecting attention from
the declining profits and returns on investments that, since the
mid-1960s, should have alerted them to the end of unlimited
growth and abundance.[32]

Welfare was an easy target, first because its rolls, and expense,
had swollen so greatly in the preceding several years and, second, because so many of its clients were unmarried black
women. Welfare, it appeared, encouraged young black women
to have children out of wedlock; discouraged them from marry-
ing; and, along with generous unemployment and disability insurance, fostered indolence and reluctance to work. Clearly, it
appeared, however praiseworthy the intentions, the impact of
the War on Poverty and the Great Society had been perverse.
They had worsened the very problems they set out to solve by
destroying families, diffusing immorality, pushing taxes unen-
durably high, maintaining crippling wage levels, and lowering
productivity.

Confronted by this resurgent conservative social criticism, liberalism's response was collapse. By narrowing their criteria for
public policy to the relation between income maintenance and
work incentives, liberals had ceded the debate before it began.

First, they failed to weave together a fresh defense of the welfare state from new definitions of rights and entitlements, emergent conceptions of distributive justice, ethnographic data about poor people, and revised historical and political interpretations of poverty and welfare. This inability to mount a broad defense of social justice and the welfare state was one price paid for the capture of poverty by economists and the new profession of public policy analysis. Second, liberals failed to relate an invigorated welfare state to economic and moral renewal; they lacked a plausible response to the intuitively interconnected problems troubling ordinary Americans: stagflation; declining opportunity; increased taxes and welfare spending; crime and violence on the streets; and the erosion of families and moral standards.

Conservative critics triumphed easily in the early 1980s because they confronted the manifold worries of ordinary Americans with a convincing interpretation. Welfare became the centerpiece of an explanation for economic stagnation and moral decay. As a causal theory this conservative criticism was largely wrong, but it was nonetheless plausible and coherent.

The modern conservative assault on the welfare state began in the 1970s with an unsuccessful attempt to deny the problem of poverty in postindustrial cities. At the peak of their influence in the first half of the decade, conservatives, like the liberals before them, focused on one of the historic preoccupations in the history of poverty and relief: the results of welfare. Only they reached different answers. Welfare, they said, hurt the poor by demoralizing them. By contrast, slicing benefits would stimulate the economy, create jobs, and force poor people into an independence that, in the long run, would leave them happier and better off. This is, of course, a very old argument. Indeed, throughout American history, most welfare reform has been a euphemism for cutting the cost of relief.[33] Conservatives thus purveyed a modern version of the classic argument against social welfare.

For centuries other conservatives had used precisely the same logic to link relief to the economy, family, and public morality. This modern version reached its zenith during the high noon of the Reagan era. Its failure was followed by a new conservativism of big government that dwelled on another historic preoccupation of welfare and poverty discourse: the nature and limits of social obligation. Throughout each of its phases, the attempt to classify poor people by moral worth—the other historical preoccupation of poverty discourse—permeated conservative thought.

In 1978, Martin Anderson, who had been a domestic policy advisor to Richard Nixon, argued that poverty was no longer a serious problem in America. His book, *Welfare: The Political Economy of Welfare Reform in the United States*, attacked the concept of a guaranteed income (he had staunchly opposed the Family Assistance Plan from within the administration) and tried to show that the combination of in-kind benefits (food stamps, Medicare, housing) with public assistance and social insurance had eliminated all but residual pockets of poverty. He recommended a scaled-back, more efficiently administered version of the existing welfare state, whose political economy, he believed, left it impervious to fundamental reform.[34]

Anderson published his study of welfare in 1978, when President Jimmy Carter's Program for Better Jobs and Income (PBJI) was before Congress. PBJI proposed to reform welfare through a form of guaranteed income similar to Nixon's abortive Family Assistance Plan. Anderson, who had opposed the Family Assistance Plan, also urged the defeat of Carter's proposal. *"The basic thrust of PBJI,"* wrote Anderson, *"is to further the idea of a guranteed income, expanding welfare into the heart of the middle class of America. It is a potential social revolution of great magnitude that could result in social tragedy* [italics in original]."[35]

Anderson presented four major arguments. First, guaranteed incomes destroyed work incentives. Extrapolating from the result of income maintenance experiments, he predicted that a guaranteed income could reduce the work effort of low-income workers by as much as 50 percent. Second, within the current welfare system, a "poverty wall" built of generous benefits and high marginal tax rates cut people off from work incentives. Third, American welfare's complex political economy would defeat any attempt at radical restructuring. Therefore, needed reforms should be made within the framework of existing programs. Anderson offered a list that would tighten requirements, reduce loads, trim costs, and increase work incentives.[36] Fourth, the success of income redistribution programs had nearly eliminated poverty in America. With in-kind benefits added to cash, very few people remained below the poverty line.

Anderson's "first thesis" states the case unambiguously:

> The "war on poverty" that began in 1964 has been won. The growth of jobs and income in the private economy, combined with an explosive increase in government spending for welfare and income transfer programs, has virtually eliminated poverty in the United States. Any Americans who truly cannot care for themselves are now eligible for generous government aid in the form of cash, medical benefits, food stamps, housing and other services [italics in original].

Americans had constructed an array of programs to attack a poverty "army" numbering between 25 and 30 million. Although the enemy had nearly disappeared, the attack went on unabated. Unlike other critics, Anderson argued that welfare's failure remained a myth. The system's many inadequacies could not obscure its achievements: "In terms of the key goals it was set up to accomplish, it has been a smashing, total success."[37]

As he reflected on this claim of Anderson and others, Michael Harrington commented: the "most astounding conservative discovery of the 1970s" was that poverty had "disappeared and no one noticed." Within only a few years, he continued, "the statistical abolition of poverty had turned into an academic cottage industry in the United States." The Reagan administration welcomed this new industry's product as scientific support for its proposed reduction of social benefits, and the media publicized the good news.[38]

Almost all academic and political attention, Harrington observed, focused on possible ways the poor had been overcounted. In fact, official poverty statistics regularly undercounted the poor in two ways. First, manipulations of the official poverty line probably excluded several million people from the ranks of the poor. Second, the Census Bureau count did not include undocumented workers, most of whom do not earn enough to escape poverty. Harrington estimated that in 1984 as many as 30 million more people—that is, roughly double the Census Bureau's count—could be labeled poor by the original official standards.[39]

Harrington and others also described the ambiguities and flaws that riddled what one scholar has called the poverty reduction literature, which rests on the growth of in-kind benefits:

1. In-kind benefits do not eliminate poverty. Although they help people already in poverty to survive, they do not make them less poor.
2. By adding in-kind benefits to the cash incomes of recipients, analysts count them twice. Most of the money actually goes to vendors who provide services. (Medicaid accounts for the largest share of the money used to compute the value of in-kind benefits.)
3. Computations confound two definitions of income. They add the value of in-kind benefits to the incomes of public assistance recipients, but exclude them from the income of everyone else. In fact, the nonpoor receive far larger government subsidies. These include (but are by no means limited to) Social Security, Medicare, and income-tax deductions for interest on home mortgages.
4. In-kind benefits are distributed unevenly among the poor. The lion's share goes to those who are elderly. Medicaid accounts for two-thirds of in-kind benefits, and 46 percent of it is spent on nursing homes and other forms of institutional care.
5. Poverty reduction literature draws on three different ways of estimating the value of in-kind benefits. Each gives a radically different count of the poor. The market-value approach estimates their worth in terms of what it would cost to purchase them on the private market. It adds up their value and distributes them evenly across the poverty population—which makes

no sense because they are, in fact, distributed differentially. This method yields the largest reduction in poverty. Another method attempts to measure their value to the recipient. What would poor people be willing to pay for the benefit? The third estimates value in terms of share of a poverty budget. It gives the lowest reduction. Neither the second nor the third method is free of unverified, questionable assumptions or from the difficulty inherent in a distribution of benefits skewed toward the aging poor.
6. The trend line implied by the poverty reduction literature is wrong. After the mid-1970s, the real value of public assistance decreased, and it represented an increasingly smaller proportion of median income. Although the cash value of Medicaid grew, its rise reflected the increased cost of health care, not a wider or improved delivery of services. Poverty rates (as pointed out elsewhere in this book) started to climb.[40]

The poverty reduction literature, as Leonard Beeghley aptly points out, confuses politics and science. Researchers believed that statistics could measure poverty objectively. In fact, because poverty defies scientific measurement, all measures inevitably reflect political judgments. Reading the poverty reduction literature, it seemed as though a social problem had disappeared "like magic." Nonetheless, the growth and persistence of poverty mocked accounts of its disappearance, and soon even conservatives could no longer base policy on the assumption that in-kind benefits had combined with public assistance to eliminate want.

By the early 1980s, the impact of in-kind benefits on poverty-level incomes was beside the point. Whatever statisticians might conclude, their arguments seemed distracting quibbles beside the mounting evidence of hunger, homelessness, and destitution. Because conservatives could not redefine poverty out of existence, they needed a fresh set of reasons for cutting social benefits. In 1981, a best-selling Book-of-the-Month Club selection, *Wealth and Poverty* by George Gilder, gave the new administration the intellectual ammunition it needed to justify an ambitious attempt to cut social spending on the poor and reduce taxes for the rich.

*Wealth and Poverty* received lavish praise from Jack Kemp, David Stockman, *Barron's*, and *The New York Times* and became, according to one reviewer, the "Bible of the Reagan administration."[41] In 1984, as Gilder's influence waned, Charles Murray's more sober and conventional *Losing Ground* provided conservatives with an authoritative argument against direct government spending to combat the undeniable growth of poverty. In the same years, those who needed a more sophisticated philosophic justification for reducing the social role of government could turn to *Anarchy, the State, and Utopia*, by Harvard philosopher Robert Nozick.[42]

More a moralist than an analyst, Gilder exalts capitalism as he mounts the barricades to defend it against its enemies, which include redistributive taxation, the welfare state, and feminism. As he rummages through intellectual history, choosing bits of conservative anthropology, economics, and theology, Gilder plays on the anti-intellectualism never far from the surface of American culture. For Gilder is not a professional social scientist. Although he often draws on their conclusions for support, social scientists emerge as the most dangerous foes—muddle-headed, arrogant, self-aggrandizing liberals whose policies have very nearly destroyed America.

Above all, *Wealth and Poverty* is a paean to capitalism. According to Gilder, the essence of capitalism is altruism, not self-interest. "Capitalism begins with giving. Not from greed, avarice, or even self-love can one expect the rewards of commerce, but from a spirit closely akin to altruism, a regard for the needs of others, a benevolent, outgoing, and courageous temper of mind." Capitalism takes the universal "gift impulse" and transforms it into "a disciplined process of creative investment based on a continuing analysis of the needs of others." Not surprisingly, Gilder's hero is the small entrepreneur, the daring risk-taker, agent of change, fountain of Schumpeter's "creative destruction."[43]

Gilder celebrates both great wealth and inequality, for they embody not only the just rewards of success, but more important, the leaven for raising the living standards of all, including the poor. Poverty results from indolence, cynicism, and the demoralizing impact of public policy. "The only dependable route from poverty," asserts Gilder, "is always work, family, and faith. The first principle is that in order to move up, the poor must not only work, they must work harder than the classes above them. . . . But the current poor, white even more than black, are refusing to work hard."

Gilder's second principle of upward mobility is the maintenance of monogamous marriage and family. Married men, "spurred by the claims of family," channel their "otherwise disruptive male aggressions" into providing for wives and and children. The increase in female-headed families therefore perpetuates the poverty of women and children and unleashes the primitive impulses of men:

> The key to lowerclass life in contemporary America is that unrelated individuals, as the census calls them, are so numerous and conspicuous that they set the tone for the entire community. . . .
> The problem is neither race nor matriarchy in any meaningful sense. It is familial anarchy among the concentrated poor of the inner city, in which flamboyant and impulsive youths rather than responsible men provide the themes of aspiration.

The demoralization of the poor is the consequence of a perverse welfare system, which "now erodes work and family and thus keeps poor people poor."[44]

This glorification of great wealth sits uneasily beside a heroic portrait of small enterpreneurs or the attack on the government bailout of the Chrysler Corporation. Nor is Gilder's equation of capitalism with distinterested public love consistent with his stress on sober self-interest as a guide to how tax policy and economic incentives actually work. Nonetheless, his relentless assault on any public policy that retards the individual pursuit of wealth does not swerve as he ranges across taxation, environmental regulation, affirmative action, and welfare. Most of his arguments are not new. His concrete criticisms of welfare, for instance, restate the classic arguments against the dole, which, as always, are couched in the best interests of the poor:

> Unemployment compensation promotes unemployment. Aid for Families with Dependent Children makes more families dependent and fatherless. Disability insurance in all its multiple forms encourages the promotion of small ills into temporary disabilities and partial disabilities into total and permanent ones. Social security payments may discourage concern for the aged and dissolve the links between generations. Programs of insurance against low farm prices and high energy costs create a glut of agricultural commodities and a dearth of fuels. Comprehensive Employment and Training Act (CETA) subsidies for government make-work may enhance a feeling of dependence on the state without giving the sometimes bracing experience of genuine work. All means-tested programs (designed exclusively for the poor) promote the value of being "poor" (the credential of poverty), and thus perpetuate poverty. To the degree that the moral hazards exceed the welfare effects, all these programs should be modified, usually by reducing the benefits.[45]

Two themes set Gilder's attack on welfare policy apart. One is the harshness of his assault on affirmative action. The other is his belief in the biological basis of sex roles. Affirmative action, he maintains, aggravates the demoralizing effects of welfare by perpetuating "false theories of discrimination and spurious claims of racism and sexism as the dominant forces in the lives of the poor." The fact of the matter is that "it would seem genuinely difficult to sustain the idea that America is still oppressive and discriminatory." Then too, based on his reading of anthropology, Gilder asserts that "female sexuality, as it evolved over the millennia, is psychologically rooted in the bearing and nurturing of children." Civilization therefore depends on "the submission of the short-term sexuality of young men to the extended maternal horizons of women." Welfare destroys constructive male values by appropriating the role of provider from husbands and fathers and giving it to the state. As a result, men are "cuckolded by the compassionate state."[46]

Gilder plays fast and loose with his sources, and often relies on proof by haphazard anecdote. Overwhelming evidence refutes most of his claims about poverty and welfare, for instance. However, whether the data support his theories does not matter all that much. For Gilder is primarily a moralist and theologian who rests his case on faith and courage in the face of a wild, unpredictable universe. More to the point, he is right about the sterility of public policy dominated by a narrow technocratic vision. Gilder, far more than any careful and responsible social scientists, spoke to the interlaced economic, personal, and moral anxieties that fueled conservatism's triumph in the era of Ronald Reagan.[47]

Gilder's paean to capitalism attacked the social and economic policies of the 1960s, but it did not engage John Rawls's philosophic defense of redistributive government or the concept of distributive justice on which it rested. Instead, the major challenge to Rawls came from his Harvard colleague Robert Nozick. Nozick's *Anarchy, the State, and Utopia* (1974) and Rawls's *Theory of Justice*, noted one reviewer, in a judgment from which few would dissent, were the "two most important books in political ethics since World War II." Together, observed another, Rawls and Nozick were "inaugurating a needed renaissance in political philosophy." Nozick, who also found a more popular audience, attracted a growing number of followers. Indeed, according to Sheldon Wolin in *The New York Times Book Review*, *Anarchy, the State, and Utopia* was "welcomed by American business journals as a ringing defense of private enterprise and a devastating critique of the welfare state."[48]

It was ironic that conservatives praised Nozick, for he did not consider himself one of them. He intended *Anarchy, the State, and Utopia* to give comfort to no political party and identified himself most closely with the libertarian position. Indeed, his argument runs directly counter to the moral authoritarian strand within contemporary conservatism. Nonetheless, readers often appropriate books for purposes other than those their author intended, and given his summary statement of his conclusions, little mystery exists about the attraction of *Anarchy, the State, and Utopia* for the political Right:

> Our main conclusions about the state are that a minimal state, limited to the narrow functions of protection against force, theft, fraud, enforcement of contracts, and so on, is justified; that any more extensive state will violate persons' rights not to be forced to do certain things, and is unjustified; and that the minimal state is inspiring as well as right. Two noteworthy implications are that the state may not use its coercive apparatus for the purpose of getting some citizens to aid others, or in order to prohibit activities to people for their own good or protection.[49]

*Anarchy, the State, and Utopia* rests on the assumption that "individuals are ends and not merely means; they may not be sacrificed or used for the achieving of other ends without their consent. Individuals are inviolable." Two major arguments follow from this radical individualist premise. The first defends the existence of the state with a hypothetical account of its origins. The second attempts to show why arguments in favor of extending the scope of the state are wrong. A final brief section delineates a libertarian utopia, whose possibility, for Nozick, makes the minimal state inspring as well as just.[50]

Like Rawls, Nozick begins with a state of nature, only its inhabitants do not make decisions behind a "veil of ignorance." Instead, they shrewdly confront dangers by creating protective associations which, over time and without prior intent, they merge into a monopoly with the essential characteristics of a state. Because it arises from a process that does not violate individual rights, the monopoly or minimal state is both necessary and legitimate. Nonetheless, with one very important exception, any extensions of its scope impermissibly violate individual rights. All major theories that attempt to legitimate these extensions are, for Nozick, fatally flawed.

He pays most attention to Rawls and to Marxism. Beyond their individual failings, both share the weakness of almost all theories of distributive justice: They are "end-state" theories, in that they advocate some optimal distribution of resources and evaluate societies on the basis of how closely they approximate it. They show little concern, however, with how distribution decisions are reached, especially with the inescapable conclusion that they are attainable only through the violation of inviolable individual rights. Nozick proposes, to the contrary, to evaluate distributions according to three criteria: "the principle of acquisition of holdings, the principle of transfer of holdings, and the principle of rectification of violations of the first two principles." Individual holdings acquired and transferred through morally permissible means are entitlements. Individuals deserve them; the state may not take them away. "Taxation of earnings from labor is on a par with forced labor." The state may not appropriate the wealth of one individual for the benefit of another. It has no moral right to coerce any person to share resources. It has no obligation to assist the poor through the public purse, nor may it intervene to prohibit behavior that does not violate the inviolable rights of others.[51]

Through the principle of rectification of violations Nozick provides a back door for an activist, redistributive state: "Although to introduce socialism as the punishment for our sins would be to go too far," he observes, "past injustices might be so great as to make necessary in the short run a more extensive state in order to rectify them." In fact, distribution patterns might be taken as "rough rules of thumb" for identifying the result of historic injustices, and "a rough rule of thumb for rectifying injustice" might be to "organize society so as to maximize the position of whatever group ends up least well-off in the society." Nozick therefore does not rule out ending up with the same practical politics as Rawls, even though he would reach them by an entirely different route.[52]

That route entails a radical and curious disjunction of method. His account of the origins of the state rests on a wholly hypothetical state of nature, whose lack of concrete historical foundation he vigorously defends. Yet he criticizes most theories of distributive justice for their ahistorical basis. As end-state theories, they remain unconcerned with how societies reach desired distributions and are thus insensitive to violations of individual rights. Only through historical accounts of the acquisition and transfer of holdings, he counters, may individuals' entitlements to their possessions be sanctioned as legitimate, or condemned as its opposite.

Despite his stress on historical process, Nozick offers no evidence that contemporary distributions of wealth are outcomes of just processes of acquisition and transfer. Nor does he provide any but the most general guide for assessing them. Indeed, using his principles, few historians would have difficulty reaching a conclusion opposite to that which he implies—namely, the entitlement of contemporary Americans to the undisturbed enjoyment of all their wealth. For evidence of fraud, collusion, violence, and the violation of individual rights abounds in America's past.

To Nozick, property seems wholly a matter of things. He enters the debate about distributive justice among philosophers and political theorists, but ignores its counterpart among legal scholars, thereby avoiding questions about the definition of property such as those raised by Charles Reich. Could he agree that property represents a relationship sanctioned by, and not antecedent to, the state? How would acknowledgment of changing forms of property affect his argument? Here, as in so much of the most interesting discourse about poverty and welfare, streams of scholarship develop parallel to, but rarely touching, each other.

However Nozick intended his arguments to be used, they lent themselves easily to the retrenchment of social benefits and the exaltation of greed fashionable in the early 1980s. It is a greatly oversimplified, distorted, and vulgar, but nonetheless comprehensible, step from Nozick's dazzling scholarship to David Stockman's assertion that no one is entitled to claim any social benefits from government. It is an even less precipitous step to Charles Murray's attack on the welfare state.

. . .

In *Losing Ground* (1984), Charles Murray quotes Robert Nozick only once. His chapter on the purposes of social welfare ("What Do We Want to Accomplish?") starts with Nozick's observation that "The legitimacy of altering social institutions to achieve greater equality of material condition is, though often assumed, rarely argued for." Like Nozick and Gilder, Murray is not an egalitarian. His slogan is, "Billions for equal opportunity, not one cent for equal outcome." The legitimacy of social inequality underpins his attack on social welfare, just as it does Gilder's defense of wealth and Nozick's concept of entitlement.[53]

Another assumption, not wholly consistent with the first, lurks just beneath the surface of Murray's argument. The first assumption justifies inequality with equal opportunity. The second assumes a harsh world of limited possibilities: "The tangible incentives that any society can realistically hold out to the poor youth of average abilities and average industriousness are mostly penalties, mostly disincentives." With public supports stripped away, as Murray wants, most people can look forward only to hard work and limited gains. Social policy must therefore emphasize the stick rather than the carrot.[54]

Murray's unambiguous argument that contemporary social welfare harms the poor updates an old position in the endless debates about poor laws, and his stance on the classification of poor people also echoes old arguments. "Some people," he writes, "are better than others. They deserve more of society's rewards, of which money is only one small part." Despite centuries of failed attempts to draw the line between the deserving and undeserving poor, for Murray the distinction between them is clear enough to serve as the basis of social policy.

One reason for the spectacular success and influence of Murray's book was his concentration on the core preoccupations within poverty discourse. Another was his style. Murray writes clearly and in the manner of a social scientist. His book bristles with graphs and quantitative data. It has none of the bizarre flights of fancy or overt antifeminism of Gilder's work. Most important, though, Murray's argument fit the Reagan agenda perfectly. At precisely the appropriate moment, it provided what appeared to be an authoritative rationale for reducing social benefits and dismantling affirmative action.

Nearly every reviewer commented on Murray's influence. In March 1985, Robert Greenstein observed: "Congress will soon engage in bitter battles over where to cut the federal budget, and *Losing Ground* is already being used as ammunition by those who would direct more reductions at programs for the poor." Murray's name, pointed out Christopher Jencks, "has been invoked repeatedly in Washington's current debates over the budget—not because he has provided new evidence on the effects of particular government programs, but because he is widely presumed to have proven that federal social policy as a whole made the poor worse off over the past twenty years." *Losing Ground*, others pointed out, was the Reagan administration's new Bible.[55]

Murray's success illustrates the role of big money in the marketplace of ideas. William Hammett, president of the conservative Manhattan Institute, read a pamphlet Murray had written and invited him to the institute, where he was supported for the two years during which he wrote *Losing Ground*.[56] Hammett invested in the production and in the promotion of Murray's book. He spent about $15,000 to send more than 700 free copies to influential politicians, academics, and journalists, and he paid for a public relations specialist, Joan Taylor Kennedy, to manage the "Murray campaign." Kennedy aggressively booked Murray on TV shows and the lecture circuit; arranged conferences with editors and academics; and contacted newspapers and magazines. The institute even organized a seminar on Murray's book with intellectuals and journalists influential in policy circles. Participants were paid honoraria of $500 to $1500 and housed at an expensive New York hotel. As Chuck Lane observes, "the quality of Murray's intellectual goods" was not the only reason for his success. Murray had generous help surmounting the expensive barriers to entry into the marketplace of ideas.[57]

The core of Murray's thesis may be restated in the form of several assertions:

• Despite massively swollen spending on social welfare after 1965, the incidence of both poverty and antisocial behavior increased.
• Neither the growth of poverty nor antisocial behavior resulted from economic conditions, which were improving.
• Black unemployment increased during the period because young blacks voluntarily withdrew from the labor market.
• Female-headed black families increased because young men and women saw less reason to marry.
• Labor market and family behavior (also criminal behavior) reflected rational short-term responses to economic incentives.
• These incentives were the perverse result of federal social policy after 1965.

All these assertions, as one commentator after another has shown, are wrong.

For one thing, welfare did not cause the rise in black out-of-wedlock births, and Murray has the facts about incentives backward. Welfare benefits, in constant dollars, fell steeply after 1972, during the very period in which Murray claims their generosity acted as a perverse incentive. (Murray nowhere mentions this 20 percent decline in AFDC benefits.) The number of black children supported by AFDC declined by 5 percent from 1972 to 1980. No correlations exist between state-level benefits and the size of AFDC rolls. Out-of-wedlock births also rose sharply among women who do not receive welfare.

Similarly, Murray confuses the relation between the growth of the economy and proverty. Poverty increased because the economy worsened after 1973. The gross national product, on which Murray relies, is an inadequate measure of either opportunity or individual well-being. Real wages declined, productivity dropped, inflation soared, and unemployment increased, partly because the economy did not grow fast enough to absorb the large number of entering workers.

Murray was wrong about the poverty rate. Christopher Jencks showed that Murray's figures rested on dubious assumptions in the work of economist Timothy Smedding. Jencks's reworking of the figures with Census Bureau statistics shows that the share of the population living below the official poverty line was almost twice as high in 1965 as in 1980, and almost three times as high in 1950 as in 1980. The reduction in poverty appears remarkable when set against the unemployment rate, which doubled between 1968 and 1980. Rising unemployment, not government programs, is one reason why the poverty rate as measured before income transfers did not drop during this period. Another reason is that many elderly people withdrew from the work force when Social Security benefits increased.[58]

As for the rationality of behavior, the relative advantage of work versus welfare increased during the 1970s, in contrast to Murray's claim that it decreased. Murray's assertion rests on the hypothetical example of a couple, Harold and Phyllis, who must choose whether or not to marry when Phyllis becomes pregnant. By 1980, claims Murray, it made less economic sense for them to marry than ever before. As Robert Greenstein shows, Murray's argument is flat wrong. First, it is based not on the nation but on Pennsylvania, where welfare benefits grew twice as fast during the 1970s as in the country as a whole. It also miscalculates income by incorrectly assuming that the family would have lost food stamp benefits had Harold worked. (Murray includes food stamps, however, in calculating the family income.)

With accurate computations, work at a minimum wage job was more profitable than welfare throughout most of the country; in the South, minimum-wage jobs often paid twice as much. Murray fails to provide a budget for Harold and Phyllis for 1980. Had he done so, it would have shown that the value of all welfare benefits packaged together had dropped by 20 percent during the 1970s. Conversely, after 1975 the earned income-tax credit increased the advantages of working. As Greenstein points out: "in 1980—even in Pennsylvania—Harold and Phyllis would have one-third more income if Harold worked than if he re-mained unemployed and Phyllis collected welfare."[59]

Murray distorts or ignores the accomplishments of social pro-grams. He does not recognize the decline in poverty among the elderly, increased access to medical care and legal assistance, the drop in infant mortality rates, or the near abolition of hunger prior to the Reagan administration's policies. He does not ob-serve the irony that without federal affirmative action programs and other antidiscrimination measures, the black economic progress, which he lauds, could not have occurred.

Murray is also wrong about most of his assertions concerning the history of poverty and social welfare in America, including federal social policy since 1965. Only because he tells the story in a contextual vacuum is he able to argue that the federal gov-ernment stumbled into a set of misguided policies that worsened the condition of the poor which, without massive public inter-vention, had started to improve.[60] For instance, he points to rising black male unemployment in the 1960s but does not con-nect it to the mechanization of southern agriculture in the 1950s that drove so many from the land and toward northern cities. His book remains innocent of any discussion of the transforma-tions within American cities described in this chapter. Murray has nothing to say about the role of shifting occupational struc-tures and spatial patterns in promoting poverty. Only by adding these omissions to his neglect of declining real wages, rising unemployment, and faulty economic and social history is Mur-ray able to assert the unmediated and demoralizing impact of federal social policy on the poor during a period of growing prosperity and opportunity.

Murray complements his statistics with what he calls "thought-experiments." These are little fictions designed to illus-trate his argument. The most famous, Harold and Phyllis, is simply wrong. Another shows the poverty of imagination that underlies his own ideas about the possibilities of policy. Murray attempts to show that a hypothetical and well-funded govern-ment campaign to reduce or eliminate smoking would inevitably fail. Yet the only examples he gives concern government action

directed toward individuals. The elimination of subsidies to to-
bacco growers, the prohibition of advertising, or very high taxes
have no place on his agenda. No government so constrained
could eliminate smoking—or, for that matter, poverty. Because
social policy is usually either futile or perverse, Murray recom-
mends draconian cuts: the elimination of virtually all social benefits except Social Security (the reasons for whose stay of
execution he does not explain) and reconstituted, limited unemployment insurance. In his view, only by cutting the cord
that binds them to the government can federal policy truly help
the poor.

Murray ascended into the policy universe with the speed of a
rocket, but his tenure was brief. No administration can persuade
Congress to dismantle the welfare state or pretend that the attendant misery, chaos, and potential violence should be endured as
a prelude to progress. Sophisticated conservatives know the
inevitability of big government in modern America. Their problem is to make it work for their ends and to set it on a plausible
theoretical and moral base. This was the task begun by Lawrence Mead, as he helped launch the third stage of conservatism.


By the mid-1980s, few conservatives still urged dismantling the
welfare state. One reason was the intractable nature of poverty,
especially among minorities in inner cities. As homelessness and
children's poverty became national issues, only the most stubborn conservative could argue that cutting social benefits would
improve the condition of poor people by prodding them toward
independence. A second reason was moral. Conservatives objected not only to government intervention in the economy,
liberal foreign policy, and decreased military spending, but to
trends they believed threatened family life and violated moral
values. As the Reagan revolution failed to check abortion, divorce, out-of-wedlock pregnancy, and drug use, conservatives
reasserted the importance of authority in public life. Because
only government had the power to prohibit or enforce behavior,

the future of conservatism necessitated its reconciliation with the state. In social policy, the first major book to justify big government in conservative terms was Lawrence Mead's *Beyond Entitlement: The Social Obligations of Citizenship*, published in 1986.

Mead does not quote Adam Smith; his preferred philosophers are Hobbes, Burke, and Tocqueville. His concern is society, not the individual, and he worries more about order than liberty. His target is permissive social policy, and his solution, enforced work obligations for the poor.

"My question," Mead writes, "is why federal programs since 1960 have coped so poorly with the various social problems that have come to afflict American society." Although his question echoes Murray, Mead's answer is different. The major problem with the welfare state, he claims, "is its *permissiveness*, not its size." By permissiveness, Mead means that federal programs "award their benefits essentially as entitlements, expecting next to nothing from the beneficiaries in return." These permissive federal social programs result partly from the structure of American government and partly from an intellectually flabby liberalism grounded in sociological explanations of poverty that deny the importance of authority and obligation.[61]

Mead believes that "functioning" in American society has declined during the last two decades. By functioning he means competence as reflected in the proportion of the population on welfare, the unemployment rate, the amount of serious crime, and SAT scores. Americans, he concludes, not only are rejecting their social obligations to one another; they are losing their ability to cope with the ordinary tasks of everyday life. The fault, Mead is very clear, does not lie with social structure or economic conditions. Its source is individual will conditioned by government programs that "shield their clients from the threats and rewards that stem from private society—particularly from the market place." Instead of "blaming people as they deviate, government must persuade them to *blame themselves*." As for the poor, Mead asserts, "the main barrier to acceptance is no longer unfair social structures, but their own difficulties in coping."[62]

With Gilder, Nozick, and Murray, Mead shares the dark view of human nature common among conservatives. Gilder's unbridled male aggression, Nozick's warlike state of nature, Murray's natural indolence and amorality, and Mead's inability to resist the snares of permissiveness all circumscribe the limits of reform and mandate public coercion. Gilder, Murray, and Mead assume that many people will always have to work hard at badly paid, dull jobs they detest. Workplace reform, high wages, the constructive use of automation to increase leisure and decrease alienation play no role in their visions of the future. Instead, they believe public policy should help Americans adapt to their gloomy prospects by lowering their expectations. Like other contemporary conservatives, Gilder, Murray, and Mead therefore reject equality of condition as a dangerous and illusory social goal. The American definition of equality, asserts Mead, does not rest on income or status. Rather, equality means "the enjoyment of equal citizenship, meaning the same rights *and* obligations as others." Mead defends his definition of equality by expedience rather than on constitutional or philosophical grounds: "The great virtue of equal citizenship as a social goal is that it is much more widely achievable than status."[63]

Mead assumes that anyone who wants a job can find one. The deindustrialization of American cities and the postindustrial economy play no more role in his argument than in Murray's. "Unemployment has more to do with functioning problems of the jobless themselves than with economic conditions." The lack of childcare, for example, does not excuse unemployment among women now supported by AFDC. A "lack of *government* child care," he claims, "seems seldom to be a barrier; most prefer to arrange care with friends or relatives." Others remain unemployed because they are unwilling to relocate, accept or remain at unpleasant and badly paid jobs, or commute more than twenty miles to work. Very simply, "disadvantaged workers are unlikely to labor regularly unless they are required to as a condition of support of society."[64]

The quality and material rewards of work remain irrelevant for Mead. "There are good grounds to think," he asserts, "that work, at least in 'dirty,' low-wage jobs, can no longer be left solely to the initiative of those who labor." For them, "employment must become a duty, enforced by public authority, rather than an expression of self interest." Low-wage work "apparently must be mandated," he writes, "just as a draft has sometimes been necessary to staff the military." Government "need not make the desired behavior worthwhile to people. It simply threatens punishment." What's more, the refusal to work is a grave act against the state. "Nonwork," asserts Mead, "is a political act" that underlines the "need for authority. . . . In an open political system rebellious actions, even if not overtly political, tend to provoke countervailing forces." With plenty of jobs available, continued unemployment reflects more than indolence; it is subversion.[65]

The primary responsibility of government is not to raise living standards, increase personal satisfaction, or even to facilitate markets. "Government is really a mechanism by which people force themselves to serve and obey *each other* in necessary ways." Obedience necessitates the enforcement of shared values. "Federal policymakers must start to ask how programs can affirm the norms for functioning on which social order depends." Because social order demands the public creation of norms, government "must take over the socializing role."[66]

Mead uses the condition of blacks to show how permissive social policy backfired. Before the civil rights movement, he claims, black society was more "coherent" than after; "at least racism did not exempt blacks from normal social demands as recent federal policy has done." With no supporting evidence, Mead asserts that the lack of accountability built into federal social programs is "among the reasons why nonwork, crime, family breakup, and other problems are much commoner among recipients [of government benefits] than Americans generally." The remedy is an "authoritative social policy" that enforces "social obligations." Because the structure of American federalism leaves the federal government the only agency capable of enforcing social obligations, Mead calls for an enhanced, even more intrusive state to recapture social policy from the soft and muddled liberal intellectuals whose influence has moved government away from the values and desires of the vast majority of Americans.[67]

Mead is nonetheless ambivalent about the scope of the state. He would assign it a key role in socialization but deny it one in employment, for he redefines employment in public works projects as just another form of dependence. Great Society training programs offered "what amounted to welfare through the allowances and other benefits." Indeed, by effectively relaxing the work obligation for many men, "the employment programs probably increased joblessness rather than reducing it." Mead, in fact, has a double standard of dependence. He does not question other forms of government largesse that sustain more affluent Americans: contracts for weapons, corporate bailouts, tax shelters, agricultural subsidies, and urban renewal money. These also shield their recipients from the discipline of the market, relax obligations to earn a profit, and lessen the need to produce efficiently. Why these also do not erode competence and fuel permissiveness remains unclear. Surely, though, obligations should rest no more on the poor than on anyone else.[68]

Mead's case rests on three major pillars: an interpretation of American history and the history of reform; an assessment of labor market trends; and a concept of citizenship. He reads the history of American social reform from about 1900 to 1965 as a progressive tradition directed toward "the elimination of barriers to the advancement of competent citizens." Reform began around 1900 with the first federal economic regulations, leaped forward during the New Deal of the 1930s, and culminated with the civil rights act of the 1960s. These reforms assumed the competence of ordinary Americans, who in fact made "good use of new opportunities with little further help from the government." Because Mead assumes these movements met their goals, he believes no major structural barriers to advancement now block the path toward prosperity or social justice. Liberals, however, remain fixated on the past, anachronisms proposing outmoded solutions, still arguing that government should do

more for people who instead need to be taught to help themselves.[69]

Only by distorting the past can Mead use history to support
his interpretation of the present. Another way to read the same
events is this: Minorities and working people, no matter how
competent, cannot without the power of the state reduce discrimination or improve their wages and working conditions.
This is as true in the present as it was in the past. America's
progressive reform agenda remains unfinished and its accomplishments vulnerable. The Wagner Act (1935), omitted from
Mead's list of progressive reforms, guaranteed labor the right to
organize freely and without fear of reprisal; Supreme Court decisions, federal legislation, and affirmative action programs advanced opportunities for blacks. These gains, however, remain
fragile. Only vigorous federal action can prevent their erosion.
The Reagan administration cut social benefits, undermined federal enforcement of civil rights, and along with big business,
successfully rolled back advances won by organized labor.

Certainly, blacks with advanced education have penetrated
the upper ranks of the occupational structure in unprecedented
numbers. However, federal cutbacks in financial aid and increased poverty have inhibited opportunities for younger blacks
to attend college. Although affluent blacks now can buy a home
in almost any suburb, escalating house prices limit the number
of potential owners. The average income of two-parent black
families now is close to that of whites, but there are fewer of
them, and most black families headed by a woman live in poverty. Nearly half of all black children live in families with incomes below the poverty line. Racism continues to flare, as
when gangs of white youths try to drive blacks from a neighborhood in Philadelphia or chase them to their deaths on Long
Island. On college campuses across the country, according to
many observers, in recent years racism has grown, not declined.
Only the most formal definition of equality and narrow criteria
support Mead's view that "formidable social barriers" no longer
block the mobility of America's poor and minorities.[70]

Mead's discussion of the balance between permissiveness and authority in American reform ignores the intrusive, authoritarian strand that runs throughout its history. Again, the consequences undermine his conclusions. Since early in the nineteenth century, American reformers have tried to regulate behavior. One example is the temperance movement, which began in the 1830s and culminated in Prohibition, mandated by the Eighteenth Amendment to the Constitution. Other reforms encouraged the state to intervene between parents and children. Like Mead, early educational reformers believed the state should compensate for the incompetence of poor parents by socializing their children. Indeed, this was one purpose of public schools, which educators and their allies managed to make compulsory, starting with Massachusetts in 1852 and ending with the southern states in the twentieth century. In the late nineteenth century, some states licensed private child protection agencies that encouraged poor neighbors to spy on one another and used police powers to break up poor families. States also reformed poor laws in ways that separated parents from their children. In the twentieth century, juvenile courts suspended children's civil liberties and deployed social workers to supervise family relations. After World War II, several states tried to alter the sexual behavior of black women by attaching "suitable home" provisions to welfare regulations.[71]

These reforms, which illustrate the intrusive, authoritarian strand in the history of American reform, also usually failed to meet their goals. Prohibition, as everyone knows, provoked lawbreaking, adulterated whiskey, and violence. Compulsory education did remove some poor children from the streets, but it had little impact on crime, poverty, or moral behavior, as its advocates had promised. Child protection agencies did not stop child abuse, and within two decades family breakup had been discredited as an object of social policy. Juvenile courts failed to stem delinquency and disappointed their founders. Welfare regulations have not changed sexual behavior. Given this history, Mead's stress on authority as the foundation of social policy emerges as neither novel nor promising.

Mead portrays the Great Society no more adequately than he does earlier reforms. His comments about community action are brief, derogatory, and inaccurate. He ignores the grassroots origins of the civil rights movement, its role as a catalyst of the War on Poverty, and the pivotal ideological and administrative position of community action. Instead, he treats the War on Poverty as a conspiracy by the elite to advance its own power and position by trapping the disadvantaged in a web of dependence.[72]

Mead argues correctly that Americans have assigned the work ethic a sacred role throughout their history. Still, questions remain. Is the American deification of work a constructive response to postindustrial society? Is work really available for all who want it? Will armies continue to toil at poorly paid, exploitive jobs? Or is it the case, as Fred Block argues, that the American economy increasingly will have more workers than it needs, even to raise productivity and remain competitive in world markets? Does the easy availability of cheap labor, as Block contends, retard technological advance and productivity? Mead, of course, denies that labor supply exceeds demand. However, this claim, the empirical centerpiece of his argument, remains unconvincing. (William J. Wilson has rebutted Mead effectively on this point.)[73]

Even if forced to concede a job shortage, Mead almost certainly would stage only a tactical retreat. For his case has a moral rather than an empirical core. It rests, that is, on his concept of citizenship and its obligations. To Mead, citizenship demands the successful discharge of social and political obligations. "The capacities to learn, work, support one's family, and respect the rights of others," writes Mead, "amount to a set of *social* obligations alongside the political ones [such as voting, paying taxes, serving in the military]." He defines a "civic society" as one in which "people are competent in all these senses, as citizens and as workers." In the social realm government programs define social expectations as other laws and the Constitution do in the political realm. As a result, the structure of benefits and requirements in the programs "constitutes an *operational definition of citizenship.*" Except in the narrow legal definition, citizenship is not an entitlement of birth; it must be earned daily through competent and responsible behavior.[74]

Mead does not explore the ambiguities inherent in his concepts of citizenship, competence, and obligation. Are social and political obligations truly equivalent? Defined by the Constitution and statutory law, political obligations are *relatively* clear. When interpretations conflict, forums exist for their resolution. Social obligations remain more ambiguous, and laws define very few of them. No one can compel someone else to learn (which is not the same as to attend school). There is no legal requirement to work. (Would Mead extend this obligation to those who live on private means?) As Mead uses it, "competence" is neither objective nor technical. Instead, it sums up the successful discharge of obligations. As the price of social benefits, competence becomes the badge of the deserving poor. In this way, Mead resuscitates the nineteenth century's easy equation of poverty with crime, ignorance, and immorality. Low SAT scores, unemployment, criminal convictions, and welfare dependence are interchangeable signals of incompetence, hallmarks of the undeserving poor, emblems of noncitizens.

Mead's concept of obligation remains asymmetrical. He tries to be very clear about what poor people owe the rest of us, and he offers even a short general list of social obligations expected of all adult Americans (these include, "fluency and literacy in English, whatever one's native tongue"). However, obligation implies mutual responsibilities, and Mead fails to ask what we, in our organized capacity as government or philanthropy, owe in return. Is it merely survival, or something more generous? Are obligations graduated? Should longer and harder work bring higher benefits? Surely, there can be no legal or moral justification for asking needy people to sign a contract whose terms remain undisclosed. If obligation is mutual, wage labor and civic competence should be considered payment for resources or services rendered by society (another of Mead's ill-defined abstractions) to its least fortunate members. Unless it provides the prerequisites of competence, society lacks a moral title to obligation. Potential citizens should expect the resources esssential for learning, work, and family life if they are to avoid low SAT scores, unemployment, adolescent pregnancy, and welfare dependence. These resources include adequate schools, affordable housing, reasonably priced day care, guaranteed health care, and decent jobs. In America's cities, poor people can count on none of these.[75]

All the poor may know is that they are obliged to work. Why is less clear. In places, Mead implies that work is necessary for self-esteem and mental health. Any work remains preferable to dependent idleness. More often, Mead assigns work a different purpose. Whether individuals like it is beside the point. The economy needs them; productivity depends on them; and the needs of society always take precedence over the preferences of individuals. If necessary, Mead would subsidize the wages of poorly paid workers rather than force their employers to pay them more. Mead does not explain why he is willing to underwrite private profits with public subsidies. Does he believe that poor people have a distinctive psychology that responds only to punishment, as contrasted with employers, who respond to incentives? The harder one pushes, the more Mead's concept of social obligation collapses into a new strategy for preserving a pool of cheap, docile labor. As such, it is a euphemism. For without mutuality, obligation becomes coercion.[76]

Mead recognizes that liberal and conservative discourse about poverty and welfare often remain trapped within a narrow band of questions bounded by the market. In contrast, he emphasizes that poverty and welfare are political and moral problems. This is the major strength of his book, and the source of its irony. Only wage labor, he argues, truly fulfills the obligations of the poor. Only as they enter paid, preferably private, employment will the poor discharge their moral duty to the rest of us. As much as for any economist, for Mead the market remains the arbiter of moral worth.

## LIBERALISM FRAGMENTED

The early 1980s belonged to the conservatives. Not only did they triumph at the polls; they set the terms of debate on social issues. For the first time in American history, "liberal" became a negative term on both the Right and Left, a badge of failed policies and stale ideas, shunned by its former champions. (Think, for instance, of George Bush's attempts during the 1988 presidential campaign to brand Michael Dukakis a liberal and the latter's efforts to avoid the label.) In the conventional wisdom, the liberal legacy was stagflation, military weakness, and a bloated, ineffective welfare state, for whose extension, or even legitimacy, no one could offer fresh or convincing arguments.

At best, these common accusations are partial truths. (Here I use "liberal" and "liberalism" loosely to signify positions favoring reliance on government to combat or alleviate poverty through income redistribution and social services.) Liberal social thought neither disappeared nor stagnated during the late 1970s and early 1980s. Rather, it fragmented. Philosophers, legal scholars, economists, and other social scientists all forged elements essential for recasting the defense of progressive social policy. However, for two major reasons they failed to assemble a powerful and popular new defense of equality and social justice. First, because they rarely spoke to each other, their contributions remained fragmented. Second, they did not link economic growth, public morality, and social benefits into a coherent argument for expanding the welfare state.

Like the resurgent conservatism of the same era, these liberal fragments of the late 1970s and early 1980s addressed the three historic preoccupations of American discourse about poverty and welfare. They classified the poor, argued over the results of welfare, and developed concepts of social obligation. Consider first the classification of the poor.

.   .   .

By the latter 1980s, both liberal and conservative poverty discourse centered on two categories that had enjoyed a recent and spectacular rise to prominence: the homeless and the underclass. Neither is any more precise than many of the old ways of talking about poor people; consensus about their existential importance masks serious differences of definition; and their membership overlaps. I will discuss each of them later, for they raise what Martha Minow calls the dilemma of difference: "how to overcome the past hostilities and degradations of people on the basis of group differences without employing—and in that sense legitimating—those very differences." Indeed, the dilemma contaminates reform because conditions of inequality or deprivation cannot be separated in discourse or policy from their social and institutional matrix. "If the goal is to avoid identifying people by a trait of difference, but the institutions and practices make that trait matter," writes Minow, "there seems to be no way to remedy the effects of difference without making difference matter yet again."[77]

Underlying categorization is the problem of definition. What exactly is poverty, and who is poor? Although liberals and conservatives often disagree, their differences on these questions concern technical rather than philosophical issues—especially, as we have seen, the role of in-kind benefits or the adequacy of the poverty line. However, the debate between them also raises the venerable and more interesting issue of objective versus relative concepts of poverty.

Is poverty an objective condition of deprivation, measured by fixed criteria? When we call people poor, do we mean they lack enough income to purchase adequate food, housing, clothing, and medical care? Or is poverty always relative, measured against contemporary expectations and living standards? Can we define poverty only when we know how most people live? Answers to these questions have a curious, shifting political history. As liberals renewed their concern with poverty in the 1960s, relative definitions seemed the defense of conservatives. After all, virtually no one in America was poor by standards of the

Third World, or even by standards that prevailed throughout much of American history. By combining a relative definition with international examples, conservatives appeared to diminish the plight of America's poor and erode the will to action. By contrast, a fixed, objective standard denoted the persistence of poverty and offered a target for social policy. (Some social scientists tried to combine the virtues of both approaches by setting the poverty line at a fixed proportion of median income. Had they prevailed, poverty would seem a much worse problem in contemporary America because the relation of the poverty line to median income has shifted downward. In 1960, the poverty line was 48 percent of the median family income for a family of four; by 1980, it had dropped to 34 percent.)[78]

Nonetheless, during the 1970s objective definitions of poverty became more appealing to conservatives. Set low, combined with in-kind benefits, objective definitions allowed conservatives to minimize the extent of poverty and relax efforts to alleviate or reduce it. At the same time, relative definitions began to shore up liberal policies because they maximized the extent and consequences of poverty. By emphasizing the importance of contextual standards, they could shake complacent assumptions of social progress and counter comparisons with the Third World.

Peter Townsend, a British social scientist, has written the major contemporary liberal defense of relative poverty. Townsend's definition shaped his design of a large national survey of poverty in Great Britain in the late 1960s. Finding conventional definitions inadequate, he argued for poverty as a form of relative deprivation. By relative deprivation he did not mean that poverty represented primarily subjective perceptions; rather, he stressed its objective base in the distributional patterns within major institutional systems: wage and salary systems of private industry and the state; assets from dividends, interest, or rent within the fiscal system; income from public social security and private employee benefits; and social services such as education and health. Poverty is "the lack of the resources necessary to permit participation in the activities, customs, and diets commonly approved by society."[79]

For Townsend, the capacity to participate in customary social, economic, and political activities defined the threshold of poverty. As resources diminish, he claimed, "there occurs a sudden withdrawal from participation in the customs and activities sanctioned by the culture." At this threshold, deprivation increases more than income falls, and withdrawal from civic and social participation escalates. It is this juncture that Townsend defined as the poverty line.[80]

Townsend measured poverty with an elaborate and ingenious questionnaire designed to elicit information about resources in each major distributional sphere. By scoring individual and family resources within spheres and summing the total, he derived both overall rankings and a poverty line. He concluded that poverty was "more extensive than is generally or officially believed and has to be understood not only as an inevitable feature of social inequality but also as a particular consequence of actions by the rich to preserve and enhance their wealth and so to deny it to others." Poverty is neither accidental nor an unavoidable part of modern industrial, or postindustrial, society; it reflects inequality deliberately perpetuated through the manipulation of wealth and power. For Townsend, therefore, the roots of poverty are political.[81]

They are also cultural, expressed in the different "styles of living" available to those with varying amounts of resources. Both the "state and market agencies" constantly seek to expand private consumption by recommending "a social style of living" for both poor and rich. For the poor, however, participation is impossible. This is serious, because, styles of living shape social acknowledgment of individual worth. Therefore, concludes Townsend, the degree of poverty reflects both unequal resource distribution and the results of shifting standards of consumption.[82]

Whether they are based on objective or relative definitions, even the methods of studying poverty fuel the process of categorization and reinforce stereotypes. Social scientists want to identify, count, and describe the poor. Their purpose is to create policies tailored to the needs and conditions of the poor and to evaluate their results. For these purposes, classification is essential. The result is that social science often unwittingly reinforces the classification of poor people into discrete categories, to which less sympathetic observers then attach moral judgments. The reason inheres in the primarily quantitative methods used to study poverty.

Quantification demands the creation of the categories without which statistical analysis is impossible. Even simple statistical manipulations require dividing people into classes, such as unmarried black mothers, unemployed young men, or elderly widows unattached to a family. More complex statistical analyses require holding variables constant in order to assess the precise influence of race, age, household status, or some other factor on a given outcome. They promote the description of individuals by single statuses defined for the convenience of census takers or social scientists and the abstraction and isolation of human attributes from their role in the complex configurations of individual lives. (Who, for instance, are we supposed to place among the homeless and who among the underclass?) Social science reifies social categories, turning poor people (and other groups) into one-dimensional cardboard cutouts neatly stacked and divided from one another.

Set beside real people, the abstractions of quantitative social science seem to be stereotypes, useful for drawing a rough topography of poverty, modeling certain processes, or even formulating public policies, but also susceptible to translation into a modern basis for old moral discriminations. Portraits of actual people or collectivities always muddy one-dimensional descriptions. They reveal the patterns of behavior and interaction submerged in classifications of convenience and suggest fluid groups unimagined by social scientists, who impose a grid constructed without reference to the lived experience of the people they study.

The method of ethnography contrasts vividly with quantitative studies of poverty. Its minimal contribution is the destruction of stereotypes; its signal achievement, in the work of its most able practitioners, is a portrait of the world from the vantage point of its subjects. The best ethnographies always break down conventional categories and reassemble the lived world of their subjects in the terms of their subjective experience. In his marvelous study of a South Chicago bar, which follows in the research tradition of Elliot Liebow and Carol Stack, Elijah Anderson, for one, shows the intricate social structure among men usually dismissed as demoralized, disorganized alcoholics.

Elsewhere, Anderson shows the intricate social interactions between poor blacks and their affluent white neighbors in a gentrifying area of a large Northeastern city, and he explores the subjective meaning of adolescent pregnancy, unemployment, crime, and other experiences collapsed into statistical rates. Earlier generations of black youths, he argues, learned from mentors within the black middle class. With racial discrimination in housing, ghettoes remained socially diverse. Unable to leave, the middle class informally supervised young people, offered adult role models, and sustained strong local institutions. The civil rights movement and affirmative action ironically unraveled these intricate local networks. As occupational and suburban housing barriers fell, ghettoes lost their middle class. Left without mentors, badly educated in city schools, unable to find work, pulled by the lure of easy money from drugs, young black men drifted into crime and away from the labor market.[83]

In *Growing Up Poor*, Terry Williams and William Kornblum also stress the importance of mentors for black youths. Williams and Kornblum followed the life histories of 900 teenagers in New York City, Cleveland, Louisville, and Meridian, Mississippi, and drew on the young people's own accounts to show the complex interaction of structural, community, and personal factors that channeled their experiences along different routes. "One way to understand the diversity of the biographies presented in this book," they observed, "is to look at the paths to maturity that the various communities offer their teenagers and young adults." Impressed by the variety among the paths young people followed, Williams and Kornblum asked why some managed to escape poverty while others remained trapped. Their answer stressed the importance of adult mentors. "The probabilities that teenagers will end up on the corner or in a stable job," they claimed, "are conditioned by a great many features of life in their communities. Of these, we believe the most significant is the presence or absence of adult mentors."[84]

Jay McLeod, in *Ain't No Makin' It*, also wanted to explain the patterns of behavior he found among teenagers, in his case only boys, living in a public housing project in a New England city. Based on a year's fieldwork among them, McLeod identified two groups of boys, Hallway Hangers and Brothers, distinguished by aspirations and behavior. The Hallway Hangers, nearly all white, acted out their low aspirations in heavy drinking, drug use, crime, hostility toward school, and intermittent work. The Brothers, all black, coupled conventional middle-class aspirations with a commitment to education, work, and respectability. For McLeod, the coexistence of these opposite patterns in the same setting illuminates a critical theoretical and political issue: the reproduction of American class structure.

His ethnographic evidence, he believes, challenges conventional theories that stress either structural or cultural factors. The key concept, for him, is aspiration: "Aspirations provide a conceptual link between structure and agency because although they are rooted firmly in individual proclivity (agency), they also are acutely sensitive to perceived societal constraints (structure)." Their diverging relationship to America's "achievement ideology" shaped the aspirations of the young people among whom McLeod worked. "The Hallway Hangers reject the achievement ideology because most of them are white. Whereas poor blacks have racial discrimination to which they can point as a cause of their family's poverty, for the Hallway Hangers to accept the achievement ideology is to admit that their parents are lazy or stupid or both. Thus, the achievement ideology not only runs counter to the experiences of the Hallway Hangers, but is also a more serious assault on their self-esteem."[85]

These ethnographies accomplish more than the destruction of stereotypes. They highlight the arbitrary and partial nature of the conventional categories used to discuss poverty. They signal the danger that even liberal poverty discourse and social science may mistake classifications for adequate descriptions of real people, rather than the abstract inventions of ideology and convenience that they are.

Throughout the Great Society era the results of welfare as well as the categorization of the poor preoccupied social scientists. Their major achievement was the design of the income maintenance experiments intended to test the impact of a guaranteed income on work and family. These massive social experiments proved ambiguous and inconclusive. When conservatives used them as ammunition against the extension of social welfare, liberals could only respond that the experiments had not caused as much harm as they claimed. In effect, they fought conservatives on well-worn turf—the relation between welfare, work incentives, and family behavior—and they seemed to lose. More recent work has qualified the negative assessment of the income maintenance experiments: Work effort declined less than conservatives concluded, and marriages did not become as unstable as earlier results suggested. Nonetheless, these liberal answers remained a narrow defense, circumscribed by the oldest preoccupation in the history of social welfare.[86]

A few radical scholars have turned the conservative argument on its head in interesting ways. Frances Fox Piven and Richard Cloward agree with conservatives that the welfare state's expansion raised wages and tightened labor markets. They point to "an emerging recognition among analysts of all political persuasions that the income-maintenance programs have weakened capital's ability to depress wages by means of economic insecurity, especially by means of manipulating the relative numbers of people searching for work." Improved unemployment and disability insurance along with food stamps increased workers' ability to refuse low wages and poor working conditions. As employers recognized the result of these commendable and progressive trends, they launched a counteroffensive against both trade unions and public social benefits.[87]

Fred Block, by contrast, argues that the conservative case

against welfare fails on its own terms. What Block terms the "realist" view of the welfare state consists of three key arguments: First, government's role in social welfare retarded productivity through disincentives to investment; second, it discouraged people from working; and third, it consumed too many resources, especially at a time of massive federal budget deficits. Block counters all three arguments. Inaccurate measures, he contends, have underestimated investment by failing to include investment in intangibles such as software, training, and other forms of human capital development and in capital-saving technology such as computers. Other inadequate measures underestimate and distort productivity by failing to account for the misallocation of resources and the appropriation of capital for nonproductive uses such as corporate takeovers and by not providing a price index for communications equipment.

Block, in fact, finds no evidence that welfare benefits have discouraged work. To the contrary, labor force participation grew rapidly during the same period that social welfare benefits expanded. By increasing purchasing power and human capital, investments in social welfare will increase more wealth than they consume. Because productivity rises fastest when output increases to meet higher levels of demand, argues Block, politicians concerned with boosting productivity should support social welfare policies that increase puchasing power.[88]

Robert Kuttner also argues against the conservative connection between low productivity and a generous welfare state. In *The Economic Illusion*, he attacks the alleged connection between social welfare and economic performance with international examples. "The economic illusion," he writes, "is the vision of static tradeoffs; the idea that we must sacrifice well-being in the present for investment in the future; social justice for economic rationality; work satisfaction for labor discipline; decent wages for international competitiveness." By comparing the relation between social policies and economic growth in several countries, Kuttner demonstrates that "policy approaches which improve equality can also improve efficiency."

Although their welfare states are more complete and expensive, economic growth in several Western European countries has exceeded America's. Clearly, as Sweden, Austria, or West Germany demonstrate, relatively generous public social benefits do not retard economic advance.[89] Nor, as other international evidence shows, has social welfare fueled adolescent pregnancy or the rise in female-headed families, as conservatives often claim. Indeed, America's rate of adolescent pregnancy remains the highest among the Western democracies, and its social benefits among the lowest.

The "realist" case remains vulnerable as history as well as theory. This is the message of *America's Hidden Success* by John Schwarz, the first liberal rebuttal to conservative claims that America lost its war on poverty. According to Schwarz:

> The government's programs to attack poverty . . . reduced poverty by more than half. They alleviated some of the grimmest conditions attendant to poverty, and they did so across the whole range of human needs pertaining to serious malnutrition, inadequate medical care, and overcrowded housing. In providing job training, they raised the economic fortunes of thousands of Americans. In providing early education to low-income children, they increased the potential of a great number of these children for success in both school and later employment.[90]

Despite the persuasive evidence that Block, Kuttner, Schwarz, and others muster, liberal commentary on the results of welfare remains incomplete. Unlike conservative attacks, liberal replies have not linked defense of the welfare state to economic revitalization and family renewal in a way intuitively sensible to ordinary Americans. Although liberals have picked at the pieces of recent conservative social thought, by no means have they shredded its popular message. The same problem inhibits the impact of most liberal discourse about the third great preoccupation in discourse about poverty and welfare: the limits of social obligation.

. . .

During the Great Society era, most liberals assumed the legitimacy of the welfare state and the desirability of its expansion.
Only legal scholars and a few philosophers reconsiderd its moral,
theoretical, or constitutional basis. In fact, the narrowly technocratic boundaries of most poverty discourse excluded all but
the most cursory attention to issues of purposes and justification.
As a consequence, when conservatives unleashed their attack
on public social programs, liberals could mount only a weak
defense.

Poverty lawyers remain the unsung liberal heroes of the late
1970s and early 1980s. Even with federal programs slashed, they
continued a vigorous defense of poor people, battling public
bureaucracies, working for the extension of civil rights from politics to economics, and representing the homeless. Nonetheless,
the body of scholarship on which poverty lawyers could draw
remained fairly thin. The flurry of debate stimulated by Charles
Reich petered out, despite the notable work of a few scholars
such as Frank Michelman of Harvard, William Simon of Stanford, and the late Edward Sparer of the University of Pennsylvania. Indeed, no liberal supporters of vigorous antipoverty
programs seized public attention with the force of George
Gilder, Charles Murray, or Lawrence Mead. Either implicitly or
explicitly, the relatively few scholars defending the expansion of
social welfare ceded vital terrain to the conservatives.

That terrain was equality. Most liberals rejected greater equality as the ground on which to attack poverty or defend the welfare state. Instead, they stressed either the immorality of
deprivation, the threat to community, or a combination of the
two. Some argued that severe deprivation violated moral and
even constitutional obligations. Others contended that poverty
inhibited participation in civic life and eroded the basis of community. As they formulated their case, however, nearly all liberal writers on poverty and welfare criticized exclusive reliance
on market models as the basis for social policy. (The major exception to this general trend is the work of Ronald Dworkin,
whose writings defend greater equality as the goal of liberal social and political policy.) [91]

Writing in the *Harvard Law Review* in 1969, Frank Michelman first developd his case for the constitutional basis of welfare in the Fouteenth Amendment. The "judicial 'equality' explosion of recent times," he observed, "has been largely ignited by reawakened sensitivity, not to equality, but to a quite different sort of value or claim which might better be called 'minimum welfare.' " Welfare's purpose, he was very clear, was not the promotion of economic equality, but "minimum protection against social hazard." The "injury" resulting from poverty, he claimed, "consists more essentially of deprivation than of discrimination," and "the cure accordingly lies more in provision than in equalization."

A decade later, Michelman added provision of the conditions for political participation to his brief on behalf of the constitutional foundation of welfare rights. Welfare rights, he asserted, are "part of constitutionally guaranteed democratic representation." Poverty, he stressed, not only disadvantaged individuals politically; it identified them as members of a group whose interests, despite their numbers, were "systematically subordinated" in the formation of political coalitions and the routine exercise of political influence. The relation between poverty and political deprivation remained especially severe for blacks. For them, meeting their "basic welfare interests" remained crucial to eliminating "vestiges of slavery from the system of democratic representation."[92]

Robert Goodin, a political philosopher, also defended government's social responsibilities as a response to a form of deprivation, which he referred to as "vulnerability." Goodin tried to break down the distinction between special and general obligations—that is, obligations to family and friends on the one side, and to strangers on the other. Contrary to common beliefs, he argues, both flow from the same conditions or sets of relations, which he calls vulnerability. Special obligations, he writes, "are generated by the vulnerability of the others rather than by any voluntary acts of will on our part." The primacy of vulnerability means that our general obligations are as great as our special ones. Because we cannot discharge many of the general obligations ourselves, government must discharge them for us. This is the moral basis of the welfare state which, he writes, "is the principal mechanism through which we discharge our collective responsibilities to protect our vulnerable compatriots." Unlike legal scholars who developed arguments for the welfare state based on constitutional entitlements, Goodin rests his case on the duty of the state rather than on the rights of individuals. "Notice," he instructs readers, "that my argument for the welfare state focuses upon the community's duties rather than upon the claimant's right."[93]

In contrast to Goodin, the contributors to *Democracy and the Welfare State*, edited by Amy Gutmann, base their arguments more on considerations of community and civic participation than on deprivation or vulnerability. "The primary focus of many of the papers in this volume," writes Gutmann, "is not individual virtue, equality, or self-realization, but democratic citizenship. The pivotal questions are: What social institutions are necessary to encourage and protect citizenship? What rights do citizens have, and what duties are required of them?" J. Donald Moon's thoughtful approach to these questions links criticism of exclusive reliance on market models to the basis of civic participation. "[The] justification for organizing economic life through the market," observes Moon, rests on "a conception of the individual as agent, capable of choice and deliberation, and entitled to certain rights and to be treated with respect." Consequently, the "justification of the market" weakens when its normal operation "deprives some people—through no fault of their own—of the very means of survival, not to mention the possibility of maintaining their well-being and dignity." Poverty's significance extends beyond the suffering it involves to embrace "an undeserved exile from society." Moon goes on to say: "There is something deeply and undeniably unjust about a social order that necessarily frustrates fulfillment of the promises it makes."[94]

For Michael Walzer too, poverty violates the basis of community. His argument derives from his concept of complex equality, developed in *Spheres of Justice* (1983), the major theoretical work on distributive justice since Rawls and Nozick. To

Walzer, the primary enemy of justice is domination rather than the inegalitarian distribution of goods. Justice is "the opposite of tyranny," and the recognition of complex equality the guarantor of democracy. Complex equality assumes the division of goods into multiple distributive spheres, each guided by its own rules, each relatively autonomous. "Every social good or set of goods," he writes, "constitutes, as it were, a distributive sphere within which only certain criteria and arrangements are appropriate." Protecting the relative autonomy of spheres requires constant policing of their boundaries.

The greatest danger of violation usually comes from the market sphere. Powerful men and women most often use the resources accrued there to invade the others; "market power," which tends to "overspill the boundaries" turns into a form of tyranny, "distorting distributions in other spheres." This need for constant vigilance enhances the importance of democracy, because it is the only political system that protects the autonomy of spheres:

> Once we have located ownership, expertise, religious knowledge, and so on in their proper places and established their autonomy, there is no alternative to democracy in the political sphere. The only thing that can justify undemocratic forms of government is an undifferentiated conception of social goods.[95]

Because citizenship is active and participatory, public policy, according to Walzer, should have as one goal empowerment, or widespread "participation in communal activities, the concrete realization of membership." Membership, Walzer contends, is "the primary social good that we distribute to one another," and the "denial of membership is always the first of a long train of abuses." Walzer's emphasis on membership raises two questions that are important here. What rights do individuals have as members of communities, and what circumstances deprive them of full membership?[96]

Poverty and prolonged unemployment deprive people of membership because they represent "a kind of economic exile,

a punishment that we are loathe to say that anyone deserves."
Poverty creates exiles by stripping people of self-respect, which
requires some substantial connection to the group; it thereby
dilutes the meaning of citizenship, and turns neighbors into
strangers.[97]

For Walzer, the public response to poverty should reflect
three principles that together demand an extensive welfare state.
Political communities should meet the needs of their members
as they are collectively understood, distribute goods in proportion to need, and honor the "underlying equality of membership." By their arrogance and the dependence they breed, public
relief programs too often adopt the worst practices of private
charity, thereby violating equality and dignity: "The old patterns
survive; the poor are still deferential, passive, and humble, while
public officials take on the arrogance of their private predeces-
sors." Public programs, therefore, should "aim at setting up the
poor on their own" through "rehabilitation, retraining, subsidiz-
ing small businesses, and so on." Because participation is so
central to citizenship, the participation of the poor in the life of
the community should not await the abolition of poverty;
"rather, the struggle against poverty (and against every other sort
of neediness) is one of those activities in which many citizens,
poor and not so poor and well-to-do alike, ought to participate."[98]

Walzer's inclusive model of community and participatory definition of citizenship rest on a presumption of human dignity.
Only an irreducible commitment to individual human worth
justifies his horror of domination and emphasis on self-respect.
Very similar assumptions underpin the most comprehensive, articulate, and humane recent dissection of the ways in which
America's economy generates poverty. I refer to *Economic Justice for All*, the Catholic bishops' pastoral letter on the U.S.
economy.

Poverty, asserts the pastoral letter, "is not merely the lack of
adequate financial resources. It entails a more profound kind of

deprivation, a denial of full participation in the economic, social, and political life of society and an inability to influence
decisions that affect one's life." For the bishops, as for Walzer,
poverty represents a violation of community, a deprivation of
citizenship, and an essential powerlessness that "assaults not
only one's pocketbook but also one's fundamental human dignity."[99]

The bishops' definition of poverty reflects their search for a
language of inclusion capable of appealing to non-Catholic au-
diences and broadly shared American social values. Their "option for the poor," they stressed, should "not mean pitting one
group against another, but rather, strengthening the whole community by assisting those who are most vulnerable." Their reluctance to use divisive or provocative language, however, did not
prevent the bishops from voicing unambiguous outrage at the
persistence of poverty in America: "That so many people are
poor in a nation as rich as ours," they wrote, "is a social and
moral scandal that we cannot ignore."[100]

The letter's brief against poverty is moral, its starting point
human dignity which, "realized in community with others and
with the whole of God's creation, is the norm against which
every social institution must be measured." Human dignity derives from the creation of humans in God's image. Because it
comes from God, it is inherent in everyone, independent of
"nationality, race, sex, economic status, or any human accom-
plishment." Dignity manifests itself "in the ability to reason and
understand"; in "freedom to shape their own lives and the life of
their communities, and in the capacity for love and friendship."[101]

The recommendations in the pastoral letter rest on important
assumptions about human rights, the conditions of human
dignity, the nature of social obligations, and the quality of
work. They assume, first, that human rights encompass economic as well as civil and political rights. In this, they reflect
the most controversial premise of contemporary poverty law,
now generally rejected by federal courts. They also assume
the *social* basis of human dignity, which cannot be realized

apart from community. By implication, therefore, they reject the individualism inherent in classical liberalism, today advocated most often by free-market conservatives or libertarians such as Nozick.

Commitment to community leads to an emphasis on social obligations, which, unlike Mead, the letter bases on reciprocity. "Social justice implies that persons have an obligation to be active and productive participants in the life of society and that society has a duty to enable them to participate in this way." Forcing people to work at unrewarding, deadening, or degrading work, as Mead would permit, clearly violates both human dignity and the reciprocity essential to the realization of community, because social justice requires organizing "economic and social institutions so that people can contribute to society in ways that respect their freedom and the dignity of their labor." Work is necessary for human fulfillment, but it "should enable the working person to become 'more a human being,' more capable of acting intelligently, freely, and in ways that lead to self-realization." (Ronald Dworkin makes a similar point: "Treating people as equals requires a more active conception of membership. If people are asked to sacrifice for their community, they must be offered some reason why the community which benefits from that sacrifice is their community.") [102]

Although the letter considers inequality in contemporary America too severe, its main goals remain the realization of community and the protection of human dignity. Indeed, in keeping with Catholic teaching, the bishops not only accept but celebrate "the private ownership of productive property." At the same time, the Church's teaching rejects the notion that a free market "automatically" produces justice. Instead the bishops, like Walzer, argue that there are some goods money cannot buy. Markets, they assert, are "limited by fundamental human rights. Some things are never to be bought and sold. This conviction has prompted positive steps to modify the operation of the market when it harms vulnerable members of society."

Nor do they prefer government as the primary agent of social justice. Instead, they advance the principle of subsidiarity, which states that, "in order to protect basic justice, government should undertake only those initiatives which exceed the capacity of individuals or private groups acting independently." Subsidiarity, much like Walzer's separate spheres, protects freedom through "institutional pluralism" and links individuals to society through "mediating structures" composed of "small- and intermediate-sized communities or institutions." Subsidiarity also implies the diffusion of moral responsibility for the poor through society and all its institutions.[103]

Reducing poverty, the letter asserts, is a moral imperative, not a luxury. Public and private action therefore should speak for the voiceless and defend the defenseless—that is, they should "assess life styles, policies, and social institutions in terms of their impact on the poor." This "option for the poor" leads the bishops to advocate a major assault on unemployment, a guaranteed minimum income, and other expanded social benefits designed to increase the security of individuals and families. "We believe," they write, "the time has come for [an] experiment in securing economic rights: the creation of an order that guarantees the minimum conditions of human dignity in the economic sphere for every person."[104]

Whether *Economic Justice for All* will become the charter of a new War on Poverty remains doubtful, given its provenance. However, its place in the contemporary intellectual history of social policy is secure. For it is the finest modern American application of the principles of distributive justice to the problem of poverty. Despite its anchor in Catholic theology, *Economic Justice for All* embodies most of the major themes in the current reconstruction of the intellectual basis of the welfare state. Like a variety of secular sources, it grounds its advocacy of expanded social benefits more in deprivation (or vulnerability) and the conditions of community than in inequality; incorporates both public and private action in the quest for social justice; relies on institutional pluralism to protect liberty; and, though it assumes the legitimacy of private property, resists the intrusion of the market beyond its appropriate sphere.

The retreat from equality, whatever its intellectual merits,

made good strategic sense. In an era when "liberal" had become
a pejorative label, a ringing defense of the welfare state as the
means with which to achieve egalitarian ends could only fail.
Nonetheless, despite the conservative triumph with which the
decade had begun, by the late 1980s public sentiment undeniably had moderated. Few could deny the increased misery, visible especially within America's postindustrial cities. But this new
concern with destitution responded to only one of the strands
within current legal and philosophic discussions of poverty and
public obligation: the unwarranted suffering caused by deprivation and vulnerability. It ignored the other, the emphasis on
democracy, community, and citizenship. Public attention focused on categories of the poor who, lacking human dignity,
remained aliens and strangers, at most objects of pity and subjects of charity, but rarely fellow citizens deprived of the means
of civic participation. Of the new categories into which more
fortunate Americans classified the casualties of urban life, the
most evocative proved to be the homeless; the most menacing,
the underclass.

# The
## Underclass? | FIVE

By THE MID-1980s, a new image dominated poverty discourse. Invoked unreflectively and automatically by commentators on poverty, the concept of the *underclass* captured the mixture of alarm and hostility that tinged the emotional response of more affluent Americans to the poverty of blacks increasingly clustered and isolated in postindustrial cities. What bothered observers most was not their suffering; rather, it was their sexuality, expressed in teenage pregnancy; family patterns, represented by female-headed households; alleged reluctance to work for low wages; welfare dependence, incorrectly believed to be a major drain on national resources; and propensity for drug use and violent crime, which had eroded the safety of the streets and the subways.

In fact, the very poor evoked two different images among affluent Americans. When they appeared pathetic, they were the homeless; when they seemed menacing, they became the under-class. Although membership among the homeless and under-class overlapped, public discourse implicitly divided them by degree of personal responsibility for their situation. As long as they remained supplicants rather than militants, objects of char-ity rather than subjects of protest, the homeless became the new deserving poor.


## THE  HOMELESS

The homeless embody the contradictions of the postindustrial city. Huddled over steam vents, in doorways, on the benches of subway and train stations, they remind us daily that economic recovery has not lessened poverty or tempered inequality. They bear the most visible cost of the transformation of American cities by urban renewal, gentrification, and downtown revitali-zation; of the dismantling of the old industrial economy; and of government's war on welfare. They show that the richest and most powerful nation in the world cannot provide all its citizens with a decent and secure place in which to live. They tell us that the billions of dollars poured into urban reform have not ren-dered archaic "the other America." The growing number of fam-ilies among them drive home the awful fact that among industrialized countries, only in America is childhood the age of greatest poverty.

Homelessness is both a condition and a category. The Stewart B. McKinney Homeless Assistance Act, passed by Congress in 1987, defines a homeless person as "one who lacks a fixed night-time residence or whose nighttime residence is a temporary shel-ter, welfare hotel, transitional housing for the mentally ill, or any public and private place not designed as sleeping accommo-dations for human beings." This innocuous and seemingly ob-jective definition begs questions: For how long does someone lack a nighttime residence before he or she becomes officially homeless? On what grounds do we exclude from the homeless those driven to beg shelter from friends or relatives? However useful this definition is as a neutral description of a condition, homelessness remains an emotionally charged social category, a frame within which we gather, observe, study, count, think about, sometimes pity or despise numbers of poor people. Although we think of them as an undifferentiated group, the homeless are different from one another, varied in age, race, gender, family condition, and history.[1]

Nobody knows how many people are homeless in America, even by the McKinney Act's definition. Counting the homeless is extraordinarily difficult for several reasons, including their transience. Many people are homeless only for a short time, and the number of homeless in the course of a year far exceeds the number without shelter on any given night. The National Alliance to End Homelessness, for instance, estimated that 735,000 people were homeless every night; between 1.3 and 2 million would be homeless for at least one night in 1988; and 6 million Americans because of the disproportionately high cost of housing, are at "extreme risk of becoming homeless." In 1982, Hombs and Snyder, two homeless advocates, estimated the number as 2.2 million; in 1984, the U.S. Department of Housing and Urban Development reported the number as between 200,000 and 300,000. Hombs and Snyder were advocates for the homeless; HUD was an agent of the Reagan administration. In fact, these studies and others are flawed. All that can be said with confidence, and it is probably enough, is that shelter operators report large increases in the numbers of people who seek their services. Between January 1983 and December 1984 the number of families in New York City's shelters rose 67 percent; in 1987, most American cities reported annual increases between 15 and 50 percent in those identified as homeless.[2]

Although families with children comprise the fastest growing subgroup among the homeless population (according to the U.S. Conference of Mayors, in 1986 they were 28 percent of all homeless people in America's 25 largest cities), most homeless people still are individual adults, a majority men, though the number of women has increased notably in recent years. The

age of the men averages between 34 and 37; the women generally
are two to six years younger. Most homeless adults have never
married and lack family to whom they can turn for help. Nearly
half have graduated from high school, and the great majority
have lived for a long time in the city that shelters them. Large
numbers are Vietnam veterans; probably about 30 percent could
be diagnosed as having some form of psychiatric disorder; and
substantial numbers have alcohol and drug problems. Other notable subgroups among the homeless are adolescents who have
run away from home or been turned out by their parents; elderly
people, whose proportion among the homeless is much lower
than among the whole population; and the rural homeless, who
remain much less visible than their counterparts in cities.[3]

The reasons why so many more Americans are homeless reflect both structural change and government policy. Homeless
people are casualties of the postindustrial city. The exit of manufacturing has removed many of the jobs at which they once
might have worked. The new jobs for which they qualify within
the service sector usually pay wages too low to meet escalating
housing costs. Urban renewal has torn down low-cost housing,
including the SRO (single room occupancy) hotels in which
unattached poor people often lived. Indeed, as it has wiped out
skid rows in cities across the country, urban redevelopment has
obliterated housing for the poor. In only a little more than one
decade, between 1970 and 1982, nearly half of all single-room
units in America, some 1,116,000, vanished. Fueled by inflation
and gentrification, rents rose rapidly in the 1970s. By 1980, 7
million households were paying more than half their income in
rent.[4]

Demographic patterns worsened the housing problem. Increased migration of minorities into cities and growing numbers
of single-parent families escalated the demand for more low-cost
housing during the very years that urban redevelopment, inflation, and gentrification lessened the supply. Government policy
exacerbated the problem in a number of ways. Its urban renewal
and transportation policies financed the destruction of low-cost
urban housing and accelerated the social and spatial transfor-

mation of cities, while its policies toward the mentally ill added to the number of people unable to support themselves and in need of housing.

For very good reasons, in the 1960s critics began to expose the flaws in public mental health systems that responded to mental illness by warehousing victims in massive and expensive institutions. In the same years, the advent of new drugs capable of controlling the behavior of the mentally ill made possible their discharge into communities. As a result, the population of mental hospitals dropped from a high of 559,000 in 1955 to a low of 130,000 in 1980. Its advocates promoted deinstitutionalization as part of a comprehensive policy that included community mental health clinics and appropriate aftercare. For the most part, it was not. Former patients, lacking work, struggled to find housing affordable on minimal incomes from disability insurance. Although the number of former patients did not grow after the great first wave of discharges, admissions declined, and many of the mentally ill who once would have been hospitalized were left on the streets, where they too joined the ranks of the homeless.[5]

Cuts in social welfare at both the federal and state levels compounded the difficulties poor people encountered finding housing. Between 1970 and 1985, the median value of AFDC benefits declined about one-third in constant dollars. At the same time, the value of General Assistance—that is, relief provided by state governments, dropped about 32 percent. In the early 1980s, the Reagan administration, as part of its war on welfare, successfully excised about 200,000 disabled people, many with psychiatric disorders, from the roles of Supplemental Social Security. It also radically reduced the role of the federal government in increasing the supply of low-cost housing. "The Reagan administration," claims Chester Hartman, wanted "to shut off the housing spigot altogether." As a result, new housing starts for all HUD lower-income housing programs dropped steadily from 183,000 in 1980 to 28,000 in 1985.

In the same years, the administration cut the Community Development Block Grant, of which about 30 percent was spent on housing rehabilitation; ended Neighborhood Self-Help De-

velopment grants, which helped communities resist housing displacement; reduced federal operating subsidies for public
housing and funds for modernizing public housing; and raised
the proportion of income to be paid by the poor for subsidized
housing. In 1985, a HUD Deputy Assistant Secretary told the
Urban League's convention: "We're basically backing out of the
business of housing, period." The administration's answer to the
problem was vouchers, a housing allowance poor people could
spend as they wished. However, without incentives to build low-
cost housing or subsidies, there was little likelihood that private
developers would construct the massive number of low-cost
units now needed; nor, without controls, was it likely that landlords would repair substandard buildings or refrain from charg-
ing excessive rents. The existing housing stock could not meet
the demand for low-cost housing; neither through direct action
nor incentives did the federal government increase the supply of
new housing; income subsidies were too low to permit poor people to afford available housing without depriving themselves of
other necessities. The result was a housing crisis of which the
homeless were but the most visible tip.[6]

We know surprisingly little about how poor people throughout
American history actually survived from day to day. Often, they
have depended on incomes that seemed too low to sustain them
and their families. The key to their survival, I suspect from what
little research there is, has been a series of complex, intersecting
networks. Some of these have centered on family. Kin have
helped each other through crises. Others have linked neighbors
in intricate chains of reciprocity, spontaneous and extraordinary
acts of generosity between poor people themselves. Still others
have been more institutional: local labor markets that awarded
jobs on the basis of friendship and patronage and, of critical
importance, local sources of credit, mainly small merchants and
landlords, who sustained people they knew through the times
they lacked cash.

My sense, and I can offer it only as a hypothesis, is that homelessness, and indeed urban poverty, has become a different sort
of problem than in the past because these networks either have

been attenuated or have disappeared. Urban redevelopment has destroyed the basis of many neighborhood networks; retailing has almost disappeared from many inner-city neighborhoods, where national chains have replaced local merchants. Jobs have moved away from where people live, and few local labor markets of any significance still exist. Finally, there is the question of family. Family members may disperse to find work; pinched by the crisis in low-cost housing, they may often lack space in which to house their kin; with AFDC available, more young, single mothers seek their own housing, for which they are able to pay very little. All these factors may have weakened the network of supports within inner cities, transforming the experience of poverty and fueling the rise of homelessness.[7]

It is a mistake to draw close parallels, as some do, between homelessness in the past and now. In the nineteenth century, workers moved often from city to city (or town to town) looking for work. Work was so irregular that they often found themselves unemployed, and before the era of cheap public transportation, they needed to live close to where they worked. Especially when workplaces remained relatively small and scattered, these factors all propelled workers toward the road, where they sometimes found themselves without money or shelter.

Although a variety of factors, especially the depression that started in 1873, increased the number of poor, wandering workers in the late nineteenth century, they did not encounter much public sympathy. Public discourse transformed the verb *tramp* into a noun that signified a lazy, dangerous, probably alcoholic man in search of a handout. Only much later did *hobo* join *tramp* as a noun with which to describe men on the move, and only as the problem abated did it acquire its colorful connotations. In fact, throughout most of America's past, unemployed men asking for relief were the quintessential undeserving poor, immediately suspect for their inablity to support themselves in the land of opportunity. By contrast, the quintessential deserving poor were the many widows with children left penniless through no fault of their own. They too often lacked homes. Less clear was the status of the destitute elderly. Old women evoked more pity than old men, who were assumed to be failures because of their inability to save for their old age. Unless old people had managed to buy a home of their own or could move in with children, they often ended their lives in wretched poorhouses. Later, in the skid rows of twentieth-century cities, old men often slept in the streets, and all categories of the homeless found shelter in cheap hotels or lodging houses.[8]

The "new homeless," as Peter Rossi labels them, differ from the old in important ways. Fewer of them are old, and many fewer old people are either poor or homeless. Indeed, today's homeless are surprisingly young. Unlike young men on the road in search of work a century ago, most of them are relatively long-term residents of the cities in which they live. Many more of the homeless now are women and families and with the demolition of skid rows and urban redevelopment, they remain scattered throughout cities rather than clustered in one or two areas. Nor, with the destruction of SROs and similar facilities, do they have as many alternative shelters. Today's homeless probably work less than their counterparts in the nineteenth century. Often, they are not between jobs; instead, they are more or less permanently unemployed, and a majority of them, now, are not white. Until World War II, great economic and demographic continuities linked the experience of generations within American cities. After the war, the transformations of economy, demography, and space that created the postindustrial city so altered the shape and content of urban life that all the familiar patterns eventually shattered. As a result, the context, meaning, implications, and future of the homelessness have altered irrevocably.[9]

Although some moral ambiguity hovers over the homeless today, their status among the very poor has improved. They are, as Mark Stern has argued, the new deserving poor. They represent a category as well as a condition. What accounts for its timing and appeal? (Sociologist Peter Rossi points out that the *Reader's Guide to Periodical Literature* listed no articles on homelessness in 1975, compared to 34 in 1984 and 48 in 1986. His own working bibliography in 1988 exceeded 60 single-spaced pages, with about three-quarters of the entries dating from 1980 or later.) The emergence of homelessness as a public problem reflects, first, its visibility. Homelessness does not take place in private, nor does it confine itself to ghetto areas where affluent persons rarely travel. On the contrary, it is defined by its public nature. Because homelessness manifests itself in public spaces, its spectacular increase has altered urban topography. As they appropriated spaces in railroad stations, subways, lobbies, and doorways, homeless people redefined urban space. They might not be helped, but they could not be ignored.

For Stern, it was the 1981 consent decree in New York City's Callahan case that initially turned homelessness into a public problem. "The decree committed the city to provide clean and safe shelter for every homeless man and woman who sought it and set standards against overcrowding in shelters." National political action reinforced events in New York City, as a coalition formed at the 1980 Democratic Convention organized demonstrations; two books, *Shopping Bag Ladies* by Ann Marie Rousseau and *Private Lives, Public Spaces* by Ellen Baxter and Kim Hopper, focused the attention of the public on the issue, and the harsh winter of 1981–82 finally forced it to the forefront of public consciousness.[10]

Stern locates the appeal of homelessness in its capacity to reestablish the "gift relationship" as the basis of public and private charity. Charity's historic role extended beyond the alleviation of poverty; it served to bind classes together and to reinforce social relations based on deference and obligation. In his great study of poverty in late nineteenth-century London, Gareth Stedman Jones wrote: "To give, from whatever motives, generally imposes an obligation upon the receiver. In order to receive one must behave in an acceptable manner, if only by expressing gratitude and humiliation." Responses to homelessness reflected the appeal of the gift relationship.[11] Plans for fighting homelessness, as Stern notes, tried to reestablish "the bond between giver and recipient" through voluntary rather than state action. Discourse on the homeless stressed "their almost saint-like spirits," and "docility and gratitude," rather than "anger and suspicion."[12]

The framing of homelessness as a problem for charity posed dilemmas for policy. First, it frustrated solutions to long-term problems because voluntarism cannot abolish homelessness. Not only does the appropriation of homelessness as a charity deflect attention away from its potential to energize a broader attack on poverty, it also inhibits direct, aggressive action by poor people on their own behalf, which is essential to the initiation of political reform. As the homeless organize unions, press their demands in demonstrations, and form coalitions with other poor people, their special appeal will fade. They will be warned that militance backfires; run into conflict with many of their liberal champions who, hurt, will retreat from their cause; and slip again into the ranks of the undeserving poor.[13]

The other problem is this: Homelessness illustrates Martha Minow's dilemma of difference. For it is a social category, not a defining quality of persons. Those poor people with nowhere to live vary greatly in their characteristics. To collapse them into one category by abstracting one aspect of their lives is to subordinate their individuality; to mark them as different, and because they need help, as inferior to the rest of us; and to leave them with a label that can turn as quickly into a stigma as into a plea for help. Yet, without the creation of this category, public sympathy on behalf of those poor people included within it would not have swelled, many fewer volunteers would have responded, and poor people would have suffered even more.

Is there a way to energize public action that does not stigmatize and isolate? Is there in America a way to foster a discourse about poverty based on human dignity and community rather than on invidious categories and market-based models of public policy? The late 1980s provided little reason for optimism. For even more than homelessness, another new category began to dominate discussions of poverty. I refer, of course, to the underclass.

# THE EMERGENCE OF THE UNDERCLASS AS A PUBLIC ISSUE

In 1987, *The New York Times* pointed to the recent discovery of an underclass by American social science:

> *Social scientists have focused new energies on an "underclass"*
> *of Americans who live in near total isolation from mainstream*
> *society, and scholars are trying to learn more about the deteriorat-*
> *ing inner-city areas where not working is the norm, crime is a*
> *commonplace and welfare is a way of life* [italics in original].[14]

Two groups—black teenage mothers and black jobless youths —dominated the images of the underclass. The former received the most attention, and antipoverty policy, redefined as welfare reform, came to mean intervening in the alleged cycle of dependency in which young, unmarried black women and their children had become trapped. Black males became less a problem for social welfare and more of one for the police. Instead of training and employment, public policy responded by putting more of them in jail. Rates of incarceration in the United States soared above those in every other Western industrial democracy. Recidivism and prison overcrowding became the equivalent of welfare dependency and escalating AFDC rolls, and the privatization of prisons worked no better as a policy response than Ronald Reagan's early expectation of turning much of public welfare over to private charity.[15]

Not only did poverty discourse pay less attention to the joblessness of black males, it virtually ignored both the majority of the poor, who were not black and did not live in female-headed families, and the explosive growth of poverty among white adult males. Most writing about the underclass reinforced these tendencies. From the work of Ken Auletta and Nicholas Lemann, for instance, as well as from the mass media, the concept emerged as imprecise, with its sources specified either inadequately or inaccurately. The underclass seemed little more than the most modern euphemism for the undeserving poor. By contrast, in his 1987 book, William J. Wilson refocused the debate on what he viewed as the major cause of black family instability: black male joblessness.

For all its menace, the underclass was a comforting discovery. However defined, it remained a minority among the poor and a tiny share of the American population. It was small and concentrated enough to be the object of effective help, and if assistance failed, to contain. Its prominence not only refocused attention on culture and behavior; it deflected it away from the more intractable, growing, and potentially subversive problems of the working poor: increasing income inequality and the bifurcation of America's social structure.[16]

Consider, as a prime example, the first major announcement of the underclass in the mass media, *Time* magazine's cover story, "The American Underclass," in its issue of August 19, 1977. "Behind [the ghetto's] crumbling walls lives a large group of people who are more intractable, more socially alien and more hostile than almost anyone had imagined. They are the unreachables: the American underclass." *Time* defined the underclass primarily by its values and behavior, which differed sharply from those of other Americans. "Their bleak environment nurtures values that are often at odds with those of the majority—even the majority of the poor. Thus the underclass produces a highly disproportionate number of the nation's juvenile delinquents, school dropouts, drug addicts and welfare mothers, and much of the adult crime, family disruption, urban decay and demand for social expenditures." As the description continued, the image became even more menacing. "Rampaging members of the underclass carried out much of the orgy of looting and burning that swept New York's ghettos during the July blackout. . . . They are responsible for most of the youth crime that has spread like an epidemic through the nation." Most persons in the underclass were "not looters or arsonists or violent criminals," admitted *Time*, but they remained "so totally disaffected from the system that many who would not themselves steal or burn only stand by while others do so, sometimes cheering them on."[17]

Like other commentators, the authors of the *Time* article failed to define the underclass clearly and consistently. For they described it not only by its behavioral pathology and deviant values, but by its relation to the process of social mobility as well. "Underclass" referred to people "stuck at the bottom, removed from the American dream," and therefore left unclear just who composed the underclass, whether its members represented a population disadvantaged by lack of mobility, in which case their numbers would include many poor people untainted by drugs, promiscuity, or criminality, or whether the term should be reserved as a label for behavior. *Time* stressed that the underclass differed from the rest of America. They were aliens, alarming strangers in our midst. Indeed, for *Time* the American underclass consisted of international outcasts: A confluence of factors—"the weakness of family structure, the presence of competing street values, and the lack of hope amidst affluence"— had created in America an "underclass unique among the world's poor people."[18]

During the next decade, mass media interpretations of the underclass changed very little. In 1986, *U.S. News and World Report*'s cover story, "A Nation Apart," reinforced the image of poor people of color in America's inner cities as strangers, aliens in their own country, defined primarily by their deviant values. A "second nation" had emerged within black America, "a nation outside the economic mainstream—a separate culture of have-nots drifting further apart from the basic values of the haves. Its growth is now the central issue in the country's urban centers." Little more than a year later, an article in *Fortune* reinforced the same interpretation. It defined "underclass communities" as "urban knots that threaten to become enclaves of permanent poverty and vice" and impose severe social and economic costs on the rest of American society, leaving business without a work force sufficiently skilled for jobs in the twenty-first century. Not so much their poverty or race as their "behavior—their chronic lawlessness, drug use, out-of-wedlock births, non-work, welfare dependency, and school failure," asserted the author, defined the underclass: "Underclass describes a state of mind and a way of life. It is at least as much a cultural as an economic condition."[19]

Social scientists did relatively little to modify the popular image of a menacing underclass defined by behavior rather than poverty. Indeed, when American social science discovered the underclass, it paid more attention to its behavior than to its origins in the transformations that intensified poverty within postindustrial cities. As early as 1969, Lee Rainwater criticized this constricted vision. Social scientists, he wrote, had neglected to analyze "the central fact about the American underclass— that it is created by, and its existence is maintained by, the operation of what is in other ways the most successful economic system known to man."[20]

Douglas Glasgow's *Black Underclass* (1980) tried to direct debate along the path urged by Rainwater and later taken by Wilson. Glasgow used the concept to frame his research on the young men who had participated in the great Watts riot of 1965. The emergence of an underclass as a "permanent fixture of our nation's social structure," he wrote, represented "one of the most significant class developments in the past two decades." By underclass, he meant "a permanently entrapped population of poor persons, unused and unwanted, accumulated in various parts of the country."[21] Blacks, disproportionately represented among the poor, remained particularly vulnerable to the magnetic force of the underclass. "Structural factors found in market dynamics and institutional practices, as well as the legacy of racism, produce and then reinforce the cycle of poverty and, in turn, work as a pressure exerting a downward pull toward underclass status."[22] Serious misconceptions, argued Glasgow, detracted attention from the obstacles confronting blacks. For example, references to statistics that pointed to improvements in blacks' economic status between 1959 and 1974 failed to note that white unemployment fell about twice as far as black, widening the unemployment gap between races, and that the proportion of blacks among the poor actually had increased. In both 1959 and 1974, blacks' poverty rate exceeded that of whites by about three times. The argument that significant numbers of blacks had moved into the middle class also misdirected interpretations of black experience. First, figures that showed increasing incomes for black families reflected the joint wages of employed husbands and wives. In fact, as individuals black men and women continued to earn less than their white counterparts, and the increasing number of single-headed black families offset the gains by those with two wage earners.[23]

Most serious were the unemployment problems of black youth. Their lack of work opportunity in the primary labor market locked many young blacks permanently into the underclass. Nor did all blacks who worked escape, because their low wages and occupational immobility trapped them in poverty despite their commitment to the work ethic. (Glasgow stressed that research has demonstrated the eagerness for work among black youths. He dismissed as a cruel myth the idea that they were unwilling to enter the labor market.) Blacks' detachment from the "standardized institutions" feeding the primary labor market reinforced their entrapment in the underclass. Indeed, this inability to escape poverty was, for Glasgow, the component that differentiated the underclass from a lower class, whose members realistically could expect mobility if not for themselves, then for their children.[24]

Therefore, "underclass" did not "connote moral or ethical unworthiness" or "any other pejorative meaning." Rather, it described a new population, "not necessarily culturally deprived, lacking in aspirations, or unmotivated to achieve," but the static poor, trapped in their situation by a variety of forces, primarily constricted opportunities and "limited alternatives provided by socialization patterns." Rejection by mainstream institutions, especially schools, fed the rage and desperation of ghetto youth. Rejection often maimed and broke them by denying their individuality and integrity. As a result, behavior considered destructive by many remained their "one great protection" against a system that assured them failure. Economic trends also trapped black youths in the underclass by eliminating entry-level jobs and reducing the need for unskilled labor. Of all the forces sustaining the underclass, however, racism remained the strongest. Despite the virtual disappearance of legal discrimination, computers now excluded people ostensibly "on the basis not of 'race' but of 'social profile.' " What, then, was the answer? What would help break up the underclass and move blacks out of poverty? The key was jobs, whose provision should be the prime goal of policies to alleviate the underclass crisis in America's cities.[25]

Glasgow's interpretation of the underclass excluded two themes that would dominate most subsequent discussion. First, he wrote only about men. Second, he scarcely mentioned black family structure. Because liberals dominated poverty discourse, discussion of black family structure still remained tainted by discredited notions of the culture of poverty and the debacle of the Moynihan Report. Within a few years, however, writers on poverty associated with the conservative political revival had reestablished culture and family structure on the agenda of social science and public policy. This new legitimacy for old concerns —feminist attention to women's poverty—and demographic trends in the 1970s served to focus even moderate and liberal poverty discourse on family and culture. In the process, "underclass" assumed a connotation quite different than Glasgow had intended. One major example is Ken Auletta's book *The Underclass* (1982), which popularized the concept and pointed to its emerging meaning.[26]

Auletta based his book on observations of an experimental supported work program funded by the Manpower Demonstration Research Corporation in New York City. Despite his cautious conclusion that the program had succeeded, others, reading his account, could reach a less sanguine verdict.

Auletta defined the underclass as a relatively permanent minority of the poor with "four distinct categories": "(a) the *passive poor*, usually long-term welfare recipients; (b) the *hostile* street criminals who terrorize most cities, and who are often school dropouts and drug addicts; (c) the *hustlers*, who, like street criminals, may not be poor and who earn their livelihood in an underground economy, but rarely commit violent crimes; (d) the *traumatized* drunks, drifters, homeless shopping-bag ladies and released mental patients who frequently roam or collapse on city streets."[27] For Auletta as well as Glasgow, lack of mobility defined the underclass. However, Auletta remained more concerned with the behavior of the underclass than its origins and focused on strategies that taught its members how to enter the mainstream working world.

Although he intended his book to be nonideological, Auletta's account fit within the historic tradition of American poverty discourse. (This, certainly, is one explanation for the book's popularity and influence. Another is its resonance with a new consensus about the source of social problems.) Like those who wrote on poverty two centuries before him, Auletta began by separating poor people into two categories and identifying one of them primarily by its deviant behavior. Economic and occupational criteria did not determine class membership. In his definition, the source of stratification lay elsewhere. The underclass was a moral, not a sociological, category. Its members were the new undeserving poor. In the tradition of nineteenth-century social critics who fused crime, poverty, and ignorance into interchangeable eruptions of moral pathology, Auletta linked disparate groups into one class. His definition subsumed women on welfare, street criminals, hustlers, and homeless drunks, drifters, and bag ladies into one interchangeable unit identified not by income or dependence, but by behavior.[28]

Despite his narrative focus on a work training program, Auletta's discussion of poverty subordinated employment. It redirected discussion to family and behavior. "The struggle to overcome poverty," he wrote, "has entered a new phase, and one of the most significant problems that has emerged is family structure." Auletta traced the role of family structure in the work of E. Franklin Frazier, Kenneth Clark, and Daniel Patrick Moynihan and recounted the subsequent attack that drove it from the agendas of social science and public policy. Increasingly, though, he reported, the black family had reappeared as a major topic in discussions about poverty, and even "some leading black officials" had "become less inhibited on the subject." Therefore, when Auletta presented thirteen "facts about poverty and the underclass" which were "undebatable and unavoidable," women and family headed the list. His first fact was, "Poverty has become feminized," and his second, "Whether family dissolution is a cause or an effect of poverty, it unquestionably cannot be overlooked." None of his facts specified joblessness as a source of poverty. Rather, his discussion ended with the observations that "the face of poverty has been altered" and that Moynihan, in his emphasis on the family, "was prescient about the changing structure of American poverty."[29]

Most subsequent commentaries on the underclass also used imprecise definitions that stressed family and behavior and rested on implicitly moral conceptions of class structure. Consider the two long and widely read articles in *The Atlantic* (1986) by Nicholas Lemann.

In "The Origins of the Underclass," Lemann describes life in the ghettoes as "utterly different" from the American mainstream. Using (without acknowledgement) a thesis first argued by William J. Wilson, Lemann laments "the bifurcation of black America, in which blacks are splitting into a middle class and an underclass that seems likely never to make it. The clearest line between the two groups is family structure." The result is the total isolation of the underclass. "As apart as all of black life is, ghetto life is a thousand times more so, with a different language, economy, educational system, and social ethic." The statistic that most accurately captures the distinction is the rise in out-of-wedlock births, which are "by far the greatest contributor to the perpetuation of the misery of ghetto life." Lemann revives the culture of poverty thesis to explain underclass behavior because he sees its "distinctive culture," rather than unemployment or welfare, as "the greatest barrier to progress by the black underclass." His argument, he stresses, "is anthropological, not economic; it emphasizes the power over people's behavior that culture, as opposed to economic incentives, can have."[30]

Lemann's idea of *underclass* remains even less precisely defined than Auletta's, but he shares Auletta's moral conception of class structure. Membership in Chicago's underclass, for instance, which contains between 200,000 and 420,000 of the city's 1.2 million blacks, is not simply a function of poverty or blocked mobility. Rather, it results from behavior that should not be sanctioned by the well-meaning relativism of white liberals or the misplaced racial pride of black militants. Underclass behavior has crystallized into a pathological and self-perpetuating culture, on which public policy should launch a major assault.[31]

Lemann explains the origins of the underclass as the product of southern blacks' migration into northern cities and of northern middle-class movement to the suburbs. "Every aspect of the underclass culture in the ghettos," asserts Lemann, "is directly traceable to roots in the South—and not the South of slavery but the South of a generation ago. In fact, there seems to be a strong correlation between underclass status in the North and a family background in the nascent underclass of the sharecropper South."[32] Unfortunately for Lemann's thesis, all the available data contradict it. Southern black migrants to northern cities have enjoyed higher employment rates, better wages, and less dependency on welfare than northern-born blacks. In the 1960s, northern-born blacks, in fact, accounted for the increased welfare rates.[33] Women, according to Gerald Jaynes, headed fewer than 10 percent of households in the rural south because sharecropping *presupposed* a family labor system. Southern-born blacks did not import an underclass culture to northern cities. The harsh experiences they encountered there—of which the most serious was the lack of employment—broke down their culture. Indeed, Jaynes argues, developments within black communities in the 1960s represented a sustained acceleration of trends rather than a new departure.[34] (In contrast to the South, the ability of black women in northern cities to support themselves has fueled the increase in female household heads among them, just as improving employment opportunities have had a similar effect among white women.)[35]

Along with Auletta, Lemann reinforced the identification of a menacing underclass with unmarried black women. The coincidence of their views with popular stereotypes distracted casual readers from their imprecision, contradictions, and weak evidence, and "underclass" swiftly became the most fashionable term in poverty discourse. Marian Wright Edelman highlights the dangers of an imprecise definition of underclass:

> References to the underclass will add nothing to our understanding of poverty, but will erode public confidence in our ability to do something about it. If applied too loosely to all who have remained persistently poor, the term underclass may reinforce the misguided belief that poverty is the product solely or primarily of individual pathology, ignoring the institutional forces in our society which help perpetuate deprivation. By implying that there are major differences in the character of the poor vis-à-vis the nonpoor, the term undermines our confidence and desire to try to help.[36]

The underclass emerged no more clearly from social science than from journalism. As they summarized their review of the social science literature on the urban underclass, Martha Gephart and Robert Pearson, Social Science Research Council staff associates to the council's urban underclass committee, concluded that definitional and conceptual problems would "undoubtedly continue to confront scholars because there are unlikely to be easily agreed-upon definitions of the underclass available to those who seek to understand it."[37]

Drastically different estimates of the size of the underclass reflected its imprecise definition. Erol R. Ricketts and Isabel V. Sawhill, using 1980 census data, estimated the underclass as about 500,000. Peter Gottschalk and Sheldon Danziger, two economists who specialize in poverty research, using different types of measures, reached an estimate of less than 1 million in

1984. By contrast, the estimate offered by two other researchers Patricia Ruggles and William P. Marton, was 8 million for 1985. Two estimates by other experts for 1979 varied between 1.8 million and 4.1 million people.[38]


# WILLIAM JULIUS WILSON
# AND THE UNDERCLASS

In 1987, the publication of William Julius Wilson's *The Truly Disadvantaged* focused even more national attention on persistent and concentrated urban poverty. It also brought more sophistication to the debate. Although he accepted its usefulness as a term, Chicago sociologist Wilson rejected explanations that traced the origins of an underclass to female-headed families and a culture of poverty. He tried to redirect debate to where he believed its origins lay: black male joblessness.

In *The Declining Significance of Race* (1978), William Julius Wilson stressed the emergence of class stratification among blacks. No longer constrained by discrimination, a black middle class had moved into both better jobs and neighborhoods, its upward mobility no longer hampered by race. The situation of blacks left behind in inner cities, however, had worsened. Wilson's thesis provoked a major controversy that centered on his description of improvements in the circumstances of the black middle class and neglected his argument about the "deteriorating conditions of the black underclass."[39]

Incorrectly labeled a conservative, Wilson, who thought of himself as a social democrat, decided to focus on the ghetto underclass and spell out the policy implications of this thesis. The result was *The Truly Disadvantaged*.[40] Wilson argues that neutral terms, such as lower class or working class, fail to address the recent transformations within American cities that resulted in dramatic increases in the concentration of poverty. The exodus of the black middle and working class left neighborhoods to the most disadvantaged, a "heterogeneous grouping of families and individuals who are outside the mainstream of the American occupational system." These include "individuals who lack training and skills and either experience long-term unemployment or are not members of the labor force, individuals who are engaged in street crime and other forms of aberrant behavior, and families that experience long-term spells of poverty and/or welfare dependency." This, for Wilson, is the underclass. As he uses it, underclass refers to "the groups that have been left behind" and are as a consequence "collectively different from those that lived in these neighborhoods in earlier years."[41]

Wilson's definition of the underclass incorporates geography, occupation, behavior, and history. It is geographical because it assigns a key role to social concentration with a distinct territory. It identifies members of the underclass by their existence outside the mainstream of the "American occupational system." It stresses the development of behaviors at variance with "mainstream patterns and norms," and it rests on a version of recent history that views the underclass as unprecedented.[42]

To Wilson, the sources of the underclass are both demographic and economic. Drawing on the work of Stanley Lieberson, he argues that vast migrations of blacks to cities aroused latent racial consciousness and spurred the creation of barriers in housing and employment. This growing black central city population was "relatively young," and "youth is not only a factor in crime; it is also associated with out-of-wedlock births, female-headed homes, and welfare dependency." Thus, the increase in the number of young people by itself explains much of what is "awry in the inner city."[43] However, changes in urban economic structure that reduced demand for unskilled labor contributed more than demography to the creation of the underclass. Earlier immigrants entered cities when manufacturing was expanding and the demand for unskilled and semiskilled labor growing. Blacks now confront the shift away from a manufacturing to a service economy. As blue-collar jobs dwindle, the service jobs that replace them demand high educational qualifications or, at the other extreme, pay little and offer minimal career opportunity. On almost every measure of the labor market, Wilson points out, the economic position of blacks has deteriorated. So serious has joblessness among black youths become that "Only a minority of noninstitutionalized black youth are employed."[44]

Population concentration further exacerbated the impact of age structure and joblessness. From 1970 to 1980, the population rose by 12 percent in the nation's fifty largest cities and the number of persons living in poverty areas increased by more than 20 percent. The total black population in "extreme-poverty" areas soared by 148 percent during these years, compared to a 24 percent rise among whites. This "growth of the high- and extreme-poverty areas," observes Wilson, "epitomizes the social transformation of the inner city."[45]

The migration of middle- and working-class families out of many ghetto neighborhoods removed a key "social buffer" that might have deflected the full impact of prolonged and increasing joblessness on behavior. When inner city neighborhoods were more socially diverse, their basic institutions (churches, schools, stores, recreational facilities) remained viable, and by their presence, mainstream role models nurtured "the perception that education is meaningful, that steady employment is a viable alternative to welfare, that family stability is the norm, not the exception."[46] Without them, social isolation—that is, "the lack of contact or sustained interaction with individuals and institutions that represent mainstream society"—has increased, with serious consequences. Because it leaves people outside job networks and fails to develop behavior essential for successful work experience, it exacerbates the difficulty of finding jobs. Because of its relation to attitudes and behavior, social isolation leads Wilson to an emphasis on culture. But unlike earlier writers on the culture of poverty, he defines culture as "a response to social structural constraints and opportunities."[47]

As Wilson realizes, *The Truly Disadvantaged* should be read as a hypothesis about inner-city poverty based on the incomplete evidence available for its analysis. Indeed, he has mounted an unprecedented research project in Chicago, which will gather data with which to test many of his ideas. Social scientists have

already begun to probe Wilson's hypotheses. Does neighborhood, they are asking, exert an independent influence on behavior? Has racial segregation ceased to be as important an
influence on black residential patterns as Wilson implies? Would
higher employment rates for black males reduce adolescent
pregnancy by encouraging or permitting family formation?
Whatever the answers to these questions turn out to be, no one
has contradicted Wilson's emphasis on the importance of black
male joblessness and its relative neglect by social science and
public policy.[48]

Wilson points out that American poverty discourse, both liberal and conservative, has neglected jobs, which are the key to
unlocking opportunities and freeing the underclass from their
ghetto neighborhoods. Debate has focused on ameliorating the
condition of disadvantaged people with income supports and
social services and on eradicating the cultural traits that retard
their economic progress. As a result, female-headed families remain more central to the poverty debate than good jobs. Indeed,
very little current poverty discourse focuses on the working poor
or on the rate of poverty among white adult males, which has
increased dramatically in contrast to the rate among female
household heads, which has remained almost static.

How should we explain the neglect of so transparently critical
a factor? Although contemporary conservatives have misread
and made selective use of economic data, liberals have been
equally negligent. Part of the reason is historic: the three major
preoccupations of American poverty discourse (classifying poor
people, debating the effects of welfare on their behavior, and
worrying about the limits of social obligations) and lack of attention to the forces that generate poverty. In this sense, contemporary debate follows well-worn grooves, which had a certain
logic before the era when technology and government gained
the capacity to transform scarcity into abundance. By slighting
the unavailability of work, poverty discourse reinforces the hostility to working-age men almost always reflected in relief policy.
The assumption that any able-bodied man could find work underlay the reluctance of welfare administrators and reformers to

grant men outdoor relief, the consignment of men to poorhouses, and the vicious war against tramps late in the nineteenth
century. Except for the Great Depression of the 1930s, even
abundant evidence that jobs were scarce failed to shake the belief that men were unemployed because they were lazy. Poverty
discourse that focuses on behavior echoes and reinforces these
old streotypes and nourishes popular preconceptions about poor
people that influence the policy directions chosen by politicians.
But it is not only because they fit popular images that policies
reflecting behavioral and cultural explanations of poverty are
politically easiest to enact. They also conflict with the fewest
vested interests because they do not require income redistribution or the sharing of power and other resources. At the
same time, they suit intellectuals. For poor people who lack the
capacity to mobilize in their own self-interest need advocates,
organizers, and therapists. All these factors connect to focus
attention on the behavior of the poor rather than on their lack
of jobs.

The relative inattention to jobs has left the social science cup-
board stocked thinly with data and prescriptions. Still, a small
but growing body of research begins to chart the problem as it
applies to black youths.

## JOBLESSNESS AND THE BLACK UNDERCLASS

The experience of young men underlines a paradox in recent
black history. Affirmative action, equal opportunity programs,
and other efforts by both the government and private sector
have reduced discrimination and raised black youths' wages relative to whites. "Young blacks," report economists Richard
Freeman and Harry Holzer, "have made advances in both occupation and education. Yet their *employment* problem has
worsened, reaching levels that can only be described as catastrophic." As high as they are, unemployment statistics do not

capture the full measure of the crisis because they are limited to active job seekers. More revealing are the statistics of labor force participation and ratios of employment to population. Between 1955 and 1984, the ratio of employment to the total population of 18- to 19-year-old black males dropped from 66 to 34; in the same period the ratio for employed white males remained nearly identical (64 and 60). In 1983, only 45 percent of black men aged 16 to 21 were employed compared to 73 percent of whites. "In many respects," Freeman and Holzer comment, "the urban unemployment characteristic of Third World countries appears to have taken root among black youths in the United States."[49]

No single, definitive explanation accounts for the employment crisis among young black men. Social scientists debate the relative influence of skills, work ethic, family background, job location and quality, and competition from women and immigrants. Sponsored by the National Bureau of Economic Research, several economists designed a survey to provide data with which to answer key questions about joblessness among young black males. They confined their survey to males because the problem is by far the most serious among them. In 1979, they interviewed 2,358 men in inner-city areas of Boston, Chicago, and Philadelphia. They also drew on the National Longitudinal Surveys of Labor Market Experience, also from 1979, for comparisons with black men living outside inner cities and with whites. The survey asked detailed questions about standard work activities, the hourly activities of these youths in a day, their desire to work, their use of drugs, their participation in illegal activities, and their perceptions of the labor market. *The Black Youth Employment Crisis* presents the major results.[50]

The findings are complex: No single factor is *the* cause of the unemployment problem. Nor do the studies based on the survey reveal patterns on which all the participating economists agree. Some findings, in fact, are much more robust than others. What unifies the studies is the finding that "black male youths are quite responsive to a number of economic incentives and to their social and family environment." In other words, "different incentives" should significantly improve the employment situation of black youths. Designing ways of changing these incentives remains the "major challenge" confronting public policy directed toward increasing employment among young black men.[51]

What do studies based on the surveys show about specific factors relating to black youth unemployment?

1. Young black men want jobs and wages comparable to whites', and their reluctance to take worse jobs lengthens their periods of unemployment. Nonetheless, they are more willing to take badly paying, dead-end jobs, although they do so only temporarily. Because young blacks model their expectations and aspirations on white society, their problem is means, not ends, and concerns about a "culture of poverty" defined by an absence of "middle-class aspirations" lack any foundation. Instead, the great problem young blacks face is "how to achieve their aspirations."[52]

2. The "dynamics of the transition to work" differ for inner-city black youths in four important and unfortunate ways. In contrast to white youths, their employment rate does not improve very much with age. As a consequence, joblessness will not disappear when they become older. Inner-city black youths remain unemployed or never employed far longer than whites. Black youths differ from white youths more in the ease with which they move into employment than in the rate at which they lose jobs. (This results primarily from the reluctance of employers to hire black youths.) Unlike whites and all black youths, however, the duration of their employment does not influence the chances that young black men from the inner city will leave work as a result of choice, layoff, or firing. The reason appears to be "the dead-end types of jobs inner-city blacks obtain."[53]

3. Black youths often do not live near the jobs for which they qualify. However, social scientists do not agree on the implications of this distance between home and potential work. The "spatial mismatch" hypothesis argues that "the outflow of people and firms has left those least able to find and commute to employment trapped far away from the areas where new jobs are

opening." Research on the NBER data dispute this explanation, but as a critic points out, the issue—which has obvious and important consequences for policy—remains far from settled.[54]

4. Women substitute for black men in the "production process." Indeed, women's entry into the labor market could be the "most important" causal factor in the declining labor force participation rates of young black men in recent decades. By contrast, neither Hispanic nor non-Hispanic immigrants have harmed the employment prospects of black men.[55]

5. The difficulties black youths encounter finding jobs may be compounded by both employers' discrimination and an absence of references. Indeed, lack of references appears to be a neglected but important barrier to employment.[56]

6. Young black men respond to the quality of jobs. When jobs pay well and confer higher status, they do not want to lose them. As a result, they less often are absent, because a high rate of absence increases the chances of being fired.[57]

7. About one-quarter of the income earned by sample members derived from crime, but a relatively small proportion of men earned most of it. These were predominantly the young men neither in work nor at school. As a group, these men were "very sensitive to economic incentives" and believed they could earn more money from crime. For this reason, between the carrot and the stick as policy responses, the carrot appears "more effective."[58]

8. Several factors influence the ability of young black men to escape from poverty. Among the most important is churchgoing. Young men who go to church often also attend school more regularly, work more frequently, and spend their leisure time more productively. The two next most important factors are "whether other members of the family work and whether the family is on welfare." The influence of the former is positive and of the latter, negative. The nature of the association between welfare and employment, however, remains cloudy. Is it causal? Does welfare dependence, that is, directly contribute to the low employment rate of young black men, or, as one commentator suggests, are welfare, dropping out of school, and poor employ-

ment "inextricably intertwined" in a complex and indeterminate manner?[59]

9. Black young men from homes with both parents present at age 14 succeed "only marginally better" than those from single-parent families. By itself, a female-headed home does not hamper "socioeconomic success."[60]

10. The relation of attitudes and aspirations to black youth employment remains uncertain. Two authors argue that attitudes and aspirations influenced the number of hours 20- to 24-year-old (but not 16- to 19-year-old) men worked in the past year and that their effect was independent of family background. The most important attitudes were the beliefs that "having a good education was very important" and that "the unemployed could find work if they wanted" and the perception that most of their friends were employed. The most important aspiration was a white collar or crafts job by age 30. The question is how to interpret these findings. The authors cannot say whether attitudes result from or determine experience or how to encourage them. The commentator on their paper believes the findings support his theory "that the labor market behavior of black youths reflects a fear that they will be trapped for life in the menial jobs that are generally open to youth in the U.S. labor market but that whites have historically left behind as they matured and blacks have not." Those relatively few young men who somehow surmount this fear may remain more willing to accept the low-wage work available to young people because they believe it leads to better jobs in the future.[61]

Cultural theories of unemployment receive little support from the available data. The crisis in black youth unemployment relates more to the labor market and discrimination than to any unwillingness to work. Offered decent jobs, young black men by and large respond. Nor has the major change in black family structure—the increase in families headed by women—by itself eroded their willingness to work. What counts is whether the adults in the family work. That is the good news. The bad news is that the labor market trends show little sign of reducing the factors that retard the employment of black men. Most jobs available to them are dead-end jobs and do not offer enticing incentives; without work histories, they lack the references they need to convince potential employers of their reliability; the longer they lack work, the harder it is for them to find a job; tainted in employers' perception by discrimination, a reputation for low skills, and poor work habits, they remain at the end of the line for hiring; when they are hired, they usually work only for a short time. As welfare regulations, poor job prospects, inadequate day care, and the lack of health insurance trap single mothers in AFDC, black young men lack the critical assistance and example of a working adult. Even more ominously, as women enter the labor force, they take the low-wage jobs that otherwise would have been available to black men.

Although research has started to clarify the reasons for joblessness among young black men, it dictates few solutions. Research remains inconclusive partly because its overwhelmingly microeconomic orientation ignores the forces that generate unemployment and poverty in postindustrial cities. Research focuses on supply-side factors: the skills and attitudes of the unemployed and where they live. The more important question may be how to reverse the trends that increasingly have made them redundant.

Four major options exist. The first is containment. Consign old industrial cities to the dustbin of history. Support their shrinking populations, including young men, with minimal welfare, build figurative walls between them and the suburbs, and patrol their boundaries with heavily armed police. However tempting it might be to turn old cities into reservations for the very poor, the strategy cannot work. Instead of dying, postindustrial cities have changed roles. They have even attracted small but significant clusters of affluent young professionals back to their cores. One result has been heightened tension between the new urban gentry and the long-term residents. Those who staff corporate headquarters, new office towers, third sector institutions, and live in urban neighborhoods demand services and protection.[62] A second strategy is authoritarian: lock up the most disruptive, cut welfare, and turn the remainder into a reserve army of labor desperate to work whatever the wages. This has been the thrust of current policy. Although this approach helps depress wages, growing street crime and social pathology have signaled its limits and dangers. A third option is incremental reform: education and training, perhaps accompanied by public sector job creation. Here the problems are twofold: high costs at a time of large deficits and the inability to predict, with confidence, that any mix of programs will work. The fourth option is to focus on the economic and political forces that generate occupational redundancy and unemployment. The tactics include the redirection of macroeconomic policy, controls on plant relocation, the stimulation of community-based economic development, the redistribution of political power, and a guaranteed income or wage supplements. No consensus exists, however, that these goals are even desirable, and, among those who think they are, no one knows exactly how to reach them.

Truly, the policy dilemmas are awesome. Nonetheless, by ignoring or subordinating the black youth employment crisis, poverty discourse has diverted attention from one of the most tragic and explosive problems of our time. The same cannot be said for the other group dominating images of the underclass, black teenage mothers. But is the rhetoric that surrounds them accurate and helpful? Or, in its own way, does it too distract attention from the major issues?

## ADOLESCENT PREGNANCY AND FEMALE-HEADED FAMILIES

In 1986, an otherwise sympathetic radio talk show host told me, "I don't mind paying to help people in need, but I don't want my tax dollars to pay for the sexual pleasure of adolescents who won't use birth control." His outrage summed up popular stereotypes about the relation among adolescent pregnancy, welfare, and the underclass:

1. Adolescent pregnancy is an epidemic which shows no signs of abating.

2. The epidemic is spreading fastest among blacks.

3. Unmarried black mothers (especially adolescents) consume most of America's social welfare budget and drain public resources.

4. America's adolescents become pregnant so often for two primary reasons: They start to have sex earlier than their counterparts in other countries, and generous welfare benefits encourage them to become parents.

5. The easy availability of contraceptives and abortions along with sex education encourages adolescents to have sex and thereby increases the risk of pregnancy.

6. Adolescents lack the maturity to use contraceptives regularly.

7. Unmarried women with children comprise the core of a new, self-perpetuating underclass.[63]

All these common stereotypes are wrong. Indeed, discourse about adolescent pregnancy and female-headed families remains riddled with misconceptions and paradoxes that obscure the situations they are supposed to illuminate and intensify the problems they are intended to reform.

What, in fact, does the best available evidence show? Recall, first, that most poor people in America do not live in families headed by adolescent mothers or even by women. In 1980, 37 percent of poor people lived in female-headed families. Poverty is not synonymous with single parents. Nor does adolescent pregnancy consume a large share of the social welfare budget or gross national product. In 1980, the money spent on AFDC represented only about 4 percent of all the costs of major public assistance and social insurance programs for the elderly, totally disabled, and all others, and only a fraction of AFDC payments go to adolescent mothers. In 1984, all means-tested cash transfer payments by federal, state, and local governments used 0.8 percent of GNP or 2 percent of the share of GNP spent by governments.[64]

Consider, next, the question of birth rates. Among blacks, adolescent birth rates have fallen; among whites they have increased. Between 1970 and 1980, the birth rate of unmarried black women dropped 13 percent, in contrast to a 27 percent increase among unmarried white women. Nonetheless, black marital fertility fell even faster (38 percent), which means that the fraction of births occurring to unmarried women increased. Among just 15- to 19-year-old black women, the nonmarital fertility rate (births per 1,000 women) rose from 76.5 in 1960 to a peak of 90.8 in 1970 and has declined since then; by 1980 it had dropped to 83.0. Among whites, the rate, always lower than blacks', has risen steadily from 6.6 in 1960 to 10.9 in 1970 and 16.0 in 1980. In other words, between 1970 and 1980, the fertility of unmarried black 15- to 19-year-old women dropped almost 10 percent, while the rate for unmarried white women of the same age increased by 48 percent. Although the black rate remained more than five times as great as the white, adolescent pregnancy is not an issue just for blacks.[65]

The American adolescent pregnancy rate soars above those of other industrialized Western countries'. For 15- to 19-year-olds, comparative pregnancy rates in 1981 were: United States, 96; Canada, 44.3; England and Wales, 45.4; France, 43.0; The Netherlands, 14.3; Sweden, 34.6. The American lead did not result from the higher birth rates of adolescent blacks, because blacks comprise a relatively small proportion of the entire population. Removing blacks, in fact, lowers the United States rate only to 83, still far above the others. Birth rates are much lower than pregnancy rates. Again, comparing 15- to 19-year-olds in 1981, the comparative birth rates were: United States, 53; Canada, 26.4; England and Wales, 28.6; France, 22.9; The Netherlands, 9.0; and Sweden, 14.3. Abortion largely accounts for the discrepancies between pregnancy and birth rates, and American abortion rates far exceed those in these other countries: United States, 43.3; Canada, 17.9; England and Wales, 16.8; France, 22.9; The Netherlands, 5.3; and Sweden, 20.1. America's high abortion rates show that its adolescent women do not want to become pregnant any more than their peers in other countries.

Indeed, the ratios of adolescent pregnancies to births in all these countries are quite similar. Despite the rise in abortion rates, unmarried adolescents surrender their children for adoption far less frequently than in the recent past. "Fifteen years ago," writes Maris Vinovskis, "perhaps as many as 50 percent of all out-of-wedlock infants were relinquished for adoption. Today, almost 90 percent of all out-of-wedlock births are kept by the mother."[66]

Among the six countries compared in a Guttmacher Institute study, France and The Netherlands tried hardest to reduce their abortion rates. They succeeded by increasing education about contraceptives and by making birth control methods and advice more widely available. They did not try to curb adolescent sex. Indeed, differences in adolescent pregnancy rates do not reflect distinctions in sexual activity. In these countries, adolescents' first sexual activity occurs at roughly comparable ages. Except for Canada, in the other countries adolescents begin to have sex a bit earlier than in the United States, but they use contraceptives more consistently. Fewer American young women use birth control pills, and American adolescents practice contraception less often and less regularly than their peers in other countries. That is why American adolescent pregnancy rates remain so high.[67]

The Guttmacher Institute study argues that America's exceptionally high adolescent pregnancy rates reflect both government policy and cultural attitudes. Unlike policies in other countries, the Reagan administration's approach to adolescent pregnancy emphasized the prevention of early sexual activity. Only in the United States is abstinence the aim of public policy. Whatever their moral views, other governments realize the futility of trying to curb adolescent sexual behavior.[68] However, among government policies, generous welfare benefits play no role in promoting adolescent pregnancy. All the countries with lower rates of adolescent pregnancy offer far more comprehensive and universal social benefits to children and families than the United States. Most also have less poverty. In fact, in the United States the poverty that results from labor market conditions, discrimination, and inadequate welfare benefits helps generate high rates of adolescent pregnancy.[69]

Attitudes toward sex also promote adolescent pregnancy in America. Young people growing up in contemporary America receive conflicting messages about sex. The media usually "extol sexual attractiveness as a good in itself," and rarely discuss the personal relationships or risks. At the same time, vocal minorities oppose "sex education in public schools and the provision of contraception to adolescents." These conflicting currents hinder contraceptive use by pressuring adolescents into sexual relations without acknowledging "that they are or want to be sexually active and to take responsibility for avoiding pregnancy or sexually transmitted diseases."[70]

On one point public perceptions are correct: The proportion of all births that occur to unmarried adolescent black women has risen. One reason is that their fertility has fallen more slowly than fertility among older and married women. The other reason is the decline in the proportion who marry. Between 1960 and 1980, the proportion of never married black 14- to 24-year-olds increased from 65 to 82 percent. (Among whites, it rose only from 63 to 69 percent.) As a consequence, many more mothers had never married. The ratio of out-of-wedlock births (number of births to unmarried women per 1,000 births) for 15- to 19-year-old black women rose from 422 in 1960 to 852 in 1980; for 20- to 24-year-olds, the increase was from 200 to 561. Ratios also rose for white women of the same age, although they remained much lower: for 15- to 19-year-olds from 72 to 322, and for 20- to 24-year-olds, from 22 to 115.[71]

These trends, of course, have increased the proportion of families headed by women. Between 1960 and 1984, the proportion of households headed by women increased from 9.0 percent to 12.0 percent for whites and from 22.0 percent to 43.0 percent for blacks.[72] More than any others, these families are likely to be poor. (In 1982, women headed 71 percent of all poor black families.) The sources of the explosive growth in female-headed families differ by race. Two leading scholars, Garfinkle and McLanahan, argue that "the increase in women's labor force participation (and the economic dependence that accompanied it)" have been the major factor precipitating the growth in female-headed families among whites. For blacks, by contrast, declining employment opportunities for males have been most important.[73]

The relation between family structure and poverty also differs by race. Changes in family structure account for only a small proportion of the increased poverty among black families, according to Mary Jo Bane. "The poverty rate in 1979," she writes, "would have been about 16 percent lower than it was had family composition remained the same as it was in 1959. Family composition changes contributed almost nothing to the increase in poverty between 1979 and 1983." Higher poverty rates "within household composition types," rather than family composition trends, account for most of the higher poverty rates among blacks. Had black and white household composition been identical in 1983, poverty rates among blacks still would have been much higher, because "55 percent of the difference between blacks and whites comes from higher poverty rates for blacks *within* household composition types."[74]

None of these trends, it is important to reiterate, result from generous welfare policies. After 1972, the number of children in female-headed households increased dramatically, while the number of children in households receiving AFDC declined. "If AFDC were pulling families apart and encouraging the formation of single-parent families," assert two researchers, "it is hard to understand why the number of children on the program would remain constant throughout a period in our history when family structures changed the most." (AFDC has permitted young women with children to move out of their parents' homes; whether or not this is a healthy development is, of course, a matter on which commentators disagree.) Nor does any relation exist between the fraction of children living in single-parent families and AFDC levels across states. Indeed, most women rely on AFDC for relatively short periods of time, although younger women seem least able to leave the rolls within a few years. "A majority of those who go on welfare will be off in less than two years," report Garfinkle and McLanahan, "but a substantial minority—and this minority accounts for the majority of the caseload at any point in time—will be dependent for a long time."[75]

Even the dynamics of the relation between household composition and poverty differ for black and white women, shows Bane. Black women usually do not become poor because of divorce or separation. More often, they already were poor. White women much more commonly become poor when their marriages break up. Black women's poverty, asserts Bane, results from "reshuffling"; white women's is more "event-driven." Of women in the Michigan Income Panel Dynamic Study: "Three-quarters of whites who were poor in the first year after moving into a female-headed or single-person household became poor simultaneously with the transition; in contrast, of the blacks who were poor after the transition, about two-thirds had also been poor before."[76]

Common stereotypes about the impact of pregnancy on the future of adolescent mothers withstand research no better than those that stress the role of welfare or the relations between household composition and poverty. In an important recent study, Frank Furstenberg and his colleagues asked what had happened to a group of adolescent mothers 17 years after the birth of their children. In 1984, 25 percent of these women did depend on welfare; another 25 percent earned less than $15,000 a year; 24 percent earned $15,000–24,999; and the remaining 26 percent more than $25,000. More than two-thirds of them had graduated from high school and nearly 30 percent had some post-high-school education. Work experience remained critical throughout these women's lives. Indeed, the women who had accumulated substantial work experience before they needed welfare remained by far the most likely to regain independence. Although their earnings undoubtedly would have been higher had they not become mothers at so young an age, the modest success enjoyed by many of them undercuts the easy equation between adolescent motherhood and a life of poverty.[77]

The real facts about adolescent pregnancy and female-headed households have important implications for debates about poverty. First, they qualify the panic about an "epidemic" of adolescent pregnancy. The issue is not the adolescent birth rate, but the response of pregnant adolescents and their marital status. Their increased resort to abortion, reluctance to marry the fathers of their children, and refusal to surrender their infants for adoption are the trends that have triggered the alarm about adolescent pregnancy and linked it to concerns about welfare policy and the emergence of an "underclass." Poverty, however, is not only a problem of adolescent pregnancy or female-headed families. Most poor people in America do not live in families headed by women. The absorption of poverty by family structure obscures the sources of poverty in the labor market, discrimination, and public policy. Conversely, American policies toward adolescent pregnancy remain perverse in a nation whose putative goals include reducing both it and abortion.

Adolescent pregnancy is not only a problem for blacks, and poverty among women of color does not result primarily from their household structure. Rather, it stems from the same structural forces that sustain joblessness among black men. Nor is their poverty the ironic result of a generous welfare system. On the contrary, an inadequate, punitive, perverse welfare system guarantees that most of them will remain poor. There is no inherent reason why women who head families should be poor. They are poor because they do not receive adequate public education, job training, or public support; because the jobs open to them pay so badly; and because of labor market trends and discrimination.

The increased share of families headed by women raises other complex and delicate issues. One is the definition of family. As Carol Stack's work shows, conventional classifications of families as either male- or female-headed reflect the convenience of census takers, not the multiple family forms among contemporary Americans, especially the dense, supportive kin networks in poor black communities. Another question concerns volition. To what extent do women head families by choice? Would an improvement in the job prospects of young black men, as William J. Wilson argues, significantly increase two-parent families? Do the same reasons explain adolescent pregnancy among blacks and whites? Have single-parent families increased among blacks and whites for similar reasons? Do trends in nonmarital fertility signal new forms of family structure?

Shifts in fertility with profound implications for family life have outrun both policy and culture before in American history. In the nineteenth century, married couples began to practice birth control to limit the size of their families and the timing of their children's births. As a result, marital fertility plummeted with remarkable speed. Although almost all government authorities and leading cultural spokesmen opposed birth control and prophesied race suicide, they remained unable to prevent married couples from creating a new domestic form: the small, intimate, intense, child-centered nuclear family.[78]

Once again, fertility trends may signify a shift in family forms no longer deniable, even by opponents. Policy cannot recapture the past. The energy spent lamenting the emergence of new family forms could more productively be directed toward ensuring young women with children a decent chance to avoid a life of poverty.[79] Unfortunately, current discourse about adolescent pregnancy, with a few notable exceptions, such as David T. Ellwood's *Poor Support*, moves in the opposite direction. Its tired moralism and worn myths obscure the routes to constructive action and, in the process, divert attention and energy from the real sources of poverty. Indeed, these dangers inhere in the emerging policy consensus that melds concerns about adolescent pregnancy, welfare, and an underclass into one vague but appealing prescription. I refer to workfare.[80]

## WORKFARE AND THE UNDERCLASS

In 1986, Nicholas Lemann observed, "President Reagan has commissioned a major study of welfare reform, which is a polite way of asking what we should do about the black underclass."[81]

Although Reagan's commission issued a tepid report, state governors and influential senators also linked welfare reform to the black underclass. Together, they helped solidify a new consensus that advocated a national program called workfare. Workfare, however, was neither a new nor unambiguous idea, and the disagreements that surfaced among its advocates revealed more than unresolved technical problems about administrative details. They reflected the divergent priorities of its sponsors and their varied definitions of the problem welfare reform was supposed to solve. Was workfare to be the first phase of a broad attack on poverty? Was it a long-term strategy for reducing the cost of AFDC and enforcing a universal obligation to work? Was it a strategy designed primarily to restore family structure? Was it a means of solving the labor force problems of the low-wage service sector? How many of these purposes could workfare serve simultaneously? Were they consistent with each other. These were questions scarcely debated in the heady days when workfare appeared to be the hitherto elusive means with which to reform America's welfare system.

Richard Nathan, an authority on welfare reform, explained the origins of the workfare consensus and its link to the growth of an underclass.[82] Nathan reluctantly accepted underclass as an "accurate and functional term" representing a "real and new condition" properly defined as a class—that is, "as a group emerging from societal conditions that affect structural changes." As used in the media, he acknowledged, underclass had become a "shorthand expression for the concentration of economic and behavioral problems among racial minorities (mainly black and Hispanic) in larger, older cities." By contrast, his explanation for the origins of the underclass resembled William J. Wilson's, on whose work he drew. Like Wilson, Nathan stressed the bifurcation of racial minorities as one outcome of the "civil rights revolution." New opportunities promoted upward mobility and drew successful blacks to the suburbs and more expensive urban neighborhoods, leaving behind the poor, now more than ever isolated and lacking "the role models of an earlier day." As a consequence, "the dangerous inner-city areas festering in our land" had become an increasingly more serious social and economic problem.[83]

The emergent underclass had provoked a new social policy synthesis combining the best features of conservative and liberal ideas. This new synthesis rejected the guilt-inspired good intentions of the Great Society that stressed compassion, empowerment, and entitlement. Instead, its key concept revealed an increased belief by both liberals and conservatives that welfare recipients should earn their benefits through work and good behavior. (In Nathan's interpretation, Lawrence Mead's stress on reciprocal social obligations became the core of the emergent consensus on welfare reform.) "We may not be doing people a favor," Nathan contended, "if we transmit signals about welfare rights and entitlements in a society that has a deep and strong Calvinist tradition that practically deifies the work ethic."[84]

Workfare is the new synthesis. In the 1970s, admitted Nathan, commentators used the term narrowly to mean the idea that people should work off their welfare grants—that is, that welfare recipients should be required to work, even in make-work jobs, in exchange for receiving their benefits. However, this punitive conception of workfare failed in the few places where it was tried. In California, for instance, when Ronald Reagan was governor, at most 3 percent of the eligible population participated in work experience programs.[85]

In its 1981 budget act, Congress allowed states to test "new employment approaches to welfare reform, officially called CWEP (Community Work Experience Programs)." This, claimed Nathan, stimulated "new-style workfare":

> New-style workfare embodies both the caring commitment of liberals and the themes identified with conservative writers such as Charles Murray, George Gilder, and Lawrence Mead. It involves a strong commitment to reducing welfare dependency on the premise that dependency is bad for people, that it undermines their motivation to support themselves, and isolates and stigmatizes welfare recipients in a way that over a long period feeds into and accentuates the underclass mindset and condition.[86]

As Fred Block and John Noakes argue, the other two events that moved new-style workfare high on the national agenda were its bipartisan support by the National Governors Association in 1985 and the introduction of welfare reform bills in both the Senate and House in 1987. New-style workfare, Block and Noakes contend, proved especially appealing to congressional Democrats who could use it to show their leadership in forging a bipartisan solution uniting compassion with efficiency and thereby solving a heretofore intractable problem. Were Republicans to accept their proposal, Democrats could champion their capacity to transcend partisan politics; were they—or the president—to resist, Democrats could attack them as recalcitrant defenders of a punitive and wasteful system. [87]

New-style workfare consisted of obligational state programs encompassing a variety of employment and training services and activities: job search, job training, education programs, and also community work experience. By the mid-1980s, more than two-thirds of the states, asserted Nathan, had experimented with new-style workfare, and an intensive study of eight by the Manpower Demonstration Research Corporation (MDRC) showed "promising—although not large and dramatic" effects on increased earnings and reduced welfare dependency. [88] Given these results, Nathan advocated the development of new-style workfare into a comprehensive government program for both female welfare family heads and unemployed young males in distressed urban areas. [89]

However, the results of new-style workfare, including those measured by the MDRC study, are more ambiguous and less hopeful than Nathan asserts. Indeed, reexamination of the study is important because its results were used, often inaccurately, by new-style workfare's congressional proponents in both the House and Senate to legitimize and support proposed legislation. MDRC's findings should not have been generalized to either House or Senate bills because, first, the study did not include women with children below the age of 6. Both House and Senate welfare reform bills called for women with children age 3 to 6 to participate in the program. This would create childcare problems not encountered by women whose children attended school. Even more, the MDRC study based its findings on new welfare applicants, and not on long-term welfare recipients. The latter, who are hardest to move into the work force, are the special target of the congressional proposals.[90]

State experiments consisted primarily of job search workshops and unpaid work experience. Although CWEP allowed states to use workers' welfare grants as wage subsidies for private employers, in practice, most participants received close to the minimum wage, worked for relatively short periods at unskilled jobs, and received no job training or remedial education. Within states, program details varied considerably, as did outcomes measured by various criteria. Six of the eight states studied by MDRC calculated work hours by dividing the AFDC grant by the minimum wage; in others, no relation existed between the grant level and number of hours worked, but the obligation to participate ended after 13 weeks. Nor did participants who found ordinary jobs receive subsidized childcare or guaranteed medical insurance after their Medicaid entitlement expired.[91]

By February 1987, MDRC, which meticulously compared participants to a control group, could report on results of three years' experience in five areas (Arkansas, San Diego, Virginia, West Virginia, and Baltimore). What it found was partially positive. Participation rates in these areas exceeded earlier demonstration programs. Participants seemed eager to work. Their employment levels and earnings were significantly higher than those of the control groups. Not surprisingly, employment increased most for women with no prior work experience. However, the programs had almost no effect on the men receiving AFDC-U assistance; nor did MDRC find positive results in West Virginia, where unemployment remained the highest in the nation. Cost-benefit analyses showed that usually programs paid for themselves within five years. Because MDRC recognized that these programs neither moved people out of poverty nor developed useful job skills, its early conclusions reflected, at best, a cautious optimism.[92]

A hard look at the data by Noakes and Block raises even more questions about the outcome of new-style workfare as practiced so far. Most of the participants still depended on AFDC for most of their annual income: in San Diego for 43 percent; in Baltimore, for 56 percent; in Arkansas, for 89 percent; in Virginia, for 56 percent; and in West Virginia, for 73 percent. This means that by and large they bounced on and off the relief rolls. At best, the programs helped state governments save some money by churning their rolls. They did not move participants into permanent self-sufficiency or even temporarily lift most of them out of poverty. The largest gain occurred among the San Diego participants. They earned an average of $7.08 per week more than the control group, or $700 during the period of their participation. Of this, they paid $371 in income taxes and an average of $3 per day for transportation, and they worried about losing their Medicaid entitlement if they did not return to AFDC.[93] A study of 61 programs in 38 states by the General Accounting Office (GAO) also stressed the limitation of obligational work programs:

> To serve more participants, programs spread their limited funds thinly, providing inexpensive services, such as job search assistance, and paying for few support services. Yet, the programs GAO examined served only a minority of adult AFDC recipients in 1985, excluding many with young children or severe barriers to employment. . . . Evaluations of the work programs have shown modest positive effects on the earnings and employment of participants. But wages were often insufficient to boost participants off welfare. Thus, programs should not be expected to produce massive reductions in the welfare rolls.[94]

As practiced so far, new-style workfare is not an antipoverty program. It gives its participants neither the skill training, wages, nor job opportunities necessary to lift them out of poverty. Nor does it address the poverty of children. Clearly, alarm at the growing poverty among children has helped stimulate interest in welfare reform. But the state and city experiments sanctioned by the administration in recent years have lifted almost none of them over the official poverty line, inadequate as it is. Even should clever and well-funded new programs miraculously move all long-term AFDC recipients out of poverty and into jobs, they will have helped only about 1 of every 16 Americans struggling to survive below the official poverty line. Clearly, new-style workfare does not address the problem of poverty in America. Indeed, one danger is that it will lull legislators and public opinion into believing they have solved the problem of which the objects of new-style workfare form but one small part.[95]

Of course, sophisticated advocates of new-style workfare realize the limitations of existing programs. They hope to use them as precedents to prove that government intervention can move welfare clients toward independence and as the basis for incremental expansions in social welfare policy. This was the major reason some liberals supported Senator Daniel Moynihan's Family Security Act of 1987, and the Family Support Act of 1988, which received final congressional approval on September 30, even though they believed the legislation inadequate and deeply flawed.[96]

Most advocates of new-style workfare believe that women with children over the age of 3 should work; they support training and expanded day care; and they recognize that health insurance, available to families supported by AFDC through Medicaid, should be extended to women leaving the welfare rolls for jobs that offer no comparable benefits. Still, important differences exist among supporters of welfare reform and workfare, especially about one key question: Should work be voluntary or compulsory? Massachusetts officials point to the success of their Employment Training Program as evidence of the superiority of voluntary programs. Voluntarism is essential, they argue, because it motivates welfare officials to locate appealing jobs and encourages employers to offer decent wages and working conditions. The Massachusetts program offers extensive job training and places clients only in jobs that pay well above the minimum wage. (Remember that women with children paid the minimum wage remain in poverty.) The Massachusetts program is unique; in most states, concerns other than education and social mobility dominate welfare reform.[97]

One of these is family instability. When he introduced his Family Security Act in July 1987, Senator Daniel Patrick Moynihan, for one, referred to it as a revolution in "the present family welfare system" that enforced the responsibilities of parents. Child-support enforcement, the first item in the Family Support Act of 1988, is in many ways its core. As Deborah Harris points out, the act builds on child-support enforcement mechanisms introduced in 1975, adding to them provisions for automatic wage withholding. Yet despite the predictions of their advocates, Harris shows, existing enforcement mechanisms have neither proved cost-effective nor helped women escape welfare. Enforcement does appear to have reduced the amount of child-support orders in many cases and to have increased countersuits for custody by men. As advocates of child-support enforcement increasingly recognized its practical limits, they shifted their ground from economic to social criteria and laid new emphasis on establishing paternity, which is a prominent part of the Family Support Act. Enforced support, it is argued, will foster the discharge of family obligations, discourage men from indiscriminately fathering children, and punish those who shirk their family responsibilities. Yet here too, no evidence whatsoever supports these claims.[98]

The stress on child-support enforcement reflects the increasing focus of conservative poverty discourse on questions of family. Thus, Stuart Butler and Anna Kondratas, in their "conservative strategy for welfare reform," argue that "cohesive families with strong family ties and loyalties are the best guarantee against poverty," and they link their stress on strengthening families with advocacy of improved child-support enforcement. "When fathers shirk their responsibilities, children suffer and society pays." No reason exists "why any of us should have to pay the cost of an illegitimate child so that a young man can boast about the number of children he has sired. The law should come down decisively and heavily on absent fathers."[99] In Butler and

Kondratas's argument, the purpose of strong sanctions emerges less as decreasing the financial responsibility of the state, improving the economic condition of women with children, or even strengthening families than as deterrence and punishment.

The belief that any work builds character and discharges social obligations also underlies compulsory workfare programs. Their advocates place priority on work experience regardless of its quality or pay. Forcing women with children into low-wage, dead-end jobs remains preferable to supporting them with public funds. Clearly, even new-style workfare cannot shed either the equation of work and virtue or the punitive heritage that has rippled through American relief and welfare practices throughout their long and sorry history.

Not only is there little evidence that compulsory workfare could reach its goals. Workfare enthusiasts, as Theda Skocpol, Margaret Weir, and Ann Shola Orloff point out in an incisive analysis, also overlook serious potential difficulties that could undercut the programs' effectiveness. They contrast the administrative complexity of workfare with politically and socially successful past policies, which have been "broadly targeted, bureaucratically unobtrusive, and administratively simple." Even more important, workfare advocates have not learned from the political success of Social Security and the political failure of AFDC. Social Security remains popular and politically unassailable because it benefits everyone. AFDC, like outdoor relief in the nineteenth century, remains despised and vulnerable because it serves—and defines—contemporary paupers. Confined to the very poor, workfare, they believe, will share the stigma of welfare.

Nor will workfare address unemployment and underemployment among men. In fact, workfare could exacerbate the political problems of the dependent poor by angering and alienating the working and near-poor. What, they ask, "are displaced heavy-industry workers to think of the free educational and job-training benefits that welfare mothers would receive from liberal workfare programs?" Workfare, argue Skocpol and her colleagues, like the Great Society before it, would leave Democratic

Party constituencies battling each other. "Economically pressed lower 'middle-class taxpayers', disproportionately white ethnics in male-headed families, could soon be pitted against impoverished public assistance recipients (or recent graduates of workfare), disproportionately women of color and their children."[100]

Even more, workfare might depress labor costs by supplementing earnings and benefits and easing labor shortages in unskilled low-wage jobs. Without the addition of equivalent programs for young black men, workfare also could intensify job competition between them and women. More ominously, should workfare for welfare mothers become a precedent for other programs, its application to unemployment insurance could depress wages and further retard collective bargaining by flooding the low-wage, unskilled labor market. A tight labor market is the precondition for any significant decrease in unemployment and rise in real wages, but its potential conflict with workfare remains undiscussed amid the excitement generated by the new consensus. Workfare is a nonresponse to the structural sources of poverty in America. It addresses the politics of poverty, not its roots.[101]

Workfare is a major example of the welfare reform strategy advocated in the 1980s even by many liberals. Universal policies, such as guaranteed incomes, they argue, stand no chance of passage. Besides, they are inefficient because they apply a single remedy to the variety of conditions and problems among dependent people. David Ellwood, for instance, points to three groups among the poor: families in which the adults are "already doing a great deal for themselves"; those individuals who are "suffering temporary difficulties because of a job loss, a change in their family's circumstances, or some personal problem"; and "the few who are healthy but who seem unable to find work on their own and need some form of long-term support." An improved welfare system, Ellwood contends, would consist of three distinct types of support reflecting the needs of each of these groups. Policy, that is, should consist of carefully targeted programs crafted to alleviate specific problems. Even former champions of guaranteed incomes, a negative income tax, or a national health insurance program, such as the leaders of the University of Wisconsin's Institute for Research on Poverty, have retreated from their support of universal strategies. As they summarized areas of consensus among the contributors to their important 1986 book assessing antipoverty strategies, Sheldon H. Danziger and Daniel H. Weinberg concluded: "Because there is no single program or policy that can eliminate poverty, categorization by target groups as well as program area is important." [102]

William J. Wilson has emerged as the most prominent critic of categorical strategies, which, he argues, undercut fundamental reform by reinforcing invidious distinctions and blocking the formation of the coalitions essential for political success. The targeted strategy advocated by the Wisconsin group and the universal approach supported by Wilson define the poles of contemporary liberal debate on welfare reform. For Wilson, "the problem of joblessness should be a top-priority item in any policy discussion focusing on enhancing the status of families," and he calls for "a macroeconomic policy designed to promote both economic growth and a tight labor market." Because, Wilson predicts, employment alone will not necessarily lift a family out of poverty in the foreseeable future, income supports and social services also remain critical. The federal government should address these through a program of welfare reform that sets national AFDC benefit levels and otherwise extends support to poor two-parent families. [103]

Wilson argues that only policies which serve a broad slice of the population garner solid popular and political support. Programs labeled welfare, such as AFDC, always carry a stigma that reduces public generosity and cripples their effectiveness. Therefore, he favors extending benefits through universal programs, what he calls a "hidden agenda," of which a universal family or child allowance, common in other Western democracies, is a key example. [104]

Among both liberals and conservatives, by the latter 1980's *underclass* and *workfare* had become the key concepts in American discourse about poverty and reform. Their transparent reasonableness obscured their multiple meanings and the varied purposes each served. Despite the care with which William Wilson and Richard Nathan tried to define it, most commentators continued to deploy underclass as little more than a crude synonym for inner-city blacks over whom they cast the old mantle of the undeserving poor.

Given the rhetoric that surrounds it, debate about the utility of the term underclass remains more than a distracting and pedantic quibble. Aside from the moral judgment it implies, the term underclass focuses debate on a subset of the poor. It deflects attention from comprehensive social policies and encourages targeted approaches that historically have isolated their beneficiaries and reinforced the stigma attached to poverty and relief. Underclass also revives discredited notions of the culture of poverty by emphasizing the behavior of poor people rather than the sources of their poverty.

It might be useful to call for a moratorium on the term "culture" as well. For culture, like underclass, is used with such imprecision and in such varied ways that it has become more a barrier than an aid to understanding. In some writing, culture emerges as little more than a residual factor, the unexplained variance when structural factors are entered in an equation. For others, it is a relatively autonomous part of social structure, a self-perpetuating set of values and behaviors. To William Julius Wilson, by contrast, culture is the set of values and behaviors that result from adaptations to social structure; he expects them to change when objective circumstances alter. Just what is included in the term "values," always introduced as an element of culture, also remains largely unexplored in the poverty literature. The point is not to avoid difficult issues, such as the sources and consequences of female-headed families, but to define isssues precisely—to speak, that is, directly of problems rather than to slip into imprecise euphemisms that, it seems, inevitably stigmatize the people to whom they are applied and excuse mean and punitive policies.

One last implication of the term underclass is even more serious: by diffusing an image of poor people as split into two sharply divided groups, underclass helps perpetuate their political powerlessness by strengthening the barriers that for so long have divided them against each other.

# Epilogue: "Them" or "Us"?

WE CAN THINK about poor people as "them" or as "us." For
the most part, Americans have talked about "them." Even in the
language of social science, as well as in ordinary conversation
and political rhetoric, poor people usually remain outsiders,
strangers to be pitied or despised, helped or punished, ignored
or studied, but rarely full citizens, members of a larger community on the same terms as the rest of us. They are, as Vice
President Dan Quayle said in his debate with Senator Lloyd
Bentsen, "those people," objects of curiosity, analysis, pruri-
ence, or compassion, not subjects who construct their own lives
and history. Poor people seem cardboard cutouts, figures in single dimensions, members of inferior categories, rarely complex,
multifaceted, even contradictory in the manner of other persons. Their poverty therefore results from some attribute, a de-
fect in personality, behavior, or human capital. Whether their

deficiencies stem from family, genes, or deprivation doesn't really matter very much. The consequences are the same. Poverty in America is profoundly individual; like popular economics, it is supply-side.

By individualizing poverty, many American social scientists have aided the mystification of its origins and obscured its politics. In much American social science, poverty remains profoundly apolitical. Discussions of how to influence the level of social benefits along a fairly narrow band of possibilities pass for political discussion. About the real politics of poverty, American social science remains largely silent. For finally, the politics of poverty are about the processes of inclusion and exclusion in American life: Who, to put the question crudely, gets what? How are goods distributed? As such, it is a question of race, class, gender, and the bases of power. Poverty is not an unfortunate accident, a residue, an indication that the great American mobility machine missed a minority of the people. On the contrary, always it has been a necesssary result of America's distinctive political economy. Although poverty hardly has been unique to America, here, as everywhere, it assumes its particular configuration as a consequence of its temporal and national context.

Relatively few writers have tried to show American poverty whole, and they have had less influence than they merit. Among the more recent, the most notable are the National Conference of Catholic Bishops in their pastoral letter on the economy, and Michael Harrington in *The New American Poverty*. The "structures of misery today," writes Harrington, "are the results of massive economic and social transformations and they cannot be understood apart from an analysis of them." The result of global economic trends, especially the international division of labor, was a new poverty "much more systematic and structured" and hence "more difficult to defeat than the indignities of twenty years ago."[1]

Like Harrington, Europeans today write about the "new poverty," which they understand in a similar way. They do not write very much about the "underclass," which highlights the peculiarly American tendency to transform poverty from a product

of politics and economics into a matter of individual behavior.
In his summary of a twelve-country survey of poverty, Graham
Room of the University of Bath points to the recent consensus
that poverty has assumed new forms within the European Community. He finds their sources in economic restructuring and
recent demographic trends that have exposed "new weaknesses
in the post-war systems of welfare provision and social security;
new lines of social division and new patterns of dependency."
With this orientation, European discussions of the "new poverty" focus on unemployment and structural dislocation far
more than on the behavior and deficits of the poor.[2]

Indeed, European scholars often find American approaches
to poverty, including those of the most respected social scientists, bizarre. In American controversies about social policy,
notes Swedish social scientist Walter Korpi, "the European ob-
server finds lively debates on issues that he or she has previously
met only in the more or less dusty pages of historical accounts
of the development of social policy at home." In his comparison
of national American and European poverty research, Korpi
points out how American social science and public policy obscure inequality by stressing only absolute measures of poverty,
in contrast to Europeans' reliance on relative ones. Unlike Europeans, American poverty researchers, he adds, neglect both
unemployment and politics. American poverty research lacks
theories that accord economic resources and political power a
central role or that explain inequality as the outcome of "conflicts over distribution." To Korpi, this silence about politics remains "striking," given the "high degree of conflict in American
society." Equally striking is the neglect by American poverty research of the consequences for the poor of extremely high levels
of unemployment throughout the postwar period. Despite living
in a "sea of unemployment," American poverty researchers have
focused their efforts on the work motivation of the poor.[3]


Both research and policy require the reconstruction of discourse
about poverty and welfare. Europeans offer important points of

departure; so do aspects of the fragmented American liberalism of the last two decades. These include:

• Moral outrage at the persistence of hunger, homelessness, inadequate medical care, and other forms of deprivation.
• The substitution of human dignity, community, and the realization of democracy in place of classification, work incentives, and the obligation of the poor as the foundation of public policy.
• Finding ways to talk about poor people as "us" that expand ideas of citizenship and transcend the stale historic preoccupations that have constricted ideas, research, and policy during the last two centuries.
• Restricting market models of human behavior and distributive justice within appropriate boundaries by defining, and defending, in Michael Walzer's phrase, "spheres of justice."
• Enhancing the political acceptability of progressive social policy by connecting it with widely shared American values: for instance, by reviving Charles Reich's concept of the "new property," which defends redistributive policies through an appeal to private property and liberty and by showing how the persistence of poverty undermines both family life and economic growth.

The main theme is very simple: By attacking poverty, America will become a better nation. As Michael Harrington predicted, "When we join, in solidarity and not in noblesse oblige, with the poor, we will rediscover our own best selves . . . we will regain the vision of America."[4]

Reconstructing the way we think about poverty is partly an intellectual challenge. As such, it draws on creative resources, in which Ameria is rich. Acting on those ideas is another matter. It requires material resources, which America also has, and political will, which it has lacked.[5] The fundamental questions are not about the details of policy or the sources of revenue; they are, rather, about the basis of community, the conditions of citizenship, and the achievement of human dignity. They are, that is, about our definition of America and just how much we are willing to do to realize it.

# Appendix: The Dimensions
# of Poverty

Poverty remains a widespread blight on America, although not a uniform one across demographic groups. Even a cursory overview of its statistics highlights its magnitude and points to some of its sources. Here I use the official poverty line developed by the federal government (see Chapter 3 for a discussion of its origin and limits) and draw on the excellent analysis in June Axinn and Mark Stern, *Dependency and Poverty*.[1]

In 1985, about 33 million people in America, or 14 percent of the population, were poor. About two of every three of them were white. Among whites, 11.4 percent of all persons were poor compared to 31.3 percent among blacks and 29 percent among Hispanics. These figures refer to posttransfer poverty, that is, poverty based on an income measure that includes government transfer programs, such as Aid to Families with Dependent Children, Social Security, and unemployment insurance. Posttransfer poverty fell from 17.3 percent in 1965 to 15.2 percent in 1983. Its low point, 11.1 percent, occurred in 1973. By contrast, pre-transfer poverty—that is, poverty measured by incomes excluding transfer programs—increased from 21.3 percent in 1965 to 24.2 percent in 1983. Its low point was 19.0 percent in 1973. Government programs successfully removed some people from poverty; they did not prevent people from becoming poor. America still generates as much poverty as it did when the War on Poverty began two decades ago.[2]

Trends in posttransfer poverty vary among age groups, races, and locations. Among children, poverty declined from 26.5 percent in 1960 to a low of 14.2 percent in 1973. By 1985, it had increased to 20.1 percent. For the elderly, it dropped steadily from 35.2 percent in 1960 to 12.6 percent in 1985, largely (although not entirely) as a result of increases in Social Security benefits. In 1985, children formed the largest age group, 37.8 percent, among the poor, compared to 10 percent for persons over 65. Poverty rates among whites remained fairly steady, around 11.3 percent from the mid-1960s to the mid-1980s; for blacks they dropped from 41.8 percent to 31.3 percent, reflecting improved employment opportunities as a consequence of the civil rights movement and affirmative action regulations. Poverty increased most in central cities between 1973 and 1983, about 31 percent, compared to 10 percent in suburbs and 8 percent in rural areas. Most of this increase resulted from cutbacks in government programs. Indeed, the increase in pretransfer poverty within central cities was lower than within suburbs. This is a very important point, because it shows that the rise in poverty within cities does not reflect fundamental shifts in culture and behavior, as much of the current commentary on the alleged growth of an urban underclass implies. (Chapter 5 discusses the idea of an underclass.)[3]

Poverty is most widespread among families headed by women. In 1985, 27.3 percent of all persons living within families headed by white women, and 45.2 percent of children within them less than 18 years old, were poor. For families headed by black women, the same figures were 51.8 percent and 66.9 percent.

These statistics are especially troubling because of the increase in families headed by women among both whites and blacks, between 1970 and 1984, 41 percent for whites and 54 percent for blacks. Nonetheless, among all blacks poverty declined by 4 percent between 1973 and 1985, compared to a growth of 11 percent among whites.[4]

The differing trajectories of poverty rates among whites and blacks point to a major trend, which Axinn and Stern refer to as convergence. Although blacks remain poor to a far greater extent than whites, differences between them are decreasing. Between 1973 and 1984, poverty among white men grew 39 percent. Among full-time adult male workers, the poverty of white men rose 45 percent compared to 9 percent for white women. Conversely, among black men it dropped 7 percent and among black women, 20 percent. (Still, the white male poverty rate, about 5.1 percent, was about half the black rate, 10.5 percent, in 1984). One reason for these converging rates is the worsening labor market experience of white men, which includes lower wages, fewer unionized jobs, the declining value of the minimum wage, the increase in involuntary part-time work, and displacement on account of plant closings and automation. They are the economic consequences of the shift to a postindustrial economy. "Although blacks continue to have higher poverty rates than whites and women a higher rate than men," write Axinn and Stern, "changes in work experience have reduced these gaps. As these trends continue to shake the economy and social structure," poverty rates will continue to converge.[5]

One result of this massive economic restructuring has been the recent growth in the number of working poor. According to Sar A. Levitan and Isaac Shapiro: "In 1985, 2 million adults—50 percent more than in 1978—worked full time throughout the year, yet they and their families remained in poverty. Another 7.1 million poor worked either in full-time jobs for part of the year or in part-time jobs."[6]

The declining effectiveness of income transfer programs also has pushed poverty rates toward convergence. "Effectiveness" refers to the proportion of the pretransfer poor income transfers lift over the poverty line. Only in one state, Alaska, does AFDC combined with food stamps boost a family to the poverty line. Looked at another way, in 1973, transfer payments lifted 24 percent of black and 28 percent of Spanish women over the poverty line; by 1983, the proportion for both had dropped to 19 percent. Among white males, the effectiveness rate also dropped, from 63 percent to 54 percent.

The declining effectiveness of transfer programs reflects the cuts in social benefits, primarily during the Reagan years. These include changing regulations that dropped women from the AFDC and Supplemental Social Security rolls and large reductions in the proportion of unemployed workers receiving unemployment insurance, which affected men with special severity. From 1975 to 1985, the proportion of unemployed persons eligible for unemployment insurance dropped from about 50 percent to less than 30 percent—that is, by about 40 percent—and the proportion unable to find jobs before their benefits expired rose to 34 percent. Because there is little reason to expect the trends in either public social benefits or economics to reverse themselves soon, there is every reason to predict that extensive poverty will disfigure the lives of tens of millions of Americans for the indefinite future and that its emerging features will be etched into the national landscape.[7]

# Notes

INTRODUCTION

1. Striking parallels between British and American ideas about poverty are evident from reading Gertrude Himmelfarb, *The Idea of Poverty: England in the Early Industrial Age* (New York: Random House, 1983).

2. There is, of course, a substantial literature assessing Americans' attitudes toward poverty, welfare, and related issues. For examples, see Linda Burzotta Nilson, "Reconsidering Ideological Lines: Beliefs about Poverty in America," *The Sociological Quarterly* 22 (Autumn 1981): 531–548; Philip Arthur AuClaire, "Public Attitudes Toward Social Welfare Expenditures," *Social Work* 29 (March–April 1984): 139–144; Charles E. Ramsey and Rita Braito, "Public Concepts of Poverty: The County Commissioners' View," *Public Welfare* 1 (Winter 1973–74): 65–80.

3. Martha Minow, *Making All the Difference*, forthcoming, manuscript p. 5.

4. Michael Ignatieff, *The Needs of Strangers: An Essay on Privacy, Solidarity, and the Politics of Being Human* (New York: Viking Penguin, 1986 [first published in Great Britain by Chatto and Windus, 1984]), p. 18.

5. Ira Katznelson, *City Trenches: Urban Politics and the Patterning of*

*Class in the United States* (New York: Pantheon, 1981), esp. pp. 5–6, 45–72; see also Ira Katznelson and Aristide R. Zolberg, eds., *Working-Class Formation in Nineteenth-Century Western Europe and the United States* (Princeton: Princeton University Press, 1986), chaps. 1, 5, 6.

ONE: FROM THE UNDESERVING POOR TO
THE CULTURE OF POVERTY

1. On the problem of need, see Deborah Stone, *The Disabled State* (Philadelphia: Temple University Press, 1984), pp. 15–20.
2. For a meditation on social obligations to strangers, see Michael Ignatieff, *The Needs of Strangers: An Essay on Privacy, Solidarity, and the Politics of Being Human* (New York: Penguin Books, 1984). On the early history of social welfare policies in America, see Walter I. Trattner, *From Poor Law to Welfare State: A History of Social Welfare in America*, 3rd ed. (New York: Free Press, 1984), pp. 1–46; David J. Rothman, *The Discovery of the Asylum: Social Order and Disorder in the Early Republic* (Boston: Little, Brown, 1971); Benjamin J. Klebaner, "Public Poor Relief in America, 1790–1860," Ph.D. diss., Columbia University, 1952; and Michael B. Katz, *In the Shadow of the Poorhouse: A Social History of Welfare in America* (New York: Basic Books, 1986), pp. 3–35.
3. For examples of criticism of settlement practices, see "Report of the Secretary of State [of New York], 1824, on the Relief and Settlement of the Poor," reprinted in David J. Rothman, ed., *The Almshouse Experience: Collected Reports* (New York: Arno Press and New York Times, 1971), pp. 967, 952. For contemporary evidence that there is little relation between the generosity of welfare benefits and the size of AFDC roles, see Kirsten A. Gronbjerg, *Mass Society and the Extension of Welfare 1960–1970* (Chicago: University of Chicago Press, 1977), pp. 51–54.
4. [Josiah Quincy] "Report of the Committee on the Pauper Laws of this Commonwealth [1821]," p. 4, in Rothman, *Almshouse Experience*.
5. Philadelphia Board of Guardians, "Report of the Committee Appointed by the Board of Guardians of the Poor of the City and Districts of Philadelphia, to Visit the Cities of Baltimore, New-York, Providence, Boston, and Salem [1827]," p. 26 in Rothman, *Almshouse Experience*.
6. Charles Burroughs, "A Discourse Delivered in the Chapel of the New Alms-House, in Portsmouth, N.H. . . . ." (Portsmouth, N.H.: J. W. Foster, 1835), p. 9, in David J. Rothman, ed., *The Jacksonians on the Poor* (New York: Arno Press, 1971).
7. Walter Channing, "An Address on the Prevention of Pauperism" (Boston: Office of the Christian World, 1843), p. 20, in Rothman, *Jacksonians*.
8. On the relation between concepts of poverty, welfare, and the labor market, see Frances Fox Piven and Richard A. Cloward, *Regulating the Poor: The Functions of Public Welfare* (New York: Vintage, 1971); on the history of the work ethic in America, see Daniel Rodgers, *The Work Ethic in Industrial America, 1850–1920* (Chicago: University of Chicago Press,

1978). For an example of the connections between poverty and the structure of social existence in antebellum America, see Christine Stansell, *City of Women: Sex and Class in New York 1789–1869* (New York: Knopf, 1986). Stansell also emphasizes the moralization of poverty in the early nineteenth century.

9. For reanalysis of data collected in the nineteenth century, see Michael B. Katz, *Poverty and Policy in American History* (New York: Academic Press, 1983), pp. 55–182.

10. Robert Hunter, *Poverty* (Harper and Row, 1965; first published, New York: Macmillan, 1904), pp. 3, 63. On scientific charity, see Katz, *Shadow*, pp. 58–84, and Paul Boyer, *Urban Masses and Moral Order in America 1820–1920* (Cambridge: Harvard University Press, 1978). Also relevant are James T. Patterson, *America's Struggle against Poverty, 1900–1980* (Cambridge: Harvard University Press, 1981), and Daniel Kevles, *In the Name of Eugenics: Genetics and the Uses of Human Heredity* (New York: Knopf, 1985).

11. E. Wight Bakke, *The Unemployed Worker: A Study of the Task of Making a Living Without a Job* (New Haven: Yale University Press, 1940); Bonnie Fox Schwartz, *The Civil Works Administration: The Business of Emergency Employment in the New Deal* (Princeton: Princeton University Press, 1984), pp. 227–228; Josephine Chapin Brown, *Public Relief 1929–1939* (New York: Henry Holt, 1941), p. 317.

12. Winifred Bell, *Aid to Dependent Children* (New York: Columbia University Press, 1965). On how the Social Security Administration preserved the distinction between social insurance and public assistance, see Jerry R. Cates, *Insuring Inequality: Administrative Leadership in Social Security, 1935–1954* (Ann Arbor: University of Michigan Press, 1983).

13. Michael Harrington, *The Other America* (New York: Macmillan, 1962; republished by Penguin Books, 1963), p. 9.

14. Oscar Lewis, *The Children of Sanchez* (New York: Random House, 1961); *La Vida: A Puerto Rican Family in the Culture of Poverty—San Juan and New York* (New York: Random House, 1966); "The Culture of Poverty," *Scientific American* 215 (1966): 19–25; "The Culture of Poverty," in Daniel P. Moynihan, ed., *On Understanding Poverty: Perspectives from the Social Sciences* (New York: Basic Books, 1969), pp. 187–220. For useful comments on the origins of the culture of poverty concept in American social science, see Lee Rainwater, "The Problem of Lower Class Culture," *Journal of Social Issues* 26 (1970): 133–137. Rainwater points to the growing emphasis on lower-class culture as one stream in social science since the 1930s. Oscar Lewis, he contends, developed his definition "somewhat independently."

15. Lewis, *La Vida*, p. xliii.

16. Lewis, *La Vida*, pp. xliii–xlv.

17. Lewis, *La Vida*, p. xlv.

18. Lewis, *La Vida*, pp. xxlv–xlvii.

19. Lewis, *La Vida*, pp. xlvii–xlviii.

20. Lewis, *La Vida*, pp. xlviii–xlix.

21. Lewis, *La Vida*, pp. li–lii.

22. Lewis, *La Vida*, p. xiii.

23. Lewis, *La Vida*, pp. xlviii, lii.

24. Lewis, *La Vida*, p. xlii.

25. Harrington, *The Other America*, pp. 22–23.

26. Frank Riessman, *The Culturally Deprived Child* (New York: Harper and Row, 1962), pp. 2–3. For criticisms of cultural deprivation as a concept in education, see Murray L. Wax and Rosalie H. Wax, "Cultural Deprivation as an Educational Ideology" and Mildred Dickeman, "The Integrity of the Cherokee Student," in Eleanor Burke Leacock, *The Culture of Poverty: A Critique* (New York: Simon and Schuster, 1971), pp. 127–139 and 140–179. For an extension of the culture of poverty to cultural deprivation and its application to social work, see Jerome Cohen, "Social Work and the Culture of Poverty," *Social Work* 9 (January 1964): 3–11.

27. Riessman, *Culturally Deprived Child*, pp. 26–30.

28. Riessman *Culturally Deprived Child*, pp. 30–35.

29. Oscar Handlin, *Boston's Immigrants: A Study in Acculturation*, rev. and enlarged ed. (Cambridge: Harvard University Press, 1959), pp. 51, 120–212; 125).

30. John W. Cell, *The Highest Stage of White Supremacy: The Origins of Segregation in South Africa and the American South* (New York: Cambridge University Press, 1982), p. 236; Stanley M. Elkins, *Slavery: A Problem in American Institutional Life*, 3rd ed. (Chicago: University of Chicago Press, 1976).

31. David C. McClelland, *The Achieving Society* (New York: Free Press, 1961), pp. 36, 43, 205. Readers should be aware that McClelland's argument is complex and detailed. I am deliberately oversimplifying it here to highlight the parallel between some of its key assumptions and other writing about dependent people in the same period.

32. I am indebted to a conversation with Ivar Berg for the hypothesis that the popularity of the culture of poverty rested in part on liberal dissatisfaction with the concept of false consciousness.

33. "Remarks of the President at Howard University, June 4, 1965," in Lee Rainwater and William L. Yancey, *The Moynihan Report and the Politics of Controversy* (Cambridge: The M.I.T. Press, 1967), pp. 127–128.

34. The full text of the report is included in Rainwater and Yancey, *The Moynihan Report*, pp. 39–125.

35. Rainwater and Yancey, *Moynihan Report*, pp. 6–7; Kenneth B. Clark, *Dark Ghetto: Dilemmas of Social Power* (New York: Harper and Row, 1965); E. Franklin Frazier, *The Negro in the United States* (New York: Macmillan, rev. ed., 1957), esp. pp. 636–637.

36. Eleanor Burke Leacock drew the connection among nineteenth-century ideas about poverty, Lewis's version of the culture of poverty, and Moynihan's report in the Introduction to her edited volume, *The Culture of Poverty*, p. 11.

37. Rainwater and Yancey, *Moynihan Report*, pp. 27, 29. Rainwater and

Yancey analyze the principal criticisms of the Moynihan report in detail and show precisely where distortions existed. See, for instance, *Moynihan Report*, pp. 220–244.

38. "The Negro Family: The Case for National Action," in Rainwater and Yancey, *Moynihan Report*, p. 43.

39. Rainwater and Yancey, *Moynihan Report*, p. 45.

40. Rainwater and Yancey, *Moynihan Report*, p. 20.

41. Rainwater and Yancey, *Moynihan Report*, p. 51.

42. Rainwater and Yancey, *Moynihan Report*, p. 75.

43. Rainwater and Yancey, *Moynihan Report*, p. 62.

44. Rainwater and Yancey, *Moynihan Report*, p. 17.

45. Rainwater and Yancey, *Moynihan Report*, pp. 66–67. Emphasis in original.

46. Rainwater and Yancey, *Moynihan Report*, pp. 67 and 71.

47. Rainwater and Yancey, *Moynihan Report*, pp. 74–75.

48. Rainwater and Yancey, *Moynihan Report*, p. 75.

49. Rainwater and Yancey, *Moynihan Report*, pp. 80–90.

50. Rainwater and Yancey, *Moynihan Report*, pp. 93–94.

51. Rainwater and Yancey, *Moynihan Report*, p. 31.

52. Rainwater and Yancey, *Moynihan Report*, pp. 142, 22–244.

53. Rainwater and Yancey, *Moynihan Report*, p. 238.

54. See the major attacks on the report by Benjamin F. Payton and William Ryan. Rainwater and Yancey, *Moynihan Report*, pp. 396, 463.

55. Edward C. Banfield, with the assistance of Laura Fasano Banfield, *The Moral Basis of a Backward Society* (New York: Free Press, 1958). Lewis introduced the culture of poverty in *The Children of Sanchez*, published in 1961.

56. Banfield, *Moral Basis*, p. 83.

57. Banfield, *Moral Basis*, pp. 8, 18–32, 40–41, 115.

58. Banfield, *Moral Basis*, p. 155; 66.

59. Edward C. Banfield, *The Unheavenly City* (Boston: Little, Brown, 1970), and *The Unheavenly City Revisited* (Boston: Little, Brown, 1974).

60. Banfield, *Unheavenly City Revisited*, pp. 2–3.

61. Banfield, *Unheavenly City Revisited*, p. 53.

62. Banfield, *Unheavenly City Revisited*, p. 56.

63. Banfield, *Unheavenly City Revisited*, p. 54.

64. Banfield, *Unheavenly City Revisited*, p. 78.

65. Banfield, *Unheavenly City Revisited*, pp. 84, 96.

66. Banfield, *Unheavenly City Revisited*, pp. 47–48.

67. Banfield, *Unheavenly City Revisited*, pp. 128–131.

68. Banfield, *Unheavenly City Revisited*, p. 135. Emphasis in original.

69. Banfield, *Unheavenly City Revisited*, p. 141.

70. Banfield, *Unheavenly City Revisited*, p. 143.

71. Banfield, *Unheavenly City Revisited*, p. 235.

72. Banfield, *Unheavenly City Revisited*, pp. 240–259.

73. Banfield, *Unheavenly City Revisited*, p. 281.

74. Charles E. Lindblom and David K. Cohen, *Usable Knowledge: Social Science and Social Problem Solving* (New Haven: Yale University Press, 1979), p. 58.


TWO: POVERTY AND THE POLITICS
OF LIBERATION

1. For a general criticism of the politics of the culture of poverty, see Hylan Lewis, "Culture of Poverty? What Does It Matter?" in Eleanor Burke Leacock, *The Culture of Poverty: A Critique* (New York: Simon and Schuster, 1971), pp. 345–363.
2. Randolf S. David, "The Sociology of Poverty or the Poverty of Sociology? A Brief Note on Urban Poverty Research," *Philippine Sociological Review* 25 (1977): 145–146, 149. Emphasis in original.
3. Alessio Colombis, "Amoral Familism and Social Organisation in Montegrano: A Critique of Banfield's Thesis," *Domination et Dependance: Situations Peuples Mediterraneans* 25 (1983): 24.
4. Alejandro Portes, "Rationality in the Slum: An Essay on Interpretive Sociology," *Comparative Studies in Society and History* 14 (1972): 269.
5. Portes, "Rationality in the Slum," pp. 274 and 272.
6. Colombis, "Amoral Familism," p. 33.
7. David, "The Sociology of Poverty," pp. 148–149.
8. Walter B. Miller, "Subculture, Social Reform, and the 'Culture of Poverty'," *Human Organization* 30 (1971): 112.
9. Chandler C. Davidson, "On the 'Culture of Shiftlessness'," *Dissent* 23 (1976): 355.
10. Eleanor Leacock, "Distortions of Working-Class Reality in American Social Science," *Science and Society* 31 (1967): 3–4.
11. See, for example, Audrey James Schwartz, "A Further Look at 'Culture of Poverty': Ten Caracas Barrios," *Sociology and Social Research* 59 (July 1975): 362–386.
12. Leonard Davidson and David Krackhardt, "Structural Change and the Disadvantaged: An Empirical Test of Culture of Poverty/Situational Theories of Hard-Core Work Behavior," *Human Organization* 36 (1977): 308.
13. Frederick S. Jaffe and Steven Polgar, "Family Planning and Public Policy: Is the 'Culture of Poverty' the New Cop-Out?", *Journal of Marriage and the Family* 30 (1968): 228–235.
14. Harland Padfield, "New Industrial Systems and Cultural Concepts of Poverty," *Human Organization* 29 (1970): 33. Some other examples of empirical studies are: Victor S. D'souza, "Socio-Cultural Marginality: A Theory of Urban Slums and Poverty in India," *Sociological Bulletin* 28 (1979): 9–23; Seymour Parker and Robert J. Kleiner, "The Culture of Poverty: An Adjustive Dimension," *American Anthropologist* 72 (1970): 516–527; David B. Miller, "A Partial Test of Oscar Lewis's Culture of Poverty in Rural America," *Current Anthropology* 17 (1976): 720–723; Hyman Rodman, *Lower-Class Families: The Culture of Poverty in Negro Trinidad* (London:

Oxford University Press, 1971); Schwartz, "A Further Look;" Gordon Ter-nowetsky, "Work Orientations of the Poor and Income Maintenance," *Australian Journal of Sociology* 12 (1977): 266–279; and Sonia R. Wright and James D. Wright, "Income Maintenance and Work Behavior," *Social Policy* 6 (1975): 24–32.

15. Rodman, *Lower-Class Families*, p. 195. Rodman developed his concept from his field work in Trinidad.

16. Elliot Liebow, *Tally's Corner: A Study of Negro Streetcorner Men* (Boston: Little, Brown, 1967), pp. 213, 208, 209, 222.

17. The discussion that follows draws on the following sources: Davidson and Krackhardt, "Structural Change"; Davidson, " 'Culture of Shiftlessness' "; David Elesh, "Poverty Theories and Income Maintenance: Validity and Policy Relevance," *Social Science Quarterly* 54 (1973): 359–373; Lola M. Irean, Oliver C. Moles, and Robert M. O'Shea, "Ethnicity, Poverty, and Selected Attitudes: a Test of the 'Culture of Poverty' Hypothesis," *Social Forces* 47 (June 1969): 405–413; Miller, "Subculture"; Padfield, "New Industrial Systems"; Jack L. Roach and Orville R. Gursslin, "An Evaluation of the Concept 'Culture of Poverty,' " *Social Forces* 45 (March 1967): 383–393; Hyman Rodman, "Culture of Poverty: The Rise and Fall of Concept," *The Sociological Review* 25, new series (1977): 867–876; Charles A. Valentine, *Culture and Poverty: Critique and Counter-Proposals* (Chicago and London: University of Chicago Press, 1968), and "Models and Muddles Concerning Culture and Inequality: A Reply to Critics," *Harvard Educational Review* 42 (1972): 97–108; Lee Rainwater, "The Problem of Lower Class Culture," *Journal of Social Issues* 26 (1970): 133–148; J. Allen Winter, ed., *The Poor: A Culture of Poverty or a Poverty of Culture?* (Grand Rapids, Mich.: William B. Eerdmans, 1971); Leacock, *Culture of Poverty*.

18. Lee Rainwater and William Yancey, *The Moynihan Report and the Politics of Controversy* (Cambridge: MIT Press, 1967), pp. 217–218.

19. Quoted in Rainwater and Yancey *Moynihan Report*, p. 130.

20. Quoted in Rainwater and Yancey, *Moynihan Report*, p. 200.

21. Rainwater and Yancey, *Moynihan Report*, p. 202.

22. Rainwater and Yancey, *Moynihan Report*, p. 16.

23. Rainwater and Yancey, *Moynihan Report*, p. 271.

24. Rainwater and Yancey, *Moynihan Report*, pp. 175–176.

25. Rainwater and Yancey, *Moynihan Reeport*, pp. 177–178; 133–135.

26. Elizabeth Herzog, "Is There a 'Breakdown' of the Negro Family," reprinted in Rainwater and Yancey, *Moynihan Report*, p. 347.

27. William Ryan, "Savage Discovery: 'The Moynihan Report,' " reprinted in Rainwater and Yancey, *Moynihan Report*, pp. 459–464.

28. Office of Policy Planning and Research, United States Department of Labor, *The Negro Family: The Case for National Action*, March 1965, pp. 13, 14. One partial exception among critics was Laura Carper, "The Negro Family and the Moynihan Report," reprinted in Rainwater and Yancey, *Moynihan Report*, p. 469. On the rise in AFDC rolls, see Frances Fox Piven and Richard Cloward, *Regulating the Poor: The Functions of Public Welfare* (New York: Vintage, 1971), pp. 183–199, and *Poor People's Move-*

*ments: Why They Succeed, How They Fail* (New York: Pantheon, 1982), pp. 264–362. See also James T. Patterson, *America's Struggle Against Poverty, 1900–1980* (Cambridge: Harvard University Press, 1981), pp. 171–184.

29. Herbert J. Gans, "The Negro Family: Reflections on the Moynihan Report," reprinted in Rainwater and Yancey, *Moynihan Report*, pp. 455–456.

30. Christopher Jencks, "The Moynihan Report," reprinted in Rainwater and Yancey, *The Moynihan Report*, p. 444.

31. Carol Stack, *All Our Kin: Strategies for Survival in a Black Community* (New York: Harper and Row, 1974), pp. 28, 30, 31, 90.

32. Benjamin F. Payton, "New Trends in Civil Rights," in Rainwater and Yancey, *Moynihan Report*, pp. 399 and 401.

33. Herbert G. Gutman, *The Black Family in Slavery and Freedom, 1750–1925* (New York: Vintage Books, 1976); Frank F. Furstenberg, Jr., Theodore Hershberg, and John Modell, "The Origins of the Female-Headed Black Family: The Impact of the Urban Experirence," in Theodore Hershberg, ed., *Philadelphia: Work, Space, Family, and Group Experience in the Nineteenth Century* (New York: Oxford University Press, 1981), pp. 435–454; Olivier Zunz, *The Changing Face of Inequality: Urbanization, Industrial Development, and Immigrants in Detroit, 1880–1920* (Chicago: University of Chicago Press, 1982); Kenneth L. Kusmer, *A Ghetto Takes Shape: Black Cleveland, 1870–1930* (Urbana: University of Illinois Press, 1976); Stanley Lieberson, *A Piece of the Pie: Blacks and White Immigrants since 1880* (Berkeley: University of California Press, 1980).

34. Stokely Carmichael and Charles V. Hamilton, *Black Power: The Politics of Liberation in America* (New York: Random House, 1967), p. 167.

35. On the early civil rights movement, see Aldon D. Morris, *The Origins of the Civil Rights Movement: Black Communities Organizing for Change* (New York: Free Press, 1984).

36. Robert L. Allen, *Black Awakening in Capitalist America: An Analytic History* (Garden City: Doubleday, 1969), pp. 27–28; see also Carmichael and Hamilton, *Black Power*, p. 50; and Jack M. Bloom, *Class, Race, and the Civil Rights Movement* (Bloomington: University of Indiana Press, 1987), pp. 164–179. For contrasting comments on Allen, see Martin Kilson, "Militant Rhetoric and the Bourgeoisie," *New York Times Book Review*, February 22, 1971, p. 28, and Anne Kelley, [review], *Black Scholar* 3 (1971): 50–54.

37. Martin Luther King, Jr., "President's Address to the Tenth Anniversary Convention of the Southern Christian Leadership Conference, Atlanta, Georgia, August 16, 1967," in Robert L. Scott and Wayne Brockriede, eds., *The Rhetoric of Black Power* (New York: Harper and Row, 1969), pp. 147–148.

38. King, "President's Address," pp. 155–158.

39. Martin Luther King, Jr., *Where Do We Go From Here: Chaos or Community?* (Boston: Beacon Press, 1968), pp. 169, 177–178.

40. King, "President's Address," pp. 159–160. On the riots, see Robert M.

Fogelson, *Violence as Protest: A Study of Riots and Ghettos* (Garden City: Anchor Books, 1971).

41. Cleveland Sellers, *The River of No Return: The Autobiography of a Black Militant and the Life and Death of SNCC* (New York: Morrow, 1965), p. 166; and Bloom, *Class, Race, and the Civil Rights Movement*, pp. 208–209. On the history of SNCC, see also Clayborne Carson, *In Struggle: SNCC and the Black Awakening of the 1960s* (Cambridge: Harvard University Press, 1981).

42. Especially important were: Harold Cruse, Kenneth Clark, and Malcolm X. Allen, *Black Awakening*, p. 6; Carmichael and Hamilton, *Black Power*, p. 2.

43. Carmichael and Hamilton, *Black Power*, pp. 16–31. For an insightful analysis of the lack of political power in cities, its implications, and its relation to urban political programs, see Joyce Ladner and Walter W. Stafford, "Black Repression in the Cities," *Black Scholar* 1 (April 1970: 39–52).

44. Frank G. Davis, *The Economics of Black Community Development: An Analysis and Program for Autonomous Growth and Development* (Chicago: Markham, 1972), pp. 6–7; Guy C. Z. Mhone, "Structural Oppression and the Persistence of Black Poverty," *Journal of Afro-American Issues* 3 (1975): 406; Charles Sackrey, "The Economics of Black Poverty," *The Review of Black Political Economy* 1 (1971): 48, 50; Wilfred L. David, "Black America in Development Perspective, Part I," *The Review of Black Political Economy* 3 (1973): 99–100; Ron Bailey, "Economic Aspects of the Black Internal Colony," *Review of Black Political Economy* 3 (1973): 62–63; Robert Heilbroner, "Introduction," in Thomas Vietorisz and Bennett Harrison, *The Economic Development of Harlem* (New York: Praeger, 1970), p. xxiii; and on growth as an idea underlying post-World War II domestic and foreign policy, Alan Wolfe, *America's Impasse: The Rise and Fall of the Politics of Growth* (Boston: South End Press, 1981). For a useful comment on Davis, see the review by Carolyn Shaw Bell, *Journal of Negro History* 57 (1972): 437–439.

45. Andre Gunder Frank, "The Development of Underdevelopment," in Charles K. Wilbur, comp., *The Political Economy of Development and Underdevelopment* (New York: Random House, 1973), pp. 94–95; Bailey, "Economic Aspects," p. 60; Wilfred L. David, "Black America in Developmental Perspective," *Review of Black Political Economy* 3 (1973): 87; Donald J. Harris, "The Black Ghetto as Colony: A Theoretical Critique and Alternative Formulation," *Review of Black Political Economy* 2 (1972): 26; Joseph N. Seward, "Developmental Economics and Black America: A Reply to Professor David," *Review of Black Political Economy* 5 (1975): 11–12; Thaddeus H. Spratlen, "Ghetto Economic Development," *Review of Black Political Economy* 1 (1971): 43–71, is a useful review of the literature.

46. Bailey, "Economic Aspects," pp. 44; Paul A. Baran and Paul M. Sweezy, *Monopoly Capital: An Essay on the American Economic and Social Order* (New York: Monthly Review Press, 1966), pp. 285–287. Baran and Sweezy's book generated considerable comment and controversy. See,

for instance, Karl de Schweinitz, Jr., "Who Decides?—Economics and Politics," *Public Administration Review* 28 (1968): 84–90; James O'Connor, "Marxist Heavyweight Division," *Nation* 202 (1966): 749–750; Howard J. Sherman, "Economic Systems: Planning and Reform; Cooperation," *American Economic Review* 55 (1966): 919–921; Henry Pachter, "The Political Economy of Fidelism," *Dissent* 14 (1967): 358–361; Harvey Magdoff, [review], *Economic Development and Cultural Change* 16 (1967): 145–149; and Myron E. Sharpe, Maurice Dobb, Joseph M. Gillman, Theodore Praeger, and Otto Nathan, "Marxism and Monopoly Capital: A Symposium," *Science and Society* 30 (1966): 461–496.

47. David, "Black America . . . Part II," p. 82; Bailey, "Economic Aspects," pp. 59–64; Robert Allen, "A Historical Synthesis: Black Liberation and World Revolution," *The Black Scholar* 3 (1972): 8; William K. Tabb, *The Political Economy of the Black Ghetto* (New York: Norton, 1970), pp. 21–24. For comments on Tabb's book, see the reviews by Joseph L. Arnold, *Journal of Negro History* 56 (1971): 294–296, and Morris Levitt, *American Political Science Review* 65 (1971): 1176–1178.

48. Davis, *Economics of Black Community Development*, pp. 5–8; Kenneth H. Parsons, "Poverty as an Issue in Development Policy: A Comparison of United States and Underdeveloped Countries," *Land Economics* 45 (February 1969): 60–61; David, "Black America . . . Part II," pp. 85–86.

49. Bailey, "Economic Aspects," pp. 64–66; Allen, "A Historical Synthesis," pp. 11–12; Baran and Sweezy, *Monopoly Capital*, p. 273; Tabb, *Political Economy*, p. 27; Seward, "Developmental Economics," p. 11; Joyce Ladner and Walter W. Stafford, "Black Repression in the Cities," *The Black Scholar* 1 (1970): 38–52; James Turner, "Blacks in the Cities: Land and Self-Determination," *The Black Scholar* 1 (1970): 11, argues that the movement toward metropolitan government had as its purpose depriving blacks of effective political power.

50. Ralph H. Metcalf, Jr., "Chicago Model Cities and Neocolonization," *The Black Scholar* 1 (April 1970): 23; David, "Black America . . . Part I," p. 91; Turner, "Blacks in the Cities," p. 10; Allen, "A Historical Synthesis," p. 8; Bailey, "Economic Aspects," pp. 4–6; Tabb, *Political Economy*, p. 23.

51. J. H. O'Dell, "Colonialism and the Negro American Experience," *Freedomways* 6 (1966): 300; David, "Black America . . . Part II," p. 98; Bailey, "Economic Aspects," p. 47; Allen, "A Historical Synthesis," pp. 9–10.

52. Bailey, "Economic Aspects," pp. 55–56; James Turner, "Blacks in the Cities: Land and Self-Determination," *The Black Scholar* 1 (1970): 25; Kwame Nkrumah, "The Mechanisms of Neocolonialism," chapter 18 in Nkrumah, *Colonialism, the Last Stage of Imperialism*, reprinted in *Freedomways* 6 (1966): 139.

53. Bailey, "Economic Aspects," pp. 45–46, 57–58; Harris, "The Black Ghetto as Colony," pp. 11–12.

54. Thomas Sowell, "Economics and Black People," *Review of Black Political Economy* 1 (1971): 16–17.

55. Seward, "Developmental Economics," pp. 198–199.

56. Sowell, "Economics and Black People," p. 16.

57. Davis, *Economics of Black Community Development*, p. 19; Guy C. Z. Mhone, "Structural Oppression and the Persistence of Black Poverty," *Journal of Afro-American Issues* 3 (1975): 417–418.
58. Turner, "Blacks in the Cities," pp. 12–13; Sackrey, "Economics and Black Poverty," 59.
59. Ira Katznelson, *City Trenches: Urban Politics and the Patterning of Class in the United States* (New York: Pantheon, 1981), p. 120.
60. My definition of cultural authority is taken from Paul Starr, *The Social Transformation of American Medicine* (New York: Basic Books, 1982), p. 13: "the probability that particular definitions of reality and judgments of meaning and value will prevail as valid and true."
61. Katznelson, *City Trenches*, esp. pp. 179–180.
62. One discussion of the decline in household manufacture is Nancy Cott, *The Bonds of Womanhood: "Women's Sphere" in New England, 1780–1835* (New Haven: Yale University Press, 1977).
63. A good statistical overview of women's employment is Lynn Y. Weiner, *From Working Girl to Working Mother: The Female Labor Force in the United States, 1820–1900* (Chapel Hill: University of North Carolina Press, 1985), which has a very useful bibliography. See also Michael B. Katz, Michael J. Doucet, and Mark J. Stern, *The Social Organization of Early Industrial Capitalism* (Cambridge: Harvard University Press, 1981), pp. 97–101.
64. For examples of women's poverty, see Stansell, *City of Women* and Katz, *Poverty and Policy*, pp. 17–54.
65. Katz, *Shadow*, pp. 58–109, and *Poverty and Policy*, pp. 57–89.
66. The most immediate political consequence of granting suffrage to women in 1920 was the Sheppard-Towner Act, which created federally sponsored free medical clinics for mothers and children. Despite the program's success, the hostility of the organized medical profession killed it late in the decade. On the Sheppard-Towner Act, see Sheila M. Rothman, *Woman's Proper Place: A History of Changing Ideas and Practices, 1870 to the Present* (New York: Basic Books, 1978), pp. 136–141; on veterans' pensions, see Ann Shola Orloff and Theda Skocpol, "Why Not Equal Protection? Explaining the Politics of Public Social Welfare in Britain and the United States, 1880s–1920s," paper presented at the annual meeting of the American Sociological Association, Detroit, Michigan, September 2, 1983, pp. 49–55, and Ann Shola Orloff, "The Politics of Pensions: A Comparative Analysis of the Origins of Pensions and Old Age Insurance in Canada, Britain, and the United States, 1880s–1930s," Ph.D. diss., Princeton University, 1985; a useful survey of Progressive era policies for children is Susan Tiffin, *In Whose Best Interest? Child Welfare Reform in the Progressive Era* (Westport, Conn.: Greenwood Press, 1982); a good discussion of mothers' pensions is Roy Lubove, *The Struggle for Social Security 1900–1935* (Cambridge: Harvard University Press, 1968), pp. 91–112; see also Katz, *Shadow*, pp. 113–145.
67. On AFDC, see Piven and Cloward, *Regulating the Poor*; Bell, *AFDC*; Patterson, *America's Struggle*; on the NWRO, see Guida West, *The Na-*

*tional Welfare Rights Movement: The Social Protest of Poor Women* (New York: Praeger, 1981); Larry R. Jackson and William A. Johnson, *Protest by the Poor: the Welfare Rights Movement in New York City* (Lexington, Mass.: Heath, 1974), and Piven and Cloward, *Poor People's Movements*, pp. 264–361; an extremely usesful source on trends in spending for social welfare programs is Committee on Ways and Means, U.S. House of Representatives, *Background Material and Data on Programs Within the Jurisdiction of the Committee on Ways and Means* (Washington, D.C.: GPO, 1985).

68. On the expansion of social welfare, see Patterson, *America's Struggle*, pp. 157–209, and Katz, *Shadow*, pp. 261–272.

69. Harrell R. Rodgers, Jr., *Poor Women, Poor Families: The Economic Plight of America's Female-Headed Households* (Armonk, N.Y.: and London: M. E. Sharpe, 1986), pp. 16–36; Irwin Garfinkle and Sara S. McLanahan, *Single Mothers and Their Children: A New American Dilemma* (Washington, D.C.: The Urban Institute Press, 1986), pp. 45–85; Robert Pear, "Poverty Rate Dips," *New York Times*, July 31, 1987, p. A12; Frances Fox Piven and Richard A. Cloward, "The Contemporary Relief Debate," in Fred Block et al., *The Mean Season: The Attack on the Welfare State* (New York: Pantheon, 1987), pp. 55–57.

70. Mary Jo Bane, "Household Composition and Poverty," in Sheldon H. Danziger and Daniel H. Weinberg, *Fighting Poverty: What Works and What Doesn't* (Cambridge: Harvard University Press, 1986), p. 211; Mark Stern and June Axinn, work in progress (1986); Community Service Society of New York, *Poverty in New York City: 1980–1985* (New York: Community Service Society of New York, 1987), pp. xi.

71. U.S. Department of Commerce, Bureau of the Census, Technical Paper 51, "Estimates of Poverty including the Value of Noncash Benefits: 1979–1982" (Washington, D.C.: GPO, 1984), p. xiv.

72. Sheldon H. Danziger, Robert H. Haveman, and Robert D. Plotnick, "Antipoverty Policy: Effects on the Poor and the Nonpoor," in Danziger and Weinberg, *Fighting Poverty*, computed from Table 3.5, p. 63, and Table 3.7, p. 66.

73. Robert Pear, "Increasingly, Those Who Have Jobs Are Poor, Too," *New York Times*, December 27, 1987, p. E5; Sar A. Levitan and Isaac Shapiro, *Working But Poor: America's Contradiction* (Baltimore: Johns Hopkins University Press, 1987).

74. Levitan and Shapiro, *Working But Poor*; Community Service Society of New York, *Poverty in New York City*; Marian Wright Edelman, *Families in Peril: An Agenda for Social Change* (Cambridge: Harvard University Press, 1987), p. 48; see also pp. 25–29. Edelman is director of the Children's Defense Fund, which has played a major role in publicizing children's poverty.

75. For examples of the literature describing the feminization of poverty, see Rodgers, *Poor Women*, and Mary Corcoran, Greg J. Duncan, and Martha S. Hill, "The Economic Fortunes of Women and Children: Lessons from the Panel Study of Income Dynamics"; Roslyn L. Feldberg, "Comparable

Worth: Toward Theory and Practice in the United States"; and Sheila B. Kammerman, "Women, Children, and Poverty: Public Policies and Female-headed Families in Industrialized Countries," in Barbara C. Gelpi, Nancy C. M. Hartsock, Clare C. Novak, and Myra H. Strober, eds., *Women and Poverty* (Chicago: University of Chicago Press, 1986), pp. 1–24, 163–180, 41–64; and Diane Pearce, "The Feminization of Poverty: Women, Work and Welfare," *Urban and Social Change Review* 10 (1978): 28–36. The latter is the article that introduced the phrase "feminization of poverty."

76. "Introduction," pp. 4–5, and Zillah R. Eisenstein, "The Patriarchal Relations of the Reagan State," in Gelpi et al., *Women and Poverty*, pp. 180–183. In the same volume, see also Muriel Nazzari, "The 'Woman Question' in Cuba: An Analysis of Material Constraints on Its Solution," pp. 65–82; and Mari H. Clark, "Women-headed Households and Poverty: Insights from Kenya," pp. 103–120.

77. Kathleen Moran, "Preface to a Feminist Theory of Poverty," Clayborne Carson with Mark McLeod, eds., *Poverty with a Human Face: Poverty, Justice, and Equality in the Contemporary United States* (San Francisco: Public Media Center, 1985), pp. 30, 32–33 (emphasis in original).

78. Only in relatively recent times have social and political forces permeated the fixed boundaries between spheres, blurred old distinctions, and shifted some power toward women. Without doubt, throughout most of Western history men have controlled economic and political power in families, workplaces, and government, and they have solidified their power through custom, law, ideology, and naked force. Nonetheless, definitions of gender and the role of women have not remained static. On the contrary, they have altered significantly throughout history. In America, the sharp division between public and private spheres on which some feminist theory draws, for instance, emerged most starkly in the nineteenth century. Even then, historians still are not clear to what extent it reflects universal experience, for most of their evidence rests on sources that describe middle-class domestic life. For a criticism of the view that the private (or domestic)/public distinction is a universal feature of gender roles see, M. Z. Rosaldo, "The Use and Abuse of Anthropology: Reflections on Feminism and Cross-Cultural Understanding," *Signs* 5 (1980): 389–417.

79. Gerda Lerner, *The Creation of Patriarchy* (New York: Oxford University Press, 1986), p. 239. Lerner defines patriarchy as: "the manifestation and institutionalization of male dominance over women and children in the family and the extension of male dominance over women in society in general." See also Rosaldo, "Use and Abuse of Anthropology," p. 417.

80. I discuss the public/private distinction in *Reconstructing American Education* (Cambridge: Harvard University Press), pp. 132–134; the ambiguous and protean nature of the distinction between the two is a major theme of two excellent books in the history of medicine, Charles E. Rosenberg, *The Care of Strangers: The Rise of America's Hospital System* (New York: Basic Books, 1987), and Paul Starr, *The Social Transformation of American*

*Medicine* (New York: Basic Books, 1982). The distinction between male and female spheres is a major topic in recent historical writing. One particularly compelling example is John Mack Faragher, *Women and Men on the Overland Trail* (New Haven: Yale University Press, 1979).

81. Sylvia Welby, *Patriarchy at Work* (Minneapolis: University of Minnesota Press, 1986), pp. 1–89; quotation, pp. 47–48; Jacqueline Jones, *Labor of Love, Labor of Sorrow: Black Women, Work and the Family from Slavery to the Present* (New York: Basic Books, 1985), pp. 12–13.

82. On the family wage issue, see Allan C. Carlson, "What Happened to the 'Family Wage'?" *The Public Interest* 83 (Spring, 1986): 3–17.

83. Joan Smith, "The Paradox of Women's Poverty: Wage-earning Women and Economic Transformation," in Gelpi et al., *Women and Poverty*, pp. 121–140.

84. Smith, p. 138; on workfare, see Chapter 5.

85. Diana M. Pearce, "Toil and Trouble: Women Workers and Unemployment Compensation," in Gelpi et al., *Women and Poverty*, p. 146. On the institutionalization of the split between public assistance and social insurance in the 1930's, see Michael B. Katz, *In the Shadow of the Poorhouse: A Social History of Welfare in America*, pp. 234–245. On the origins of the split between social insurance and public assistance, see Margaret Weir, Ann Shola Orloff, and Theda Skocpol, eds., *The Politics of Social Policy in the United States* (Princeton: Princeton University Press, 1988).

86. Barbara Ehrenreich and Frances Fox Piven, "The Feminization of Poverty: When the Family Wage System Breaks Down," in Irving Howe, ed., *Alternatives: Proposals for America from the Democratic Left* (New York: Pantheon, 1984), pp. 41–60.

87. Barbara J. Nelson, "Women's Poverty and Women's Citizenship: Some Political Consequences of Economic Marginality," in Gelpi et al., *Women and Poverty*, pp. 230–231.

88. Douglas Glasgow, "The Black Underclass in Perspective," in National Urban League, *The State of Black America 1987* (Washington, D.C.: National Urban League, 1987), pp. 135–136.

89. See also Karin Stallard, Barbara Ehrenreich, and Holly Sklar, *Poverty in the American Dream: Women and Children First* (New York: Institute for New Communications and Boston: South End Press, 1983) and Ruth Sidel, *Women and Children Last: The Plight of Poor Women in Affluent America* (New York: Penguin Books, 1986).

90. Michael Harrington, *The New American Poverty* (New York: Holt, Rinehart, and Winston, 1984).

91. Daniel Patrick Moynihan, *Family and Nation* (New York: Harcourt, Brace, Jovanovich, 1986). See also Stuart Butler and Anna Kondratas, *Out of the Poverty Trap: A Conservative Strategy for Welfare Reform* (New York: Free Press, 1987).

92. Moynihan, *Family and Nation*, pp. 167–176. For a definitive rebuttal of the epidemic argument, see Maris A. Vinovskis, *An "Epidemic" of Adolescent Pregnancy? Some Historical and Policy Considerations* (New York: Oxford University Press, 1988).

93. Frank F. Furstenberg, Jr., J. Brooks-Gunn, and S. Philip Morgan, *Adolescent Mothers in Later Life* (New York: Cambridge University Press, 1987).

THREE: INTELLECTUAL FOUNDATIONS OF
THE WAR ON POVERTY

1. There are several useful books that deal with the War on Poverty and Great Society. They include: Henry J. Aaron, *Politics and the Professors: The Great Society in Perspective* (Washington, D.C.: Brookings Institution, 1978); Daniel Knapp and Kenneth Polk, *Scouting the War on Poverty: Social Reform in the Kennedy Administration* (Lexington, Mass.: Heath/Lexington Books, 1971); Daniel P. Moynihan, *Maximum Feasible Misunderstanding: Community Action in the War on Poverty* (New York: Free Press, 1969), *The Politics of a Guaranteed Income: The Nixon Administration and the Family Assistance Plan* (New York: Random House, 1973); ed., *On Understanding Poverty: Perspectives from the Social Sciences* (New York: Basic Books, 1969); Robert A. Levine, *The Poor Ye Need Not Have With You: Lessons from the War on Poverty* (Cambridge: MIT Press, 1970); James L. Sundquist, ed., *On Fighting Poverty: Perspectives from Experience* (New York: Basic Books, 1969); Sar A. Levitan, *The Great Society's Poor Law: A New Approach to Poverty* (Baltimore: Johns Hopkins University Press, 1969).
2. Henry Cohen in "Poverty and Urban Policy: Conference Transcript of 1973 Group Discussion of the Kennedy Administration Urban Poverty Programs and Policies," Kennedy Archives, p. 51. See also pp. 46, 91, 93. Michael Harrington, *The Other America: Poverty in the United States* (New York: Macmillan, 1962); John Kenneth Galbraith, *The Affluent Society* (Boston: Houghton Mifflin, 1958); Dwight McDonald, "Our Invisible Poor," *New Yorker*, January 19, 1963, pp. 82–132.
3. "Poverty and Urban Policy," p. 359.
4. Frederick Hayes, Richard Boone, and Adam Yarmolinsky, "Poverty and Public Policy," pp. 164, 255, 242.
5. Interview with Paul Ylvisaker for the Ford Foundation Oral History Project, Cambridge, Massachusetts, September 27, 1973. Interviewer: Charles T. Morrissey, Session Number One, p. 54.
6. Daniel Capron in "Poverty and Public Policy," p. 176; see also p. 139.
7. "Mobilization for Youth, Inc. General Support," in Ford Foundation, Grant No. 62-369, accepted proposals, docket excerpts, June 21–22, 1962, p. 1; Ylvisaker interview, Session Number Two, October 27, 1973, p. 58.
8. Adam Yarmolinsky in "Poverty and Urban Policy," p. 193.
9. Richard Cloward and Daniel Capron in "Poverty and Urban Policy," pp. 160–161.
10. Adam Yarmolinsky in "Poverty and Urban Policy," pp. 162–163.
11. Daniel Capron in "Poverty and Urban Policy," pp. 167–168.

12. David Zarefsky, *President Johnson's War on Poverty: Rhetoric and History* (University, Ala.: University of Alabama Press, 1986), pp. 43–44.
13. Frances Fox Piven and David Hackett in "Poverty and Urban Policy," pp. 198 and 202; Piven, "Great Society," pp. 275–276.
14. Frances Fox Piven and Adam Yarmolinsky in "Poverty and Urban Policy," pp. 392, 395.
15. David Austin in "Poverty and Urban Policy," p. 184.
16. Daniel Capron in "Poverty and Urban Policy," p. 170.
17. David Hackett in "Poverty and Urban Policy," pp. 260–262.
18. Zarefsky, *President Johnson's War on Poverty*, pp. 22–23.
19. Zarefsky, *President Johnson's War on Poverty*, pp. 23–24.
20. Zarefsky, *President Johnson's War on Poverty*, pp. 26–36.
21. Robert Lampman quoted in Allen J. Matusow, *The Unraveling of America: A History of Liberalism in the 1960s* (New York: Harper and Row, 1984), p. 220; Zarefsky, *President Johnson's War on Poverty*, pp. xi–xii.
22. David Austin in "Poverty and Urban Policy," p. 147.
23. [Lyndon Johnson] *Economic Report of the President Transmitted to the Congress January 1964 Together with the Annual Report of the Council of Economic Advisors* (Washington: GPO, 1964), pp. 14–17; Daniel Capron in "Poverty and Urban Policy," p. 140.
24. [Council of Economic Advisors], "The Problem of Poverty in America," in *Economic Report of the President*, pp. 55, 57, 76.
25. "The Problem of Poverty in America," pp. 62–69.
26. "The Problem of Poverty in America," pp. 72–78.
27. Adam Yarmolinsky in "Poverty and Urban Policy," pp. 286–288.
28. On the nature and prevalence of the concept of growth in both international and domestic policy during the 1960s, see Alan Wolfe, *America's Impasse: The Rise and Fall of the Politics of Growth* (Boston: South End Press, 1981).
29. Margaret Weir, "The Federal Government and Unemployment: The Frustration of Policy Innovation from the New Deal to the Great Society," in Margaret Weir, Ann Shola Orloff, and Theda Skocpol, eds., *The Politics of Social Policy in the United States* (Princeton: Princeton University Press, 1988), pp. 169, 171. Weir's essay offers a persuasive and sophisticated account of the forces defeating a coherent macroeconomic employment policy since the 1930s.
30. Daniel Capron in "Poverty and Urban Policy," pp. 149–150; W. Willard Wirtz, memorandum to Honorable Theodore Sorenson, January 23, 1964, Sorenson papers, Kennedy Library.
31. Adam Yarmolinsky in "Poverty and Urban Policy," pp. 286–288. I discuss the outcome of the income maintenance plan (Heineman Commission) below.
32. Weir, "The Federal Government and Unemployment," pp. 172, 186.
33. David Hackett in "Poverty and Urban Policy," p. 24; Frances Fox Piven, "The New Urban Programs: The Strategy of Federal Intervention," in Richard A. Cloward and Frances Fox Piven, eds., *The Politics of Tur-*

*moil: Essays on Poverty, Race, and the Urban Crisis* (New York: Pantheon, 1972), p. 311, fn. 14.

34. Richard A. Cloward and Lloyd Ohlin, *Delinquency and Opportunity: A Theory of Delinquent Gangs* (New York: Free Press, 1964), p. x. On the panic over juvenile delinquency in the 1950s, see James Gilbert, *A Cycle of Outrage: America's Reaction to the Juvenile Delinquent in the 1950s* (New York: Oxford University Press, 1986).

35. *Delinquency and Opportunity*, pp. 20–32.

36. *Delinquency and Opportunity*, pp. 33, 78, 86.

37. *Delinquency and Opportunity*, pp. 194–211.

38. Two case studies of how community action became a new form of social control are Ira Katznelson, *City Trenches: Urban Politics and the Patterning of Class in the United States* (New York: Pantheon, 1981), and Joseph H. Helfgot, *Professional Reforming: Mobilization for Youth and the Failure of Social Science* (Lexington, Mass.: Lexington Books, 1981).

39. Mobilization for Youth, "A Proposal for the Prevention and Control of Delinquency by Expanding Opportunities," June 10, 1962 (mimeo, Ford Foundation Archives, grant 62-369), pp. 3–4.

40. Piven, "The Great Society," p. 311.

41. Jane Addams, *Democracy and Social Ethics* (New York: Macmillan, 1907), p. 220.

42. William Cannon and Daniel Capron in "Poverty and Urban Policy," pp. 178, 146–147. See also pp. 144 and 244–245.

43. Adam Yarmolinsky in "Poverty and Urban Policy," p. 285.

44. Lloyd Ohlin and Fred Hayes in "Poverty and Urban Policy," p. 270; see also p. 285.

45. Zarefsky, *President Johnson's War on Poverty*, pp. 45–46. William Cannon in "Poverty and Urban Policy," p. 244.

46. Daniel Capron in "Poverty and Urban Policy," pp. 144 and 148.

47. Adam Yarmolinsky in "Poverty and Urban Policy," pp. 248 and 260; see also pp. 149, 218–219, 252–253, 275–278.

48. Adam Yarmolinsky in "Poverty and Urban Policy," pp. 284–285. See also pp. 153–154 and 238–239.

49. Vincent J. Burke and Lee Burke, *Nixon's Good Deed: Welfare Reform* (New York: Columbia University Press, 1974), p. 14.

50. Robert H. Haveman, *Poverty Policy and Poverty Research: The Great Society and the Social Sciences* (Madison: University of Wisconsin Press, 1987), p. 82

51. *Poverty amid Plenty*, p. 48.

52. *Poverty amid Plenty*, pp. 72, 52–55, 62–63.

53. Burke and Burke, *Nixon's Good Deed*, pp. 92–93.

54. The opposition to the Family Assistance Plan is a major theme of Burke and Burke, *Nixon's Good Deed*, and of the excellent analysis in Christopher Leman, *The Collapse of Welfare Reform: Political Institutions, Policy, and the Poor in Canada and the United States* (Cambridge: MIT Press, 1980). On Social Security, Martha Derthick, *Policymaking for Social Security*

(Washington, D.C.: Brookings Institution, 1979); Jerry R. Cates, *Insuring Inequality: Administrative Leadership in Social Security, 1935–1954* (Ann Arbor: University of Michigan Press, 1983); W. Andrew Achenbaum, *Social Security: Visions and Revisions* (New York: Cambridge University Press, 1986); Jill Quadagno, *The Transformation of Old Age Security: Class and Politics in the American Welfare State* (Chicago: University of Chicago Press, 1988); Ann Shola Orloff, "The Political Origins of America's Belated Welfare State," and Edwin Amenta and Theda Skocpol, "Redefining the New Deal: World War II and the Development of Social Provision in the United States," in Weir, Orloff, and Skocpol, *The Politics of Social Policy*, pp. 37–122. On food stamps, an excellent overview, which contains valuable references, is Kenneth Finegold, "Agriculture and the Politics of U.S. Social Provision: Social Insurance and Food Stamps," in Weir, Orloff, and Skocpol, *The Politics of Social Policy*, pp. 199–234. See also Nancy Amidei, "Food Stamps: The Irony of Success," *Public Welfare* (Spring 1981): 15–21; Robert J. Fersh, "Food Stamps: Program at the Crossroads," *Public Welfare* (Spring 1981): 9–14. On the origins of Medicare and Medicaid, see Paul Starr, *The Transformation of American Medicine* (New York: Basic Books, 1982).

55. Frances Fox Piven and Richard Cloward, *Poor People's Movements: Why They Succeed, How They Fail* (New York: Pantheon, 1977), pp. 264–361; *Poverty amid Plenty*, pp. 121–122; Guida West, *The National Welfare Rights Movement: The Social Protest of Poor Women* (New York: Praeger, 1981); Larry R. Jackson and William A. Johnson, *Protest by the Poor: The Welfare Rights Movement in New York City*, (Lexington, Mass.: Heath, 1974); James T. Patterson, *America's Struggle Against Poverty 1900–1980* (Cambridge, Mass.: Harvard University Press, 1981); Isaac Shapiro and Robert Greenstein, *Holes in the Safety Nets: Poverty Programs and Policies in the States* (Washington, D.C.: Center on Budget and Policy Priorities, 1988); C. R. Winegarden, "The Welfare 'Explosion': Determinants of the Size and Recent Growth of the AFDC Population," *American Journal of Economic Sociology* 32 (1973): 244–256; R. Richard Ritti and Drew W. Hyman, "The Administration of Poverty: Lessons From the 'Welfare Explosion' 1967–1973," *Social Problems* 25 (December 1977): 158–175; Gilbert Y. Steiner, "Reform Follows Reality: The Growth of Welfare," *Public Interest* 34 (1974): 47–65.

56. Rand E. Rosenblatt, "Legal Entitlement and Welfare Benefits," in David Kairys, ed., *The Politics of Law: A Progressive Critique* (New York: Pantheon, 1972), p. 263.

57. Rosenblatt, "Legal Entitlement," pp. 266, 269–270.

58. Charles Reich, "The New Property," *Yale Law Journal*, 73 (April 1964): 771, 738, 734–737, 733; William H. Simon, "The Invention and Reinvention of Welfare Rights, " *Maryland Law Review*, 44 (1985): 28.

59. Reich, "The New Property," pp. 785–786.

60. John Rawls, *A Theory of Justice* (Cambridge: Harvard University Press, 1971), p. 11.

61. Rawls, *Theory of Justice*, pp. 60 and 75.

62. Rawls, *Theory of Justice*, pp. 73–74, 100–101.

63. Rawls, *Theory of Justice*, pp. 102, 281.

64. Rawls, *Theory of Justice*, p. 275.

65. Especially useful here is Patterson, *America's Struggle Against Poverty*, pp. 157–184. On the origins of and distinctions between Medicare and Medicaid, see Starr, *Transformation of American Medicine*, pp. 264–265.

66. See John E. Schwarz, *America's Hidden Success: A Reassessment of Twenty Years of Public Policy* (New York: Norton, 1983).

67. Peter Marris and Martin Rein, *Dilemmas of Social Reform: Poverty and Community Action in the United States* (London: Routledge and Kegan Paul, 1967); Allen J. Matusow, *The Unraveling of America: A History of Liberalism in the 1960s* (New York: Harper and Row, 1984); Sanford Kravitz, "The Community Action Program," in Sundquist, ed., *On Fighting Poverty*, pp. 52–69; Sar A. Levitan and Robert Taggart, *The Promise of Greatness* (Cambridge: Harvard University Press, 1976), pp. 169–187; Moynihan, *Maximum Feasible Misunderstanding*; Paul E. Peterson and J. David Greenstone, "Racial Change and Citizen Participation: The Mobilization of Low Income Communities through Community Action," in Robert Haveman, ed., *A Decade of Federal Antipoverty Programs: Achievements, Failures, and Lessons* (New York: Academic Press, 1971), p. 263; Guida West, *The National Welfare Rights Movement: The Social Protest of Poor Women* (New York: Praeger, 1981).

68. Frances Fox Piven and Richard Cloward, *Regulating the Poor: The Functions of Public Welfare* (New York: Pantheon, 1971); *Poor People's Movements: How They Succeed, Why They Fail* (New York: Pantheon, 1977); *The New Class War: Reagan's Attack on the Welfare State and Its Consequences* (New York: Pantheon, 1982); Patterson, *America's Struggle Against Poverty*, pp. 180–184; Jack L. Roach and Janet K. Roach, "Mobilizing the Poor: Road to a Dead End," *Social Problems* 26 (December, 1978): 160–167; Larry Isaac and William R. Kelly, "Racial Insurgency, the State and Welfare Expansion: Local and National Level Evidence from the Postwar United States," *American Journal of Sociology* 86 (May, 1981): 1348–1386; Edward T. Jennings, "Racial Insurgency, the State, and Welfare Expansion: A Critical Comment and Reanalysis," *American Journal of Sociology* 88 (May, 1983): 1220–1236; Joyce Gelb and Alice Sardell, "Strategies for the Powerless: The Welfare Rights Movement in New York City," *American Behavioral Scientist* 17 (March–April 1974): 507–530; Michael Betz, "Riots and Welfare: Are They Related?" *Social Problems* 21 (June 1974): 345–355.

69. Mollie Orshansky, "Counting the Poor: Another Look at the Poverty Profile," first published in the *Social Security Bulletin*, 1965, reprinted in Mollie Orshansky, *The Measure of Poverty: Technical Paper I Documentation of Background Information and Rationale for Current Poverty Matrix* Washington: GPO, 1977), pp. 19–20.

70. Mollie Orshansky, "Children of the Poor," first published in the *Social Security Bulletin*, July 1963, reprinted in Orshansky, *The Measure of Poverty*, p. 10; Orshansky, "Memorandum for Dr. Daniel P. Moynihan Sub-

ject: History of the Poverty Line," July 1, 1970, p. 234; "Who's Who Among the Poor: A Demographic View of Poverty," first published in the *Social Security Bulletin*, July 1965, reprinted in *The Measure of Poverty*, pp. 50, 68–69; "Perspectives on Poverty 2: How Poverty is Measured," (1968), reprinted in *The Measure of Poverty*, p. 245.

71. Orshansky, "Counting the Poor," p. 24; "Who's Who Among the Poor," p. 50; "Perspectives on Poverty 2," p. 245; "Poverty Thresholds," in *The Measure of Poverty*, p. 276.

72. Mollie Orshansky, "Measuring Poverty: A Debate," *Public Welfare* (Spring 1978): 47. On the measurement of poverty, see Michael Harrington, *The New American Poverty* (New York: Holt, Rinehart and Winston, 1984), pp. 69–71 and 84–85; Harrell R. Rodgers, Jr., *The Cost of Human Neglect* (Armonk, N.Y.: M. E. Sharp, Inc., 1982), pp. 15–30; Sidney E. Zimbalist, "Replacing Our Obsolete Poverty Line," *Public Welfare* 35 (Fall 1977): 36–41 and "Drawing the Poverty Line," *Social Work* 9 (July 1964): 19–26; John B. Williamson and Kathryn M. Hyer, "The Measurement and Meaning of Poverty," *Social Problems* 22 (June 1975): 652–663; Marie Withers Osmond and Mary Durkin, "Measuring Family Poverty," *Social Science Quarterly* 60 (June 1979): 87–95; James H. Hauver, John A. Goodman, and Marc A. Grainer, "The Federal Poverty Thresholds: Appearance and Reality," *Journal of Consumer Research* 8 (June 1981): 1–10; Theo Goehart, Victor Halberstadt, Arie Kapteyn, and Bernard Van Praag, "The Poverty Line: Concept and Measurement," *Journal of Human Resources* 12 (1977): 503–520; Sheldon Danziger and Peter Gottschalk, "The Measurement of Poverty: Implications for Antipoverty Policy," *American Behavioral Scientist* 26 (July–August 1983): 739–756; Donald E. Chambers, "Another Look at the Poverty Lines in England and the United States," *Social Service Review* 55 (September 1981): 472–483, and "The U.S. Poverty Line: A Time for Change," *Social Work* 27 (July 1982): 354–358; Leonard Beeghley, "Illusion and Reality in the Measurement of Poverty," *Social Problems* 31 (February 1984): 322–333; and Christopher Jencks, "The Politics of Income Measurement," in William Alonso and Paul Starr, eds., *The Politics of Numbers* (New York: Russell Sage Foundation, 1987), pp. 83–131. The entire book is an excellent and authoritative source on the politics of numbers in contemporary American social science.

73. Robert H. Haveman, *Poverty Policy and Poverty Research: The Great Society and the Social Sciences* (Madison: University of Wisconsin Press, 1987).

74. Haveman, *Poverty Policy*, pp. 51–52.

75. Haveman, *Poverty Policy*, pp. 32–34.

76. Elizabeth Evanson, "A Brief History of the Institute for Research on Poverty," *Focus* 9 (Summer, 1986): 2–7; [anon.] *A Description* (University of Wisconsin-Madison: Institute for Research on Poverty, 1986).

77. See Greg Duncan et al., *Years of Poverty, Years of Plenty: The Changing Economic Fortunes of American Workers and Families* (Ann Arbor: Institute for Social Research, University of Michigan, 1984).

78. Haveman, *Poverty Policy*, p. 192; Philip K. Robins et al., *A Guaranteed*

*Annual Income: Evidence from a Social Experiment* (New York: Academic Press, 1980).

79. Haveman, *Poverty Policy*, p. 167.

80. Haveman, *Poverty Policy*, p. 236. See also Charles E. Lindblom and David K. Cohen, *Usable Knowledge: Social Science and Social Problem Solving* (New Haven, CT: Yale University Press, 1979).

FOUR: INTERPRETATIONS OF POVERTY IN
THE POSTINDUSTRIAL CITY

1. These and subsequent figures on poverty in this chapter represents persons or families with incomes below the official poverty lines. They are taken from U.S. Bureau of the Census, Current Population Reports, Series P-60, No. 160, *Poverty in the United States: 1986* (Washington, D.C.: G.P.O., 1988). The numbers in this paragraph are from Table 1.

2. *Poverty in the United States*, Tables 2 and 6.

3. *Poverty in the United States*, Tables 6 and 17.

4. Fred Block, *Revising State Theory: Essays in Politics and Postindustrialism* (Philadelphia: Temple University Press, 1987), p. 27.

5. Frank Levy, *Dollars and Dreams: The Changing American Income Distribution* (New York: Russell Sage Foundation, 1987), p. 87, Table 5.2; Emma Rothschild, "The Reagan Economic Legacy [II]," *New York Review*, July 21, 1988, p. 37.

6. John D. Ksarda, "Jobs, Migration, and Emerging Urban Mismatches," in Michael G. H. McGeary and Laurence E. Lynn, eds., *Urban Change and Poverty* (Washington, D.C.: National Academy Press, 1988), p. 170, Table 9.

7. Ksarda, "Jobs," pp. 174–175.

8. Ksarda, "Jobs," pp. 176–177.

9. Levy, *Dollars and Dreams*, p. 93.

10. Levy, *Dollars and Dreams*, pp. 3–4, 63, 6.

11. Rothschild, "Reagan Economic Legacy," pp. 33, 37–38.

12. Rothschild, "Reagan Economic Legacy," pp. 37–38.

13. Sar A. Levitan and Isaac Shapiro, *Working But Poor: America's Contradiction* (Baltimore: Johns Hopkins University Press, 1987), pp. 4, 7, 16.

14. Levy, *Dollars and Dreams*, pp. 182, 198.

15. John D. Ksarda, "Urban Change and Minority Opportunities," in Paul Peterson, ed., *The New Urban Reality* (Washington, D.C.: The Brookings Institution, 1985), p. 33; Levy, *Dollars and Dreams*, p. 105; Ksarda, "Jobs," p. 152.

16. Ksarda, "Jobs," p. 151.

17. Ksarda, "Urban Change," p. 52, Table 5.

18. Sara McLanahan, Irwin Garfinkle, and Dorothy Watson, "Family Structure, Poverty, and the Underclass," in McGeary and Lynn, eds., *Urban Change and Poverty*, pp. 102, 105. For more discussion of female-headed families and adolescent pregnancy, see Chapters two and five.

19. McLanahan et al., "Family Structure," pp. 112–114.

20. John H. Mollenkopf, *The Contested City* (Princeton: Princeton University Press, 1983), p. 13.

21. On the relation of home, work, and transportation costs, see Theodore Hershberg et al., "The 'Journey-to-Work,': An Empirical Investigation of Work, Residence, and Transportation, Philadelphia, 1850 and 1880," in Theodore Hershberg, ed., *Philadelphia: Work, Space, Family, and Group Experience in the 19th Century* (New York: Oxford University Press, 1981), pp. 128–173. On suburbanization, see Kenneth T. Jackson, *Crabgrass Frontier: The Suburbanization of the United States* (New York: Oxford University Press, 1985); Peter O. Muller, *Contemporary Suburban America* (Englewood Cliffs, N.J.: Prentice-Hall, 1981); Herbert J. Gans, *The Levittowners: Ways of Life and Politics in a New Suburban Community* (New York: Vintage Books, 1967); Bennett M. Berger, *Working Class Suburb: A Study of Auto Workers in Suburbia* (Berkeley: University of California Press, 1960); Carol A. O'Connor, *A Sort of Utopia: Scarsdale, 1891–1981* (Albany: SUNY Press, 1983); Barry Checkoway, "Large Scale Builders, Federal Housing Programs, and Postwar Suburbanization," in William K. Tabb and Larry Sawers, eds., *Marxism and the Metropolis: New Perspectives on Political Economy*, 2nd ed. (New York: Oxford University Press, 1984), pp. 152-173.

22. See David Ward, *Cities and Immigrants: A Geography of Change in Nineteenth-Century America* (New York: Oxford University Press, 1971); Olivier Zunz, *The Changing Face of Inequality: Urbanization, Industrial Development, and Immigrants in Detroit, 1880–1920* (Chicago: University of Chicago Press, 1982); Ian Davey and Michael Doucet, "The Social Geography of a Commercial City ca. 1853," Appendix One, Michael B. Katz, *The People of Hamilton, Canada West: Family and Class in a Mid-Nineteenth-Century City* (Cambridge: Harvard University Press, 1975), pp. 319–342.

23. Gans, *Levittowners;* Jackson, *Crabgrass Frontier*, pp. 231–245.

24. Susan S. Fainstein and Norman I. Fainstein, "Economic Change, National Policy, and the System of Cities," in Susan S. Fainstein et al., *Restructuring the City: The Political Economy of Urban Redevelopment*, rev. ed. (New York: Longman, 1987), p. 14.

25. Gary Orfield, "Minorities and Suburbanization," in Rachel G. Bratt et al., *Critical Perspectives on Housing* (Philadelphia: Temple University Press, 1986), pp. 224–225 (includes excerpts from Mt. Laurel Decision, pp. 225–226).

26. Fainstein and Fainstein, "Economic Change," p. 14. For many examples of the process at work, see Robert A. Caro, *The Power Broker: Robert Moses and the Fall of New York* (New York: Random House, 1974).

27. Fainstein and Fainstein, "Economic Change"; Alan Wolfe, *America's Impasse: The Rise and Fall of the Politics of Growth* (Boston: South End Press, 1981), p. 88; R. Allen Hayes, *The Federal Government and Urban Housing: Ideology and Change in Public Policy* (Albany: SUNY Press, 1985).

28. John H. Mollenkopf, "Post-War Politics of Urban Development," *Politics and Society*, 5 (1975): 282; Martin Anderson, "The Federal Bulldozer," and Herbert J. Gans, "The Failure of Urban Renewal," in James Q. Wilson, ed., *Urban Renewal: The Record and the Controversy* (Cambridge: M.I.T. Press, 1966), pp. 494–495; 539.

29. Brian J. L. Berry, "Islands of Renewal in Seas of Decay," in Peterson, *New Urban Reality*, pp. 71–73.

30. David T. Ellwood, *Poor Support: Poverty in the American Family* (New York: Basic Books, 1988), p. 202. See also William Julius Wilson, *The Truly Disadvantaged: The Inner City, The Underclass, and Public Policy* (Chicago: University of Chicago Press, 1987), p. 58; Mary Jo Bane and Paul A. Jargowsky, "Urban Poverty Areas: Basic Questions Concerning Prevalence, Growth and Dynamics," unpublished manuscript, Center for Health and Human Resources Policy, John F. Kennedy School of Government, Harvard University, February 29, 1988, pp. 292, 31, 71–72.

31. I have described the components of the war on welfare in *In the Shadow of the Poorhouse* (New York: Basic Books, 1986), chap. 10.

32. Katz, *Shadow*, p. 278; on the sources of conservatism, I have found useful: Barry Bluestone and Bennett Harrison, *The Deindustrialization of America* (New York: Basic Books, 1982); Ramesh Mishra, *The Welfare State in Crisis: Social Thought and Social Change* (New York: St. Martin's Press, 1984); Thomas Byrne Edsall, The New Politics of Inequality (New York: Norton, 1984); Thomas Ferguson and Joel Rogers, *Right Turn: The Decline of the Democrats and the Future of American Politics* (New York: Hill and Wang, 1986); Frances Fox Piven and Richard A. Cloward, *The New Class War: Reagan's Attack on the Welfare State and Its Consequences* (New York: Pantheon, 1982).

33. For examples, see Katz, *Shadow*, pp. 46–52 and 285–289.

34. Martin Anderson, *Welfare: The Political Economy of Welfare Reform in the United States* (Stanford, Cal: Hoover Institution Press, 1978).

35. Anderson, *Welfare*, p. 169.

36. Anderson, *Welfare*, pp. 43–44, 87, 133.

37. Anderson, *Welfare*, pp. 15, 38.

38. Michael Harrington, *The New American Poverty* (New York: Holt, Rinehart, and Winston, 1984), pp. 77, 79–80.

39. Harrington, *New American Poverty*, pp. 81–84.

40. Leonard Beeghley, "Illusion and Reality in the Measurement of Poverty," *Social Problems*, 31 (February 1984): 327–331; Harrington, *New American Poverty*, pp. 85–87; Sheldon Danziger and Peter Gottschalk, "The Measurement of Poverty," *American Behavioral Scientist*, 26 (July–August 1983): 739–756; U.S. Bureau of the Census, Technical Paper 56, *Estimates of Poverty Including the Value of Noncash Benefits: 1985* (Washington, D.C.: U.S. Government Printing Office, 1986).

41. George Gilder, *Wealth and Poverty* (New York: Basic Books, 1981; Bantam edition, 1982), pp. xi, 221–222; Leonard Silk, "A Walk on the Supply Side," *Harvard Business Review* (November–December 1981), p. 44; Richard Hofstadter, *Anti-Intellectualism in American Life* (New York: Knopf,

1963). For other commentary on Gilder, see Robert Lekachman, "Right Wisdom," *Dissent* 29 (Summer, 1981): 373–374; Joseph Sobran, "The Economy of Faith," *National Review* 33 (February 6, 1981): 104–105; Michael Kinsley, "Tension and Release," *New Republic*, February 7, 1981, pp. 25–31; Gordon Tullock, "Two Gurus," *Policy Review* (Summer 1981–Spring 1982): 137–144; Kendall P. Cochran, [review], *Social Science Quarterly* 63 (December 1982): 793–794; Robert Higgs, [review], *Journal of Economic History*, 41 (December 1981): 957–959; [anon.], "Blessed Are the Money-Makers," *The Economist*, March 7, 1981, pp. 87–88; Vera Shlakman, [review], *Social Work*, (March 1982): 198; Richard N. Farmer, [review], *Business Horizons*, 24 (July–August 1981): 90–93; Alan Ryan, "Three Cheers for Capitalism," *Partisan Review*, 50 (Spring 1983): 300–303; Barry Gewen, "Gilder's Capitalism Without Tears," *New Leader*, March 23, 1981, pp. 17–19; Ronald A. Krieger, "Supply-Side Economics," *Choice*, 19 (November 1981): 341–347.

42. Gilder, *Wealth and Poverty*; Robert Nozick, *Anarchy, State, and Utopia* (New York: Basic Books, 1974); Charles Murray, *Losing Ground: American Social Policy 1950–1980* (New York: Basic Books, 1984).

43. Gilder, *Wealth and Poverty*, pp. 23, 34, 103–106, 278–279.

44. Gilder, *Wealth and Poverty*, pp. 82, 87, 89, 90–91, 153.

45. Gilder, *Wealth and Poverty*, pp. 135–136.

46. Gilder, *Wealth and Poverty*, pp. 153, 155, 90, 139–140.

47. Gilder, *Wealth and Poverty*, pp. 304–315.

48. George R. Geiger [review], *Antioch Review* 36 (Summer 1978): 377; Ernest Van Den Haag, "The Libertarian Argument," *National Review* 27 (July 4, 1975): 729; Michael Sean Quinn, "Defense of a Minimal State," *Southwest Review* 60 (Summer 1975): 312; Sheldon Wolin, [review], *The New York Times Book Review*, May 11, 1975, p. 31. For other comments on Nozick, see: Virginia Held, "John Locke on Robert Nozick, *Social Research* 43 (Spring 1976): 169–195; R.P.M., [review], *Review of Metaphysics* 30 (Spring 1976): 134–135; Francis Canavan, "False Individualism, Reasons for Hope, Backward Glances," *America*, July 19, 1975, p. 37; Tibor R. Machan, "The Minimal State," *Modern Age* (Fall 1975): 434–435; George Kateb, "The Night Watchman State," *American Scholar* 45 (Winter 1976): 816–826; Raziel Abelson, "Is There a Public Interest," *The New Leader*, April 14, 1975, pp. 19–21; Douglas Rae, [review], *The American Political Science Review* 70 (1976): 1289–1291; Steven Lukes, "State of Nature," *New Statesman*, March 14, 1975, pp. 343–344; Christopher Lehmann-Haupt, "Hard Book That Must Be Read," *New York Times*, August 5, 1975, p. 29; Michael Harrington, "Misconception of Society," *Commonweal*, November 7, 1975, pp. 534–536; Bernard Williams, "The Minimal State," *Times Literary Supplement*, January 17, 1975, pp. 46–47; Peter Witonski, "New Argument," *New Republic* 172 (April 26, 1975): 29–30; Peter Singer, "The Right to Be Rich or Poor," *New York Review of Books* 22 (March 6, 1975): 19–24.

49. Nozick, *Anarchy, the State, and Utopia*, pp. ix–xii.

50. Nozick, *Anarchy, the State, and Utopia*, p. 31.

51. Nozick, *Anarchy, the State, and Utopia*, pp. 153, 169.

52. Nozick, *Anarchy, the State, and Utopia*, p. 231.

53. Murray, *Losing Ground*, p. 196.

54. Murray, *Losing Ground*, pp. 233, 177.

55. Robert Greenstein, "Losing Faith in Losing Ground," *New Republic*, March 25, 1985, p. 14; Christopher Jencks, "How Poor Are the Poor?" *New York Review* 32 (May 5, 1985): 41.

56. Chuck Lane, "The Manhattan Project," *The New Republic*, March 25, 1985), pp. 14–15.

57. Lane, "The Manhattan Project."

58. Jencks, "How Poor Are the Poor?", p. 46; Greenstein, "Losing Faith," p. 14.

59. Greenstein, "Losing Faith," pp. 12–13.

60. It would require far too much space for me to present the counterhistorical evidence to Murray's assertions here. I offer much of it throughout my books, *In the Shadow of the Poorhouse* and *Poverty and Policy in American History* (New York: Academic Press, 1983).

61. Mead, *Beyond Entitlement*, pp. 1, ix.

62. Mead, *Beyond Entitlement*, p. 7.

63. Mead, *Beyond Entitlement*, 12. Mead's central themes—distrust of human nature, the need for lowered expectations, a more authoritarian government, and a rejection of equality of condition—are precisely those ascribed by Peter Steinfels to contemporary "neoconservatives." Steinfels, *The Neoconservatives, passim.*

64. Mead, *Beyond Entitlement*, pp. 7, 9, 10, 18–19, 24, 74, 69.

65. Mead, *Beyond Entitlement*, pp. 13, 84–85.

66. Mead, *Beyond Entitlement*, pp. 200, 6, 10, 87.

67. Mead, *Beyond Entitlement*, pp. 67, 9, 12.

68. Mead, *Beyond Entitlement*, pp. 62–63, 41.

69. Mead, *Beyond Entitlement*, pp. 18–21, 49.

70. Evidence on the extent and demographics of black poverty is presented elsewhere in this book.

71. I have written about some of these more authoritarian reforms and their outcomes in *In the Shadow of the Poorhouse* and *Reconstructing American Education* (Cambridge: Harvard University Press, 1987).

72. Mead, *Beyond Entitlement*, p. 60. On community action, see Chapter 3.

73. Fred Block, "Rethinking the Political Economy of the Welfare State," in Fred Block et al., *The Mean Season: The Attack on the Welfare State* (New York: Pantheon, 1987), pp. 109–160; "The Obligation to Work and the Availability of Jobs: A dialogue between Lawrence M. Mead and William Julius Wilson, *Focus* 10 (Summer 1987): 11–19. On the work ethic in American history, see Daniel Rodgers, *The Work Ethic in Industrial America, 1850–1920* (Chicago: University of Chicago Press, 1978).

74. Mead, *Beyond Entitlement*, pp. 6–7.

75. Mead, *Beyond Entitlement*, pp. 242–243.

76. For the idea that welfare policy assumes a psychology differentiated by class, I am indebted to Piven and Cloward, *The New Class War*, p. 39.

77. Martha Minow, *Making All the Difference*, forthcoming, manuscript pp. 80 and 145.

78. Leonard Beeghley, "Illusion and Reality in the Measurement of Poverty," *Social Problems* 31 (February 1984): 335. For another attempt to combine the best features of relative and objective definitions of poverty, see Irwin Garfinkle and Robert H. Haveman, *Earnings Capacity, Poverty, and Inequality* (New York: Academic Press, 1977).

79. Peter Townsend, *Poverty in the United Kingdom: A Survey of Household Resources and Standards of Living* (Berkeley: University of California Press, 1979), p. 88.

80. Townsend, pp. 57, 271.

81. Townsend, p. 893.

82. Townsend, pp. 921–922.

83. Elijah Anderson, *A Place on the Corner* (Chicago: University of Chicago Press, 1978); "Race and Neighborhood Transition," in Paul Peterson, ed., *The New Urban Reality* (Washington, D.C.: The Brookings Institution, 1985), pp. 99–125; "Of Old Heads and Young Boys: Notes on the Urban Black Experience," unpublished manuscript, University of Pennsylvania, 1986; "The Inner-City Black Youth Sex Code," unpublished manuscript, University of Pennsyslvania, 1988.

84. Terry M. Williams and William Kornblum, *Growing Up Poor* (Lexington, Mass.: Lexington Books, 1985), p. 104.

85. Jay McLeod, *Ain't No Makin' It: Leveled Aspirations in a Low-Income Neighborhood* (Boulder, Colo.: Westview Press, 1987), pp. 148, 129–130.

86. David T. Ellwood, *Poor Support: Poverty in the American Family* (New York: Basic Books, 1988), pp. 40, 42.

87. Frances Fox Piven and Richard Cloward, *The New Class War: Reagan's Attack on the Welfare State and Its Consequences* (New York: Pantheon, 1982), pp. 31–32.

88. Fred Block, "Rethinking the Political Economy of the Welfare State," in Block et al., *The Mean Season*, pp. 109–160.

89. Robert Kuttner, *The Economic Illusion: False Choice Between Prosperity and Social Justice* (Boston: Houghton Mifflin, 1984), p. 8.

90. John E. Schwarz, *America's Hidden Success: A Reassessment of Twenty Years of Public Policy* (New York: Norton, 1983), p. 57.

91. See, for example, Ronald Dworkin, "Why Liberals Should Believe in Equality," *New York Review* 30 (February 3, 1983): 32–34.

92. Frank I. Michelman, "On Protecting the Poor Through the Fourteenth Amendment," *Harvard Law Review* 83: 7 (1969): 9, 13; "Welfare Rights in a Constitutional Democracy," *Washington University Law Quarterly* 3 (Summer 1969): 678. The latter includes an appendix summarizing important Supreme Court decisions bearing on welfare rights and a commentary on Michelman's argument by other scholars.

93. Robert E. Goodin, *Protecting the Vulnerable: A Reanalysis of Our*

*Social Responsibilities* (Chicago and London: University of Chicago Press, 1985), pp. 145–146.

94. Amy Gutmann, "Introduction," p. 6, and J. Donald Moon, "The Moral Basis of the Democratic Welfare State," pp. 28–29, in Amy Gutmann, ed., *Democracy and the Welfare State* (Princeton: Princeton University Press, 1988). See also J. Donald Moon, ed., *Responsibility, Rights and Welfare: The Theory of the Welfare State* (Boulder and London: Westview Press, 1988).

95. Michael Walzer, *Spheres of Justice: A Defense of Pluralism and Equality* (New York: Basic Books, 1983), pp. 316, 10, 105, 303. For useful discussions of Walzer's book, see: Ronald Dworkin, "To Each His Own," *New York Review* 30 (April 14, 1983): 4–6; Michael Walzer and Ronald Dworkin, " 'Spheres of Justice': An Exchange," *New York Review* 30 (July 21, 1983): 43–46; Nancy L. Rosenblum, "Moral Membership in a Postliberal State," *World Politics* 36 (July 1984): 581–596; Ronald Kahn, [review], *The American Political Science Review* 78 (1984): 289–290; Francis Kane, [review], *America*, October 27, 1984, pp. 258–260; Brian Barry, "Intimations of Justice," *Columbia Law Review* 84 (1984): 806–815.

96. Walzer, *Spheres of Justice*, pp. 92, 31, 62.

97. Walzer, *Spheres of Justice*, pp. 278, 84, pp. 92–93.

98. Walzer, *Spheres of Justice*, pp. 92–93. See also Walzer, "Socializing the Welfare State," in Gutmann, *Democracy and the Welfare State*, pp. 13–26.

99. National Conference of Catholic Bishops [hereafter cited as NCCB], *Economic Justice for All: Pastoral Letter on Catholic Social Teaching and the U.S. Economy* (United States Catholic Conference, Washington, D.C., 1986), p. 93.

100. NCCB, *Economic Justice*, pp. xi, 8. I am indebted to David Hollenbach for an explanation of the background and intent of the pastoral letter.

101. NCCB, *Economic Justice*, pp. 12, ix, 32.

102. NCCB, *Economic Justice*, pp. 36–37, Dworkin, "What Liberals Should Believe," pp. 33–34.

103. NCCB, *Economic Justice*, pp. 57–58, 4–5, 62, 51, 153.

104. NCCB, *Economic Justice*, pp. 83, x, 49.

FIVE: THE UNDERCLASS?

1. Committee on Health Care for Homeless People [hereafter referred to as CHCHP], Institute of Medicine, *Homelessness, Health, and Human Needs* (Washington, D.C.: National Academy Press, 1988), p. 137. Other useful sources include: Jon Erickson and Charles Wilhelm, eds., *Housing the Homeless* (New Brunswick, N.J.: Center for Urban Policy Research, 1986); Richard D. Bingham, Roy E. Green, Sammis B. White, *The Homeless in Contemporary Society* (Newbury Park, Cal: Sage Publications, 1987); Peter Marcuse, "Neutralizing Homelessness," *Socialist Review* 18 (January–March, 1988): 69–96; Peter H. Rossi, "First Out: Last In: Homelessness in America," unpublished lecture, August 1988; F. Stevens Redburn and

Terry B. Buss, *Responding to America's Homeless: Public Policy Alterna-tives* (New York: Praeger, 1986); Robert A. Rosenthal, "Homeless in Para-dise: A Map of the Terrain," Ph.D. diss., University of California, Santa Barbara, 1987; Joel Blau, "The Homeless of New York: A Case Study," Ph.D. diss., Columbia University School of Social Work, 1987.

2. CHCHP, *Homelessness*, p. 4; Charles D. Cowan, William R. Breakey, and Pamela J. Fischer, "The Methodology of Counting the Homeless," in CHCHP, *Homelessness*, pp. 169–182; Jon Erickson and Charles Wilhelm, "Introduction," in Erickson and Wilhelm, eds., *Housing the Homeless*, p. xxvi.

3. CHCHP, *Homelessness*, pp. 5–18. An excellent recent overview of homelessness in one state is Phyllis Ryan, Ira Goldstein, and David Bartelt, *Homelessness in Pennsylvania: How Can This Be?* (Philadelphia: Coalition on Homelessness in Pennsylvania and The Institute for Public Policy Stud-ies, Temple University, 1989).

4. Kim Hopper and Jill Hamberg, "The Making of America's Homeless: From Skid Row to New Poor, 1945–1984," in Rachel G. Bratt, Chester Hartman, Ann Meyerson, eds., *Critical Perspectives on Housing* (Philadel-phia: Temple University Press, 1986), pp. 23, 21.

5. CHCHP, *Homelessness*, p. 28. On the political and economic factors contributing to deinstitutionalization, see Andrew T. Scull, *Decarceration* (Englewood Cliffs, N.J.: Prentice-Hall, 1977). Most of the authors who write about the homeless cite similar statistics and include policy toward the mentally ill as a contributing factor.

6. CHCHP, *Homelessness*, p. 28; Katz, *Shadow*, ch. 10; Chester Hartman, "Housing Policies Under the Reagan Administration," in Bratt, Hartman, and Meyerson, *Critical Perspectives on Housing*, pp. 362–374.

7. For examples of neighbor-based support networks early in the twentieth-century, see Michael B. Katz, *Poverty and Policy in American History* (New York: Academic Press, 1983), pp. 17–54, and "The History of an Impudent Poor Woman in New City from 1918 to 1923," unpublished manuscript. On an earlier period, see Christine Stansell, *City of Women: Sex and Class in New York 1789–1860* (New York: Knopf, 1986). For the more recent period, see Carol Stack, *All Our Kin: Strategies for Survival in a Black Community* (New York: Harper and Row, 1974).

8. On internal migration, see Michael B. Katz, Mark J. Stern, and Michael J. Doucet, *The Social Organization of Early Industrial Capitalism* (Cam-bridge: Harvard University Press, 1981), pp. 102–130. On tramps, see Erik Monkonnen, *Walking to Work: Tramps in America, 1790–1935* (Lincoln: University of Nebraska Press, 1984) and Katz, *Poverty and Policy*, pp. 157–182; the latter also, on pp. 55–89, discusses the demography of poorhouses.

9. Rossi, "First Out; Last In," esp. pp. 9–16.

10. Mark J. Stern, "The Emergence of Homelessness as a Public Problem," in Erickson and Wilhelm, *Housing the Homeless*, p. 113. Rossi, "First Out: Last In," p. 2.

11. Stern, "The Emergence of Homelessness," pp. 118–119; Gareth Sted-

man Jones, *Outcast London* (London: Oxford University Press, 1971), p. 253.

12. Stern, "The Emergence of Homelessness," p. 120.

13. Stern, "The Emergence of Homelessness," p. 121; on the necessity for poor people to take an active role in winning public policies that promote their interests, see Frances Fox Piven and Richard Cloward, *Poor People's Movements: Why they Succeed and How they Fail* (New York: Pantheon, 1977).

14. Isabel Wilkerson, "New Studies Zeroing In On Poorest of the Poor," *New York Times*, December 20, 1987, p. 26 [emphasis in original].

15. Elliot Currie, *Confronting Crime: An American Challenge* (New York: Pantheon, 1985). Comparative rates of prisoners per 100,000 population in the early 1980s were: Norway 45; Sweden 55; West Germany 60; Denmark 63; France 67; Great Britain 80; United States 217.

16. Bennett Harrison and Barry Bluestone, *The Great U-Turn* (New York: Basic Books, 1988); Sar A. Levitan and Isaac Shapiro, *Working But Poor: America's Contradiction* (Baltimore: Johns Hopkins University Press, 1987); Frank Levy, *Dollars and Dreams: The Changing American Income Distribution* (New York: Russell Sage Foundation, 1987).

17. "The American Underclass," *Time*, August 29, 1977, pp. 14, 15.

18. "The American Underclass," pp. 14, 16.

19. David Whitman and Jeannye Thornton, "A Nation Apart," *U.S. News and World Report*, March 17, 1986, p. 18; Myron Magnet, "America's Underclass: What to Do?" *Fortune*, May 11, 1987, p. 130.

20. Lee Rainwater, "Looking Back and Looking Up," *Transaction* 6 (February 1969): 9. A very good discussion of the origins of the underclass concept in American social science is in Robert Aponte, "Conceptualizing the Underclass: An Alternative Perspective," paper presented at the annual meeting of the American Sociological Association, August 26, 1988. The Aponte paper is also one of the two best criticisms of the concept I have read. The other is Nicky Gregson and Fred Robinson, "The Casualties of Thatcherism," paper presented at the annual meeting of the Association of American Geographers, March 20, 1989. For a summary of the most recent social science research on the underclass, see William J. Wilson, ed., "The Ghetto Underclass: Social Science Perspectives," special issue, *Annals of the American Academy of Political and Social Science* 501 (January 1989).

21. Douglas G. Glasgow, *The Black Underclass: Poverty, Unemployment, and Entrapment of Ghetto Youth* (New York: Random House, 1980), p. 3. Glasgow is a former dean of the School of Social Work at Howard University and vice president of the National Urban League's Washington Operations Office. For his later formulation of the issue, see his "The Black Underclass in Perspective," in National Urban League, *The State of Black America 1987* (Washington: National Urban League, 1987), pp. 129–144.

22. Glasgow, *Black Underclass*, p. 4.

23. Glasgow, *Black Underclass*, pp. 5–6.

24. Glasgow, *Black Underclass*, pp. 7–8, 178.

25. Glasgow, *Black Underclass*, pp. 9–11, 173.

26. Some of the definitions of underclass current in late 1987 are listed in Wilkerson, "New Studies"; Ken Auletta, *The Underclass* (New York: Random House, 1982).

27. Auletta, *Underclass*, p. xvi.

28. For a similar example from the nineteenth century, see Michael B. Katz, *Poverty and Policy in American History* (New York: Academic Press, 1983), pp. 134–156.

29. Auletta, *Underclass*, pp. 260–268.

30. Nicholas Lemann, "The Origins of the Underclass," *The Atlantic Monthly* 257 (June 1986): 31–61, and 258 (July 1986): 54–68. Quotations from pp. 257, 32–33, 35, 258, 59, 61. William J. Wilson points out Lemann's belatedly acknowledged debt to his work in William J. Wilson, *The Truly Disadvantaged: The Inner City, the Underclass, and Public Policy* (Chicago and London: University of Chicago Press, 1987), pp. 197–198, fn. 72.

31. Lemann, *Underclass*, 257, p. 40; 258, p. 68.

32. Lemann, *Underclass*, 257, p. 35.

33. Wilson, *Truly Disadvantaged*, p. 55.

34. Gerald Jaynes, seminar comments, PARSS seminar on the city, University of Pennsylvania, December 15, 1986. See also, Andrew Billingsley, "Black Families in a Changing Society," and Glasgow, "Black Underclass," in National Urban League, *State of Black America*, pp. 105–106 and 132–133.

35. Janice Madden, seminar comments, PARSS seminar on the city, University of Pennsylvania, December 15, 1986.

36. Marian Wright Edelman, *Families in Peril: An Agenda for Social Change* (Cambridge: Harvard University Press, 1987), p. 73.

37. Martha A. Gephart and Robert W. Pearson, "Contemporary Research on the Urban Underclass," *Items* 42 (June 1988): 3.

38. Wilkerson, "New Studies," Erol R. Ricketts and Isabel V. Sawhill, "Defining and Measuring the Underclass," unpublished manuscript, December 1986.

39. William Julius Wilson, *The Declining Significance of Race: Blacks and Changing American Institutions* (Chicago: University of Chicago Press, 1978; 2nd edition, 1980). On the controversy, see Joseph R. Washington, ed., *The Declining Significance of Race? A Dialogue among Black and White Social Scientists* (Philadelphia: Joseph R. Washington, Jr., 1979).

40. Wilson, *Truly Disadvantaged*, pp. vii–viii.

41. Wilson, *Truly Disadvantaged*, pp. 7–8.

42. Wilson, *Truly Disadvantaged*, pp. 7, 8.

43. Wilson, *Truly Disadvantaged*, pp. 33–37; Stanley Lieberson, *A Piece of the Pie: Black and White Immigrants Since 1880* (Berkeley and Los Angeles: University of California Press, 1980).

44. Wilson, *Truly Disadvantaged*, pp. 49–56.

45. Wilson, *Truly Disadvantaged*, pp. 46 and 55.

46. Wilson, *Truly Disadvantaged*, p. 56. See also Elijah Anderson, "Of Old

Heads and Young Boys: Notes on the Urban Black Experience," unpublished manuscript, University of Pennsylvania, 1986.

47. Wilson, *Truly Disadvantaged*, pp. 60–61. Wilson had very little data with which to test his concepts of concentration and isolation, and others have argued that the existing literature does not support his contentions about their impact. However, Wilson developed a large and complex research project with which to test the hypotheses in his book, and the early results appear to confirm them. Wilson, remarks to Senior Seminar, Urban Studies Program, University of Pennsylvania, November 9, 1988.

48. Christopher Jencks, "Deadly Neighborhoods," *New Republic*, June 13, 1988, pp. 23–32; Christopher Jencks and Susan Mayer, "The Social Consequences of Growing Up in a Poor Neighborhood," unpublished manuscript, Center for Urban Affairs and Policy Research, Northwestern University, April 5, 1988; Mark Testa et al., "Employment and Marriage among Inner-City Fathers," in Wilson, ed., *Annals*, pp. 79–91; Douglas S. Massey and Mitchell T. Eggers, "The Ecology of Inequality: Minorities and the Concentration of Poverty 1970–1980," unpublished ms., Population Research Center NORC, University of Chicago, January 1989.

49. Richard B. Freeman and Harry J. Holzer, "The Black Youth Employment Crisis: Summary of Findings," in Richard B. Freeman and Harry J. Holzer, eds., *The Black Youth Employment Crisis* (Chicago and London: University of Chicago Press, 1986), pp. 3 and 7 (emphasis in original); Wilson, *Trurly Disadvantaged*, Table 2.88, p. 43.

50. Freeman and Holzer, "Employment Crisis," pp. 4–6.

51. Freeman and Holzer, "Employment Crisis," pp. 6–7.

52. Harry J. Holzer, "Black Youth Nonemployment: Duration and Job Search," in Freeman and Holzer, *Black Youth Employment Crisis*, p. 65.

53. John Ballen and Richard B. Freeman, "Transitions between Employment and Nonemployment," in Freeman and Holzer, *Black Youth Employment Crisis*, pp. 97–99.

54. David T. Ellwood, "The Spatial Mismatch Hypothesis: Are There Teenage Jobs Missing in the Ghetto," and Jonathan S. Leonard, "Comment," in Freeman and Holzer, *Black Youth Employment Crisis*, pp. 147–190.

55. George J. Borjas, "The Demographic Determinants of the Demand for Black Labor," in Freeman and Holzer, *Black Youth Employment Crisis*, p. 225. The finding that women substitute for black men in employment appears robust and supported by other research.

56. Jerome Culp and Bruce H. Dunson, "Brothers of a Different Color: A Preliminary Look at Employer Treatment of White and Black Youth," and Paul Osterman, "Comment," Freeman and Holzer, pp. 233–260. I phrased this conditionally because the findings, based on a very small sample, are very tentative.

57. Ronald Ferguson and Randall Filer, "Do Better Jobs Make Better Workers? Absenteeism from Work Among Inner-City Black Youths," in Freeman and Holzer, *Black Youth Employment Crisis*, pp. 291–293.

58. W. Kip Viscusi, "Market Incentives for Criminal Behavior," in Freeman and Holzer, *Black Youth Employment Crisis*, pp. 343–344. James W. Thompson and James Cataldo point out in their comment on this paper that Viscusi's is one of the first studies not based solely on an offender population (p. 347).

59. Richard B. Freeman, "Who Escapes? The Relation of Churchgoing and Other Background Factors to the Socioeconomic Performance of Black Male Youths from Inner-City Tracts"; Robert B. Lerman, "Do Welfare Programs Affect the Schooling and Work Patterns of Young Black Men?" and Samuel B. Myers, Jr., "Comment," in Freeman and Holzer, eds., *Black Youth Employment Crisis*, pp. 372–374 and 403–441.

60. Freeman, "Who Escapes?", p. 374.

61. Linda Datcher-Loury and Glenn Loury, "The Effects of Attitudes and Aspirations on the Labor Supply of Young Men," and Michael J. Piore, "Comment," in Freeman and Holzer, *Black Youth Employment Crisis*, pp. 377–401.

62. Elijah Anderson, "Race and Neighborhood Transition," in Paul E. Peterson, ed., *The New Urban Reality* (Washington, D.C.: The Brookings Institution, 1985), pp. 99–127.

63. Some of the items in this list of misconceptions come from Elise F. Jones et al., *Adolescent Pregnancy in Industrialized Countries*, A Study Sponsored by the Alan Guttmacher Institute (New Haven and London: Yale University Press, 1986), pp. 298–299.

64. David T. Ellwood and Lawrence H. Summers, "Poverty in America: Is Welfare the Answer or the Problem?" in Sheldon H. Danziger and Daniel H. Weinberg, *Fighting Poverty: What Works and What Doesn't* (Cambridge: Harvard University Press, 1986), p. 85; Gary Burtless, "Public Spending for the Poor: Trends, Prospects, and Economic Limits," in Danziger and Weinberg, *Fighting Poverty*, pp. 23 and 40.

65. David T. Ellwood and Lawrence H. Summers, "Poverty in America: Is Welfare the Answer or the Problem?" in Danziger and Weinberg, *Fighting Poverty*, p. 94. An excellent discussion of birth rates, and of other issues raised in this section, is David T. Ellwood, *Poor Support: Poverty in the American Family* (New York: Basic Books, 1988), pp. 45–80.

66. Maris A. Vinovskis, An *"Epidemic" of Adolescent Pregnancy? Some Historical and Policy Considerations* (New York and Oxford: Oxford University Press, 1988), p. 30; Jones, *Adolescent Pregnancy*, pp. 24–30, 34, 43.

67. Jones et al., *Teenage Pregnancy*.

68. Jones et al., *Adolescent Pregnancy*, pp. 64–65, 239–240; Vinovskis, *Epidemic*, p. 211. Vinovskis (p. 212) believes historical precedent shows it is possible to reduce the amount of adolescent sexual activity through an unambiguous, strong moral position on the part of parents and cultural authorities; for another analysis of the problem and an approach different from Vinovskis', see Edelman, *Families in Peril*, pp. 51–66.

69. Jones et al., *Adolescent Pregnancy*, p. 227.

70. Jones et al., *Adolescent Pregnancy*, pp. 64–65.

71. William Julius Wilson and Kathryn M. Neckerman, "Poverty and Fam-

ily Structure: The Widening Gap between Evidence and Public Policy Issues," in Danziger and Weinberg, *Fighting Poverty*, pp. 236 and 238.

72. Harrell R. Rodgers, Jr., *Poor Women, Poor Families: The Economic Plight of America's Female-Headed Households* (Armonk, New York, and London, England: M.E. Sharp, Inc., 1986), p. 26.

73. Irwin Garfinkle and Sara S. McLanahan, *Single Mothers and Their Children: A New American Dilemma* (Washington, D.C.: The Urban Institute Press, 1986), p. 45.

74. Wilson and Neckerman, "Poverty and Family Structure," p. 240, Mary Jo Bane, "Household Composition and Poverty," in Danziger and Weinberg, *Fighting Poverty*, pp. 214–215 (emphasis in original).

75. Ellwood and Summers, "Is Welfare the Answer or the Problem," pp. 93–97; Robert Pear, "Young Mothers Said to Be on Welfare Longer," *New York Times*, September 10, 1986, p. A 28; Garfinkle and McLanahan, *Single Mothers*, p. 38.

76. Bane, "Household Composition and Poverty," p. 227.

77. Kathleen Mullan Harris, "Adolescent Childbearing and Welfare Experience: The Transition Out of Dependency," paper presented to Seminar on Race and City, PARSS Program, University of Pennsylvania, February 16, 1987, p. 27, and Table 3; Frank F. Furstenberg, Jr., J. Brooks-Gunn, S. Philip Morgan, *Adolescent Mothers in Later Life* (New York: Cambridge University Press, 1987), pp. 29, 40–43, 48–76.

78. Michael B. Katz and Mark J. Stern, "History and the Limits of Population Policy," *Politics and Society* 10 (1980): 225–45; Mark J. Stern, *Society and Family Strategy: Erie County, New York 1850–1920* (Albany: State University of New York Press, 1987); Viviana A. Zelizer, *Pricing the Priceless Child: The Changing Value of Children* (New York: Basic Books, 1985).

79. For sensible and realistic suggestions for policy based on the best current data, see Furstenberg, Brooks-Gunn, and Morgan, *Adolescent Mothers in Later Life*, pp. 145–154.

80. Ellwood, *Poor Support*, pp. 75–79.

81. Lemann, "Origins of the Underclass," 257, p. 34.

82. Richard Nathan, "Will the Underclass Always Be with Us?," *Society*, 24 (March–April 1987): 57–62. Nathan is professor of public and international affairs at the Woodrow Wilson School, Princeton University, and chairman of the board of the Manpower Demonstration Research Corporation.

83. Nathan, "Underclass," pp. 57–58.

84. Nathan, "Underclass," pp. 60–61.

85. Nathan, "Underclass," p. 61.

86. Nathan, "Underclass," p. 61.

87. Fred Block and John Noakes, "The Politics of New-Style Workfare," unpublished paper prepared for PARSS Seminar on Work and Welfare, January 1988, pp. 14–19.

88. Nathan, "Underclass," pp. 61–62.

89. Nathan, "Underclass," p. 62; Robert Pear, "Sweeping Welfare Revision Plan Stresses Responsibility of Parents," *New York Times*, July 19, 1987,

pp. 1 and 21; John Herbers, "Governors Ask Work Plan for Welfare Recipients," *New York Times*, February 22, 1987, p. A30; "A Hopeful New Consensus Emerges For Welfare Reform," *Philadelphia Inquirer*, February 22, 1987, p. 6-E.

90. Block and Noakes, "Politics of New-Style Workfare," pp. 24 and 27.

91. Judith M. Gueron, "Reforming Welfare with Work," unpublished manuscript, Manpower Demonstration Research Corporation, February 1987, pp. 13–14.

92. *"The programs led to relatively modest increases in employment, which in some cases translated into even smaller welfare savings. Nonetheless, the changes were usually large enough to justify the programs' costs, although this finding varied by state and target group."* Gueron, "Reforming Welfare with Work," pp. 15–28; quote, p. 28; italics in original.

93. Block and Noakes, "Politics of New-Style Workfare," p. 33, Table III; p. 34; p. 36, Table IV.

94. United States General Accounting Office, "Work and Welfare: Current AFDC Work Programs and Implications for Federal Policy," GAO/FHRD87-34, Washington, D.C., GPO, January, 1987, p. 3.

95. Block and Noakes, "Politics of New-Style Workfare," p. 42.

96. "Family Security Act of 1987: Section-by-Section Summary," mimeo, July 21, 1987. An opposing statement is: Fred Block and Frances Fox Piven, "Statement on Senate Bill 1511" and accompanying letter, mimeo, October 12, 1987. For a variety of statements about Moynihan's bill and the somewhat different version of welfare reform in the House, see, "Why It's So Tough to Get Welfare Reform," *New York Times*, December 6, 1987, p. 32; *Congressional Quarterly*, October 8, 1988, pp. 2825–2831.

97. Department of Public Welfare, Executive Office of Human Services, Commonwealth of Massachusetts, "The Massachusetts Employment and Training Choices Program: Program Plan and Budget Request FY88," mimeo, February 1987. For an elaboration of the rationale influential in developing the Massachusetts program, see David T. Ellwood, "The Hope for Self Support," in Manuel Carballo and Mary Jo Bane, eds., *The State and the Poor in the 1980s* [a book that examines the Massachusetts situation] (Boston: Auburn House, 1984), pp. 19–48. See also Pear, "Sweeping Welfare Revision," pp. 1, 21, and David L. Kirp, "The California Work/Welfare Scheme," *The Public Interest* 83 (Spring 1986): 34–38.

98. Deborah Harris, "Child Support for Welfare Families: Family Policy Trapped in Its Own Rhetoric," unpublished paper, PARSS seminar on work and welfare, University of Pennsylvania, November 21, 1988 (quote on p. 32). The case for child-support enforcement and a history of the child-support amendment are in Garfinkle and McLanahan, *Single Mothers*, pp. 136–137; 181–183.

99. Stuart Butler and Anna Kondratas, *Out of the Poverty Trap: A Conservative Strategy for Welfare Reform* (New York: Free Press), pp. 148 and 154.

100. Theda Skocpol, Margaret Weir, and Ann Shola Orloff, "Why Welfare Reform Won't Work—and What Would," *Baltimore Sun*, February 22, 1987, 1M and 3M.

101. Rebecca M. Blank and Alan S. Blinder, "Maroeconomics, Income Distribution, and Poverty," in Danziger and Weinberg, *Fighting Poverty*, pp. 180–208; Block and Noakes, "Politics of New-Style Workfare," p. 43.
102. Danziger and Weinberg, *Fighting Poverty*, p. 16.
103. Wilson, *Truly Disadvantaged*, pp. 105, 151–152.
104. Wilson, *Truly Disadvantaged*, pp. 153–154.

EPILOGUE: "THEM" OR "US"?

1. Michael Harrington, *The New American Poverty* (New York: Holt, Rinehart and Winston, 1984 [Viking Penguin, 1985]), pp. 8–11.
2. Graham Room, "The 'New Poverty' in the European Community: A Summary of Twelve National Reports Prepared for the European Community," unpublished report, Centre for the Analysis of Social Policy, University of Bath, May 1987, pp. 1, and 2.
3. Walter Korpi, "Approaches to the Study of Poverty in the United States: Critical Notes from a European Perspective," in Vincent T. Covello, ed., *Poverty and Public Policy: An Evaluation of Social Science Research* (Cambridge: Shenkman, 1980), pp. 287, 299, 307.
4. Harrington, *New American Poverty*, p. 13.
5. National Conference of Catholic Bishops, *Economic Justice for All: Pastoral Letter on Catholic Social Teaching and the U.S. Economy* (Washington, D.C.: United States Catholic Conference, 1986), p. 144.

APPENDIX

1. June Axinn and Mark J. Stern, *Dependency and Poverty: Old Problems in a New World* (Lexington, Mass.: Lexington Books, 1988).
2. Axinn and Stern, *Dependency and Poverty*, pp. 64, 83.
3. Axinn and Stern, *Dependency and Poverty*, pp. 64, 66.
4. Axinn and Stern, *Dependency and Poverty*, pp. 80–81.
5. Axinn and Stern, *Dependency and Poverty*, pp. 88, 109.
6. Sar A. Levitan and Isaac Shapiro, *Working but Poor: America's Contradiction* (Baltimore: The Johns Hopkins University Press, 1987), p. 3.
7. Axinn and Stern, *Dependency and Poverty*, pp. 115–116, 25.

# Index

ABOUT THE AUTHOR

Michael B. Katz is Professor of History and Director of the
Urban Studies Program at the University of Pennsylvania.
Author of seven books and many articles, he has been a
visiting member of the Institute for Advanced Study, the
Shelby Cullom Davis Center at Princeton, a Guggenheim
Fellow, and a visiting scholar at the Russell Sage
Foundation.